IN VOGUE

Sixty years of
international celebrities and fashion
from British Vogue

GEORGINA HOWELL

SCHOCKEN BOOKS

NEW YORK

First published by SCHOCKEN BOOKS 1976

Copyright © The Condé Nast Publications Ltd, 1975

Second Printing

———————————————

Research by Sheila Murphy
Design by Martin Bassett and Philip Clucas,
DP Press Limited, Sevenoaks

———————————————

Printed in Great Britain

Library of Congress Cataloging in Publication Data
Howell, Georgina, 1942–
    In Vogue.

    Bibliography: p. 338
    Includes index.
    1. Costume—History—20th century.   I. Vogue
(London) II. Title.
GT596.H68   1976   391'.009'04 .   75–42970

CONTENTS

ON THE SOFA 1916   Maurice Beck & Macgregor 1926   1938

AT THE WHEEL 1919   1923   Helmut Newton 1965

IN THE AIR   Steichen 1926   Anton Bruehl 1937   William Klein 1961   Helmut Newton 1967

WITH ESCORTS   Pollard 1924   Eric 1936   Norman Parkinson 1960   David Bailey 1965

THE CHILDREN

PREFACE

BEATRIX MILLER
Editor of *Vogue*

In October 1976, British *Vogue* celebrates its Diamond Jubilee,
60 years of reporting fashion, beauty, people, plays,
decoration, manners and attitudes.

According to James Laver's Time Spirit Theory,
that the forms of dress, apparently so haphazard,
so dependent on the whims of the designer,
have an extraordinary relevance to the spirit of the age, so,
browsing through old copies you catch the mood of the moment,
that moment. Mr I.S.V. Patcévitch, for 28 years President
and Chairman of Condé Nast, said, 'each issue of *Vogue*,
this fragile and transitory product, performs a certain function.
It holds a mirror up to its times, a small mirror perhaps,
but a singularly clear, brilliant and revealing one.'

In a sense women and *Vogue* are synonymous and the role
women play is continuously reflected, albeit in a limited stratum
of society. The 60 years mirrored here embrace some of the most
crowded changes in social history and, in particular, the part
that women take in society and the world. So it is as natural
now to publish discoveries in science that affect people, men
and women, as it is to report on the latest Paris Collections.
Today, with a readership of over 2½ million, *Vogue*'s continuing
strength lies in its adherence to the original formula, maintaining
a constant viewpoint of style, quality and specialization while
continually evolving with the spirit of the time. Thus each issue
of the magazine is the tip of an iceberg of information,
creative intuition and research that has built up
over the years, just as this book is only one of
a potential hundred more.

1916-1923

The Great Escape

LUCILE

The Great War changed everything: way of life, attitudes, society, politics, people themselves mentally and physically. No war had ever involved so many civilians. Fashion in clothes and much else was turned upside down and no longer flowed in natural progressions and reactions. With hindsight, we know that World War 1 emancipated fashion, but while it was happening the breeches of 'farmerettes' and land girls, the trousers and overalls of the women munition workers and tram conductors, the uniforms of the nurses and postwomen were not considered part of fashion and scarcely surfaced to the pages of *Vogue*. Fashion dawdled in its tracks and simultaneously hopped a decade. Some people assumed that after the war there would be a rush of exaggerated impractical clothes as a reaction to serge suits and sensible proofed trenchcoats, others that women who had once known the freedom of trousers would never look back. Both were right. Fashion didn't catch up with itself until the mid-twenties. In the meantime sports clothes and jerseys took women forwards, crinolines, pagoda hips and tapered hems took them back. The cross currents brought to *Vogue* perhaps the oddest silhouette in the history of fashion. A woman might wear a hat of vulture quills two feet tall, a calf-length dress under a tunic dropping two points to touch the ground, the whole swathed with a tempest of monkey fur bands. In the evening she might wear a brocade tunic over a sagging nappy of chiffon, or a short crinoline in tiers of fur and lamé.

Coming out bang in the middle of the war, British *Vogue* was full of references to hard times and reduced incomes, but each issue was full of the fashion news from Paris. Under headlines such as 'Paris makes a brave show in spite of guns', or 'Paris lifts ever so little the ban on gaiety', *Vogue* managed to show the most extravagant of morale-boosting fashions. Once or twice a year there would be a page on 'A wardrobe for the woman war-worker . . . for the ten thousand women who are driving ambulances, working in canteens and nursing the wounded'. There were a few features on war topics: the Citroën munitions factory, an eyewitness's account of a night with a convoy, the new ambulances. *Vogue* recommended gifts for soldiers – horsehair gloves, air pillows and National War Bonds – and gave much space to the charity matinées that combined worthy war-work with society spectaculars. Lady Duff Gordon was photographed as 'the personification of the mystery and power of Russia' at the Ten Allies Costume Ball, Miss Fay Compton as a rose and Miss Viola Tree as a 'tall bramble' at the 'Our Day' matinée, Ethel Barrymore as Flanders at the Allied Nations pageant on Long Island. 'Dressing on a war income' was a regular feature, but not as helpful as it might have been, recommending that women should slim in order to use less fabric, and suggesting 'cleverly contrived neck arrangements' to change the look of a plain dress. In 1917 *Vogue* reported that the French government had banned jewels and evening dress at the Opéra,

Left: Miss Irene Hart, portrait by Hoppé, 1917

1. Oriental evening dress, shot silver tissue and orange tulle, 1919.

the Odéon and the Comédie Française until the end of the war and had appealed to the public not to buy new dresses, and showed on the same page Doucet's irresistible evening wrap of rose panne velvet finished with skunk and tassels. There was a feature on 'Leave trousseaux' with adjuncts to 'make it [your] business to see that he carries away with him on his return to duty a refreshing vision of loveliness, and in particular to avoid the masculine', in other words the wartime innovations of 'service suits', waterproofs, wool underwear, thick stockings, tailored Viyella shirts, trenchcoats and suits of uniform cloth copied from the soldiers' coats of black rubber or serge.

The first women to wear trousers and dungarees wore them because they went with the job – dirty, hard jobs that women were taking over from the soldiers, train driving, plumbing, factory work, electrical engineering, window cleaning, farm labouring. Working clothes weren't considered part of fashion at all, just a temporary necessity like uniform, and *Vogue* reflected the attitude with one or two pages a year on equipment for ambulance drivers, compared with the main body of Paris fashion in every issue. Nevertheless short skirts and trousers became part of the vocabulary of fashion, and two coat designs arrived that stayed for good. The British Warm became the standard overcoat for men and women alike, with its deep revers, its epaulettes and buckled belt. From the mud of the front line came the trenchcoat, just as useful for landgirls or even commuters in taxiless cities. In rubberized cloth, it had double breasting, epaulettes and cuffstraps, an envelope flap across the shoulder fastening, and a button-on chin protector.

Society beauties had their portraits taken for *Vogue* by Hoppé, Hugh Cecil and Bertram Park. Ideally they were photographed in uniform, like Countess Bathurst in Red Cross outfit, or the Marchioness of Londonderry in the uniform of the Women's Service Legion. Failing that, they compensated in other ways. Mrs

Kermit Roosevelt's caption refers to her baby, and the career of her husband at the Front. The Duchess of Wellington is photographed knitting a sock. Mrs Vincent Astor, photographed in a garden hat, has the intention of opening a convalescent home near Paris where wounded American soldiers may be nursed back to health. Lady Randolph Churchill 'has organized some very beautiful tableaux vivants for the matinée', and Miss Lucile Baldwin took 'active part, last autumn, in the Tuxedo Horticultural Society, which gave an exhibition for the Red Cross'. Musical comedy actresses and starlets did their bit, too. Lily Elsie appealed for cigarette papers for the Red Cross with a new photograph in *Vogue*, Doris Keane told *Vogue* she was going to put all her fan letters from soldiers into a book and sell it in aid of the Red Cross.

Vogue was packed with patriotic advertisements, all urging the public to spend money in the line of duty. 'In too many homes . . . these are the times of the darkest clouds. Yet assuredly it is true, and the old saying is justified of its belief, that every cloud has a silver lining. It is the writer's opinion the bright relief is the keeping up of the home . . . at Jelk's you can obtain the best furniture at the lowest prices.' There were appeals to women to think of their complexions: '. . . comes the remembrance of bitterly cold days when you were driving an Army Car, of hours spent in heated factories, and the wonder of what effect either has had on your complexion, hands and hair. Your mirror reassures you, Colleen Shampoos so soon restore lustre and life to the hair . . .' or, in a higher tone, 'It is lamentable that the far-famed beauty of the Englishwoman must suffer from the terrible strain her beloved country is undergoing. It is her duty to use every means in her power to prevent the effect on her beauty . . . You are urged to take one treatment at the elegant and most up-to-date "Cyclax" Salons.'

The soldiers came home from the trenches different men.

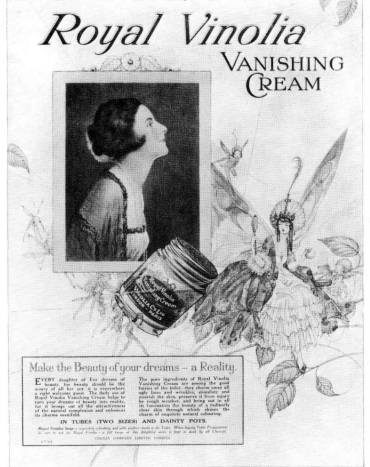

Royal Vinolia
VANISHING CREAM

Make the Beauty of your dreams – a Reality.

EVERY daughter of Eve dreams of beauty, for beauty should be the dowry of all her sex. It is everywhere a right welcome guest. The daily use of Royal Vinolia Vanishing Cream helps to turn your dreams of beauty into reality, for it brings out all the attractiveness of the natural complexion and enhances its charms manifold.

The pure ingredients of Royal Vinolia Vanishing Cream are among the good fairies of the toilet—they charm away all ugly lines and wrinkles, stimulate and nourish the skin, preserve it from injury by rough weather, and bring out in all its fascination the beauty of a radiantly clear skin through which shines the charm of exquisite natural colouring.

IN TUBES (TWO SIZES) AND DAINTY POTS.

Royal Vinolia Soap is exquisitely refreshing and adds another charm to the Toilet. When buying Toilet Preparations be sure to ask for Royal Vinolia—a full range of this delightful series is kept in stock by all Chemists.

VINOLIA COMPANY LIMITED, LONDON.

Many were suffering from shell shock with nightmares and vivid daydreams, and if they recovered now they would probably go down with nervous breakdowns in 1921 or 1922. They were out of temper with Lloyd George and his Coalition government. They'd been promised a life fit for heroes at the end of the struggle, but they came home to an impoverished country in a state of confusion, and their jobs had been filled by women or men who had managed to avoid conscription. Officers, the husbands of *Vogue* readers, were given no unemployment benefits and high prices were followed by a slump. There was plenty to escape from.

Women had grown more confident, more independent, and had begun to earn their own living in factories and offices. They no longer wanted to be cooks, nurses, maids or dressmakers: as Dorothy Parker wrote in 1919, 'that sort of thing simply isn't being done, any more; it is considered positively unfeminine'. The war had killed one out of every seven eligible men, and seriously injured another, so marriage was not inevitable. Women were in better shape after years of rationed butter and sugar, and with the popularity of hockey and tennis. The hourglass figure of the old Gaiety girls now looked comic. Laced whalebone corsets had been superseded by camisole bras and rubber girdles. The flapper had arrived. The expression, which began as 'backfisch' in Germany in the 1890s, had meant a very young tart before the war, but had come to mean the popular heroine of the munitions factory, a girl who rode on the flapper bracket of a motorbicycle, swore, smoked cigarettes publicly and sold flags with brazen flirtatiousness. This figure had little to do with the refined dignified dresses in *Vogue*, which regretted the fact in 1921: 'One cannot help wishing for a less independent, less hard, more feminine product than the average 20th. century girl.'

The new society had a new etiquette. At the end of 1918 class distinctions were temporarily relaxed. An aristocratic woman

might marry even into the labouring class as long as the man had a good war record. The 'new rich', the war profiteers, were hated by the new poor. Women were smoking in public, but the cigarettes had to be Egyptian and Turkish, not Virginian. It was considered all right to smoke in the restaurant car of a train, but vulgar on the top of a bus. Some women smoked in restaurants, and a waiter in one knocked a cigarette out of a lady's mouth. In 1919 new dance clubs and halls opened for tea dances, practice dances, subscription and victory dances. You could dance before lunch in private houses in London and the country. Before the war women danced the tango with hands on hips and pelvis thrust forward, faces white with rice powder, eyes blackened with kohl, called mascara. After the war they danced the kikikari or the shimmy with deadpan faces, a touch of lipstick, in a backless dress . . . 'I wish I could shimmy like my sister Kate, she shakes it like a bowl of jelly on a plate.' A clergyman in 1919 wrote, 'If these up-to-date

Fish

dances, described as the "latest craze", are within a hundred miles of all I hear about them, I should say that the morals of a pig-sty would be respectable in comparison.' *Vogue*, appealing to the mothers, found a tone of voice that combined tolerance with disapproval: 'a formal "coming out" seems to have gone the way of formal visits . . . Personally, one may feel that too much ease is being used too easily, particularly by people for whom formality might have served in place of those traditions which they lack . . . In any event, girls will grow up, bless them!' Debutantes in 1920 were sending out invitations in their own names to dances where there would be no chaperones. Girls were often invited to bring their own man.

Women's place was a debatable subject. As a reward for war services they were given the vote over thirty, but the government was counting on half the female population being too vain to give away their age, and the other half to put in 'safe' votes. 'From the princess to the humblest of munitions workers, the womanhood of Britain emerges from the ordeal with credentials which the future will acclaim', but many of the women who'd been praised for going out to work to help their country had their jobs snatched back in peacetime by Trades Unions: the soldiers wanted their work back again. Where women hung onto their jobs their pay was two-thirds that of a man. 'Votes for Women' gave way to 'Equal pay for Equal work'. The Sex Disqualification (Removal) Act of 1919 admitted women to many professions including the bar, and was followed up by acts to recognize women as morally responsible persons. In 1921 *Vogue* published 'Women and Education – a real Oxford for Women', to help appeal for funds for Oxford women's colleges. It was timed to accompany the announcement that the Queen would accept an honorary degree at Oxford. *Vogue* said, 'The women's part of the university will never possess the spirit which alone justifies Oxford's existence, until it has acquired the same freedom, intellectual as well as social, which characterizes the men's part.'

Oxford had admitted women to full membership in 1919, but Cambridge had refused with scenes of amazing ungallantry, hoisting high above the streets a female dummy in bloomers riding a bicycle, and was consequently in disgrace.

In 1919 a terrible epidemic of septic influenza swept through Europe and on round the world killing twenty-seven million people in all – twice as many as the war itself. In the United Kingdom there were 200,000 deaths, and people went about in public in antiseptic gauze masks. The dogs that accompanied them were muzzled, too: there had been an outbreak of rabies. There were high prices and strikes, peasouper fogs, and precious little coal. Even if your family were alive and together again, there was plenty to escape from and plenty to escape to. There was the light, bright note of the theatre – 'It will be a long time before the theatre can be serious again' – there was the cinema, there were cocktails and dancing, fancy dress balls, cabarets, weekend motoring and Fridays-to-Mondays. In summer families flooded to the seaside for their first holiday in five years: three hundred thousand visitors went to Blackpool, and women and children had to sleep in police cells while men slept out on the beaches and cliff tops. By the winter continental holidays were possible again for those who could afford them, and St Moritz was the place to go. *Vogue* ran a five-page feature on the right clothes to wear for skiing.

Of all escape valves, the films allowed you to live vicariously with the least effort. By 1919 half the population of Britain went

Ochsé Collection

Ira L. Hill

Rita Martin

1. Aquascutum's skiing suit, 1923: slate blue wool, double breasted, with strapped cuffs and military pockets.
2. Lillian Gish as she starred in David Griffith's *Hearts of the World*, 1918.
3. Sarah Bernhardt in her apartment in the Boulevard Péreire.
4. Florence Walton, famous dancer usually partnered by her husband Maurice. She wore gold and silver tissue dresses by Callot for her performances — when she was in New York they sent her one a week.
5. Gina Palerme, 1918. Delightful French musical comedy star who appeared in London at the Palace Theatre and the Duke of York's. Off stage, she might wear a chinchilla cape to the ground, with saluki dogs for accessories, or a velvet tam o'shanter and men's riding breeches.

to the pictures twice a week. Charlie Chaplin who had been slated by the British press in 1915 as a young Englishman who was not doing his bit, was on everywhere, with Mary Pickford, whose baby ringlets and childish prettiness were much copied. *Vogue* published a pageful of the starlets who were trying to look like her. Her antithesis was wicked wicked Theda Bara, first of the vamps, an aggressive *femme fatale* launched on the first big publicity wave. She went to press interviews in a white limousine with Nubian footmen, primed with what she had to say: her name was an anagram of 'arab death', her nationality was to be revealed as French-Egyptian – she was really a Miss Goodman from Ohio. Her 'Kiss me, my fool' became a catch phrase. There was Clara Kimball Young, Tarzan's Jane, and sylph-like Lillian Gish, who starred in D. W. Griffith's *Birth of a Nation*, a four-hour film that consolidated the success of films as a new art form independent of the spoken word. She appeared in *Vogue* in 1918 in pictures from Griffith's war epic *Hearts of the World*, filmed in France in the recently recaptured village of Ham. Most often in *Vogue* was Geraldine Farrar, a beautiful opera singer who signed up with Samuel Goldwyn at $10,000 a week: in 1916 *Vogue* showed stills from Cecil B. De Mille's 'photo-drama' *Joan of Arc*, in which she took the starring part. Norma Talmadge was in almost every issue, a teenage leading lady at Vitagraph who went on to manage her own film company. For ultra-escapism there was Gloria Swanson, who appeared in a Sennett comedy as early as 1916. She was sensationally fashionable in all her films: De Mille insisted on it. In films like *For Better For Worse* (1919) and *The Affairs of Anatol* (1921) she staggered under the weight of jewels, furs and ostrich plumes. *Vogue* considered her a prime example of movie bad taste, but she made a tremendous hit with the British public.

The subtitles to films brought American slang to Britain, and it was much relished and disapproved of: 'Beatrix Esmond goes nix on the love-stuff' and 'You've dribbled a bibful, baby' were read out aloud by the audiences. *Vogue* wrote a piece on the murder of the English language. An American revue which came to London with Noël Coward in the cast had its name changed from *Oh Boy!* to *Oh Joy!* The feeling that Hollywood was hardly respectable meant that only a few screen stars were included in the magazine, although everyone who was anyone in the theatre could be seen in *Vogue* constantly.

Paris set the fashion, and the musical comedy and vaudeville actresses from London, Paris and Broadway wore the clothes to perfection. They were photographed as models if they were just beginning, as themselves when they'd arrived, and finally, when they were famous, in their own clothes from Callot and Poiret, Vionnet and Lanvin. Stars like Florence Walton and Gina Palerme were the staple diet of Paris designers. Yvonne Printemps took 80

1

de Givenchy

2

Lanvins to New York, and Florence Walton was sent a Callot dress a week. *Vogue* showed drawings of many of them.

Except for a brief falling-off in audiences in 1921 when a coal strike turned theatres into refrigerators, the stage had never done better or set more fashions. Costume design for important productions was always undertaken by couturiers, so that theatre design was naturally absorbed into fashion and new productions were scanned for fashion pointers. *Vogue* showed the best stage costumes from Hindu dancers' to Poiret's extravagant Oriental designs for *Agfar* at the Pavilion. There were sentimental comedies like *Paddy, the Next Best Thing* which ran for three years, and *Chu Chin Chow* which ran for five. There was Ibsen for problem plays, Galsworthy and Shaw revivals, Oscar Wilde, Gilbert & Sullivan and *Charley's Aunt*. Birmingham repertory theatre produced *Cymbeline* in modern dress, with warriors in khaki. In 1923 Cochran brought Eleanora Duse to England for the first time in seventeen years and began a migration of foreign plays and players to London. There was Sacha Guitry's *Grand Guignol* season and Carel Čapek's *R.U.R.* Somerset Maugham's *Our Betters* was too shocking, and *The Circle* was openly booed. Noël Coward's *The Young Idea* had only a short run in 1922. Public taste at this period was for something a little more sugary.

If the actresses showed *Vogue* readers how to look in the new clothes, it was the society queens who personified fashion for the designers themselves. Beauties whose portraits appeared and who really lived the life for which Paris fashion was designed were the Duchesse de Gramont (Madame Vionnet said that if she wanted to tell if a dress were right she had only to try it on the Duchesse); wealthy socialites Mrs Vanderbilt, Mrs Hatch and Countess Torby; Lady Lavery, a red-haired Irish-American from Chicago who married the painter Sir John Lavery in 1910 and became a well-known figure in London society. Her portrait was incorporated into her husband's design for Irish pound notes. There were the Duchess of Marlborough, the Queen of Spain, Lady Elizabeth Bowes-Lyon who was to become Queen, Princess Victoria, the Duchess of Sutherland, Mrs Dudley Ward who was seen everywhere with the Prince of Wales, and Mrs Ogden Mills, one of his hostesses in the U.S.A.

Bridging the gap between aristocrat and popular figure, Lady Diana Cooper was the daughter of the Duke of Rutland, a Red Cross nurse from the war, and the star of Max Reinhardt's *The*

Miracle. A natural bohemian with a great appetite for life, she captured the public imagination, and her delicious blonde beauty together with the pastel colours she always wore were much copied. *Vogue* showed her portrait by Ambrose McEvoy, and her photograph taken by Bertram Park on the announcement of her marriage to Duff Cooper of the Grenadier Guards. Thousands of factory girls turned out to see her wedding.

Society life was much the same on both sides of the Channel, with lunches, art shows, theatre, concerts, cocktails, dancing, fancy dress balls, dinners. In London Dame Nellie Melba was singing at the Albert Hall, Madame Suggia playing the cello, John Goss singing, and Stravinsky performed at Wigmore Hall. According to *Vogue*'s critic the audience was full of 'poseurs and sycophants'. Under the headline 'Humours and Irrelevancies of the Nursery Music of Igor Stravinsky' he wrote, 'The first was a quasi-barbaric dance, only a few bars in length, but long enough, or short enough, to make people smile openly; at the second people laughed; at the third, a very solemn and ominous composition, people laughed still more.'

The first public appearance of *Façade* in 1923 brought the Sitwells into *Vogue* for the first time with a cautiously favourable review by Gerald Cumberland. Hidden behind a curtain painted by Frank Dobson, Edith Sitwell 'half sang, half shouted' her musical poetry through a Sengerphone. 'Her voice, beautiful in tone, full, resonant and clear, could, with effort, be heard above the decorative din of the music' by William Walton. This is Osbert Sitwell's own description of the reception: 'The front rows,

3. Shining at a private view, drawn by Fish.
4. Lady Lavery, 1916.
5. Tamara Karsavina in Caucasian costume, 1920

6. Lillah McCarthy in the dress and setting by the Omega Workshops for Israel Zangwill's farce *Too Much Money*, 1918.

Hoppé

Instead

6

Hugh Cecil

especially, manifested their contempt and rage, and, albeit a good deal of applause countered the hissing . . . nevertheless the atmosphere was so greatly and so evidently hostile that at the end of the performance several members of the audience came behind the curtain to warn my sister not to leave the platform until the crowd had dispersed.' The first book reviews in the magazine discussed David Garnett's *Lady into Fox*, Michael Arlen's *These Charming People*, D. H. Lawrence's *Kangaroo*, Clive Bell's *On British Freedom* and Vita Sackville-West's *Grey Wethers*.

Vogue's reception of contemporary painting was far from adventurous. Modigliani, Matisse, Picasso and Vlaminck were found 'disappointing', but clearly worrying. 'Wanted,' wrote the critic, 'a revival of national art. The artists . . . foregathered in their little coteries, apart from the world, ply their esoteric mysteries more and more out of touch and sympathy with the great Heart of the People,' and he concluded, damningly, 'The ultimate standard of art must be the breadth of its appeal.' He turned with relief to Sickert: 'One is glad and grateful to have been given this opportunity to study the work of one of the most honest, original and talented of English painters.' *Vogue* showed two wartime etchings of Nevinson, *The Road to Ypres* and *Flooded Trench on the Yser*; Nevinson remarked, 'the public is more interested in the war than it is in art.' All the leading painters and sculptors appeared in *Vogue*, and the more academic their approach the better reviewed they were. For the guidance of readers, *Vogue* produced a humourous guide illustrated by Fish, 'Shining at a Private View': suggested useful phrases were 'What rhythmic movement!' 'What green! What red! What yellow!' or failing anything else, 'How very brave.' Marie Laurençin, Laura Knight and Nina Hamnett were the women painters *Vogue* preferred, and Marie Laurençin was to draw covers for the magazine in the 1920s. In the field of applied arts, furniture from the Omega Workshop was shown, simple chairs and chests painted in confused colours described by a contemporary as being 'like a dragon's miscarriage'.

The greatest influence of all on fashion was the great and continuing inspiration of the Russian ballet. It was one consolation for the Russian Revolution that it had left half the Imperial Ballet permanently exiled abroad. Osbert Sitwell in *Great Morning* wrote, 'decoration was in the air . . . the currents that showed were mostly foreign, and reached life through the theatre . . . every chair-cover, every lamp-shade, every cushion reflected the Russian Ballet, the Grecian or Oriental visions of Bakst and Benois.' The barbaric beauty of the costumes and settings, the dancing of Karsavina, Lopokova, Pavlova, Nijinsky, Massine and the music of Rimsky-Korsakov, Balakirev, Debussy, Tchaikovsky combined in the most majestic and romantic of escapist fantasies. There was some doubt from *Vogue*'s theatre critic as to how one should react to them: 'There is really something a little incongruous in the Russian Ballet serving as a popular entertainment in a country which has begun to rage against wealth and leisure', and more doubts as to the audience's understanding of it: 'It is useless to pretend that the thousands who throng to see these ballets have the remotest idea as to what they really represent or signify.'

There was no fashion designer who had not been set off in a new direction by the Russian ballet, but perhaps those most influenced were Poiret, who took the whole thing in at a gulp, Callot, Dœuillet, Lucile, Redfern, Idare and Chanel in her embroideries.

1. Slav influence: white
crepe de chine dress with
beaded waist, 1921.
2. Lucile's marguerite costume
for the Ziegfeld Follies, 1919.
3. Tea gown of gold tissue, 1919.

LUCILE

Geometric prints, trellised and striped furs, silver and gold lace, brilliant linings, bead and silk embroidery, velvets and furs, boots, cockades and storms of feathers, glittering dragonfly lingerie and butterfly evening dresses with trains and wing sleeves, all that was most beautiful and extraordinary in Oriental fashion came straight off Diaghilev's stage. Until his death in 1929 there was nothing on the stage to rival the excitement his seasons aroused, although the original company had long since dispersed. The ballerinas naturally appeared very often in *Vogue*, and the next generation of dancers that had learnt from them: Mlle Rambert, who had learnt eurhythmics with Jacques Dalcroze and classical ballet with Nijinsky, and Madame Donnet, who founded the Ballet Philosophique. The passion for every kind of dancing was in the air. *Vogue* showed the schools of Marian Morgan and Margaret Morris, and photographed Isadora Duncan in America, with barefoot Woodland Dancers 'all born in Arcadia' responding freely to the open fields and sky.

In violent reaction to hard times and sensible clothes, the longing for escape and glamour brought a wave of fantastic fashion follies into *Vogue*. The theatrical came into the forefront of fashion. The modern woman in the gaiter suit turned into a beautiful barbarian in the evening, in a costume that might have been designed by Bakst. All Paris came out with evening dresses in tiers of shot tulle or silver lace and tea-rose brocade, with Turkish trousers of looped chiffon, lamé jackets, wings and trains of sparkling chiffon, turbans and fountains of ostrich feathers. Lucile's evening dresses, négligées and tea gowns are hardly different from her designs for the Ziegfeld Follies, and *Vogue* is filled with Egyptian gandouras, Caucasian waistcoats over dresses of metal bead embroidery, chains of gold and nets of pearls, butterfly sleeves of golden gauze, earrings dropping to the breast and head-dresses of shooting feathers. Oriental tea gowns, originally made to be worn between hunting and dressing for dinner, were worn now for informal dinners. Ida Rubinstein's dress by Worth looked like the saris of the Indian dancer Roshanara – who turned out to

be English. The Oriental influence came to an end in 1923 with a splendid 'Chinese Ball' in Paris, the French couturiers competing to dress the leading society figures.

If the greatest single influence on fashion was Oriental, the second was American. Both were enjoyed as a relief from wartime problems and restrictions, The prestige of America was never higher. The States had lost one-fiftieth of proportionate British losses in the war, yet had the glory of deciding the issue and bringing an end to the struggle. America came out of the war richer than before, whereas France and Britain were impoverished, Germany bankrupt, Austria destitute. Americans gave the lead in all social fashions, and brought jazz, films, coloured nail polish, rouge, cocktails, smoking and money into Europe. British *Vogue* was full of American social life, American cars, Venetian palaces erected

VIONNET

4. The Chinese Bal de l'Opéra in Paris, 1923: The
Duchess de Gramont costumed by Vionnet.

in Florida, American architect's houses, American resorts. Tourists
from all over the States arrived in Britain from 1919 to buy up
books, art, and sometimes houses wholesale. Agecroft Hall in
Lancashire and Great Lodge in Essex were transported brick by
brick and rebuilt in America. In return we got syncopated music,
and what to do to it – the Baleta, the Maxina, the Twinkle, the Jog
Trot, the Vampire, the Missouri Walk, the Elfreda. These new
dances were practised in the restaurant-clubs that opened when the
Licensing Act of 1921 allowed people to drink and dine at the same
place. There was the Kit-Cat Club where you might see the Prince
of Wales, the '43 where you might see Augustus John, Carpentier

Rehbinder

the boxer, or Chang the dope-gang king. To show how all the new
dances should be done there were the Castles, Americans naturally,
the first of a line of polished dancing couples that would include
Maurice and Leonora Hughes, and Fred and Adèle Astaire. The
Castles danced in hotels, cabarets and private soirées as well as on
the stage. Mrs Vernon Castle, beautiful, vivacious and chic,
appeared countless times in *Vogue*, lending her charm and elegance
to fur coats, tennis dresses, riding habits, evening dresses, wedding
dresses and every shape of hat.

Whatever was a source of inspiration and energy in any field was
caught and turned into fashion in Paris – even when in 1923 Lord
Carnarvon discovered the unrifled tomb of Tutankhamen at Luxor,
and Ancient Egypt suddenly became fashionable. From 1916 to at
least the mid-twenties the most important feature in any issue of
Vogue was the 'Seen in Paris' fashion lead, and it was the great
French designers whose clothes were drawn, photographed in the
Bois, and seen on actresses, film stars and socialites the world over.
Nine of the couture houses had kept open during the war, even
presenting their collections while Big Bertha was showering the
city with shells, or when the guns were audible not fifty miles away.
Clothes were generally shown on mannikins, and in 1918 *Vogue*
wrote, 'We were amused because the mannikins wore hats which
were selected to suit their dresses, and consequently looked like
real women of the world whom one might meet on a walk in the
Bois'. Women ordered their clothes from sketches, or from examples shown on inanimate figures, and it was a great advance in
1919 when houses began to show their clothes on women who
walked and turned around to demonstrate the look in action.

Best-established couture houses in Paris during the war were
Worth, Doucet, Lanvin, Paquin and Poiret. Charles Frederick
Worth had set the pattern for the *haute couture* by becoming dressmaker to the Empress Eugénie. He made for her the crinolines we see
in Winterhalter portraits, the first ever tailor-made suit, introduced
the train and then the bustle. His house carried on with splendid

9

and luxurious fashion. Jacques Doucet who trained Poiret, made restrained and elegant clothes, and was a connoisseur and patron of the arts. He was one of the first to buy paintings by the Impressionists, Picasso, and to collect Negro sculpture. Paul Poiret burst onto the scene in the first decade of the century, a megalomaniac, a dazzling designer of theatrical costume, and an inconsistent fashion dictator who urged women to abandon corsets on the one hand and on the other threw a lassoo round their ankles, in the form of hobble skirts. Trained by Doucet, he dressed Ida Rubinstein, Isadora Duncan, Eleanora Duse, Sarah Bernhardt, and in 1919 was making a comeback after a disastrous war (a law had to be passed specially for his benefit, forbidding soldiers to design their own uniforms). As the twenties approached his importance waned: he was never quite able to translate what was successful on the stage into clothes in which post-war women would be comfortable. He was the first couturier to launch perfumes and open a house for interior decoration; he initiated live models for fashion shows, the sunken bath, nail polish in Paris, and the private bar.

Jeanne Lanvin's reputation was made by the clothes she designed for her daughter, who became Comtesse de Polignac. Her love of Botticelli, stained glass windows and Impressionist paintings was reflected in her romantic clothes. She dressed the Princesse de Lucinge and Sasha Guitry's four wives.

Madame Paquin dressed the Queens of Belgium, Spain and Portugal and the queens of the *demi-monde*. A good businesswoman, she was elected chairman of the *haute couture* of Paris. Her contemporaries the Callot sisters introduced the fashion for lace blouses and silver and gold lamé evening dresses, and had to their credit trained Madeleine Vionnet, perhaps the greatest of all

Lachman

3   Delphi

the designers mentioned yet, who was a kind of architect of fashion. She designed a unique dress for each woman rather than a look, studying the client's proportions first on a wooden mannikin made to the exact dimensions. She chose the fabric and the line for the client's looks and character, and then cut with a mathematical precision. She invented cutting on the bias which changed the fit of clothes forever. Her clothes look nothing off, but come to life on the body. She only enjoyed dressing beautiful women, and didn't even care to dress herself particularly well: 'I was always short and I hate small women.' Her favourite client was the most elegant woman in Paris, the Duchesse de Gramont.

Gabrielle Chanel was the other great designer whose influence still affects fashion today. From a poor family, she cut up her aunt's curtains to dress a doll, and grew up into a designer with an instinct for what was just about to happen in fashion. A realist, she came up with just the thing people wanted to wear time and time again. 'Chanel' came to mean a whole look from sailor hat down to beige and black slingback shoes, even the scent in the air. She opened a millinery shop in the rue Cambon, nursed in a Deauville hospital during the war, and opened her own boutique afterwards. She made jersey chic in simple grey and navy dresses that were quite unlike anything women had worn before. She made blue pullovers and pleated skirts for the women who were replacing men in offices and factories, turned sports clothes into everyday clothes, made trousers elegant, and gave costume jewellery an intrinsic value of its own.

In London there were branches of Worth, Redfern and Paquin, there was Reville & Rossiter, and there was Lucile, the only famous house which made clothes specifically for smart London life. Lady

4
PAQUIN   Taponier

1. Chic interior, 1916: the rose and gray Paris dining room of the actress Eve Lavallière, decorated by Jils Garrine.
2. Ida Rubinstein, 1918. She came to Paris with Diaghilev and stayed. With her own company she staged gigantic spectacles incorporating ballet, opera and tragedy. For *Le Martyre de Saint Sébastien* she took the lead, D'Annunzio wrote the libretto, Bakst designed the costumes and sets, and Debussy composed the score. In the most fantastic trains and hats that Poiret could devise, she would walk down the middle of roads stopping the traffic all the way.
3. Society at L'Oasis, Poiret's nightclub in his garden, 1919.
4. Lina Cavalieri in pink and silver evening dress, 1916.

1

Lallie Charles

Duff Gordon ran her Lucile establishments in London, Paris, New York and Chicago. She closed the Paris branch during the war, returning from America to reopen in 1918. The sister of Elinor Glyn, she trained Molyneux. Lucile dresses were Oriental arabesques, dragonflies, pure enchantment: they were leisure clothes for escapists.

By 1920, the woman they dressed had a different shape. The hourglass figure from before the war had changed into a suppressed bosom and a slimmer, straighter torso. Pre-war underclothes had consisted of a bust-to-thigh whalebone corset with suspenders laced up over a drawstring shift and French drawers, and they were worn from the age of thirteen. After the war, with its shortages of butter and sugar, its work at the factory, its hockey and tennis, this was gradually simplified to a shapeless camisole bra and a girdle which reached from just above the waist to cover the hips. An American tourist in London was heard to say, 'Men won't dance with you if you're all laced up', and there were plenty of dances you couldn't do in corsets.

A curious anomaly in the simplified state of underclothes were the bathing suits worn right into the middle of the twenties – elaborate wrapover jersey dresses and baggy pants to the knee, or petal skirts and embroidered knickerbockers, worn over a brassière-cum-corset in rubber sheeting, with a turban on the head.

Sports clothes were the thin end of the wedge in making all kinds of fashion easier to move and work in. Comparing the elaborate fantasies of evening clothes with the pullover and pleated skirt of the golfer, or the cotton smock and trousers of the gardener, it's difficult to realize they were contemporary. Out of sports clothes came a garment which women could make at home, and which became the bread-and-butter fashion of the British – the jersey. It was new in 1919, and by the following year everyone had it: men soon followed with pullovers. These brisk and businesslike fashions, rather than the romantic extravagant ones, showed the direction of fashion for the following decade.

Women's looks had changed, too. '. . . and I heard, though I did not, myself, witness this,' reported *Vogue* in 1919, 'that during luncheon, at a well-known restaurant recently, a mutual friend of ours – it is not necessary to mention any name – was seen, not only to powder her nose in full view of everybody, but to redden her lips!' During the war, most women wore a touch of powder and a little eyelash dye, but nothing more until American tourists began flooding into Europe after the war, bringing with them lipstick, rouge, mascara and eyebrow pencil. Poiret was the first couturier to market his own scents and cosmetics: powder, lotion, cream, talcum, coloured nail polish, make-up base, rouge, eye shadow and stage make-up, but these were ahead of their time. Barbara Cartland describes herself in 1919: 'fair hair fluffed over the ears . . . red lips, subject of much criticism and many arguments, and a clear skin helped by chalk-white face powder. There were only three shades obtainable, dead white, yellow and almost brown!' The important beauty houses of Elizabeth Arden, Cyclax and Helena Rubinstein were among the first to advertise in British *Vogue*, but their products were complexion creams, not yet make-up.

Vogue's wartime issues show a marked difference between the looks of musical comedy actresses and society ladies: women on the stage, particularly Americans, knew how to use make up and weren't ashamed of wearing it. But everyone's hair, when photographed hatless, shows roughened, broken ends from too many permanents or too much marcel waving with hot tongs. Everyone wanted as much hair and as many curls as possible, and in 1917 *Vogue* showed a page of London actresses in the style of the young ideal, Mary Pickford. The higher and higher hats needed a good

Bertram Park

cushion of hair for anchorage, and there were advertisements in every issue for postiches and toupées 'absolutely impossible to detect'. Henna was still the only reliable way to brighten the colour of your hair, for although peroxide had been used for ten years, its effect on the hair was difficult to gauge and dangerous to repeat too often. In 1922 beauty suddenly became a fully fledged business, with the first ever articles on beauty farms and electrical massage. As the slim silhouette took over, the emphasis was on sport and beauty exercises.

After the curls and the Grecian chignons that were part and parcel of the fashion for all kinds of big hats, the small fitted cloche brought in the bob, which became the 'shingle' or the 'bingle' of the twenties, and finally the Eton crop. 'My dear, your hair is too beautiful,' says a bobbed girl to her long-haired friend in *Punch*. 'You really ought to have it cut off.' The first bob appears in *Vogue* in 1918, but this is two or three years before it became popular. By 1923 Benito is drawing a dozen variations of the same cut.

In 1923 *Vogue* showed the first sunlamp, as was to be found in the surgical wards of Princess Mary's Hospital – and a healthy tan began to be fashionable.

1. Society women are almost innocent of make up during the war years, and do not pluck their eyebrows. Hair is damaged from constant curling with hot tongs.
2. When Somerset Maugham first met Gladys Cooper in 1910 he said, 'She's the loveliest thing I've ever seen in my life.' Golden-haired, blue eyed, irresistibly the English rose, she was perfection in Reville's early costumes, and later in Molyneux: she almost always has an ostrich feather fan or boa at this time.
3. Here, Cherry Constant, from the chorus of *Theodore and Co.* at the Gaiety Theatre, 1916.
4. Black taffeta and embroidered tan silk bathing dresses belted over bloomers with bandanna handkerchiefs for turbans, 1920.

Bertram Park

1

ADY DIANA COOPER

n *Vogue* Bakst said, 'Diana is the ideal woman, the belle of the hour', talking of the Goddess but intending a compliment to Lady Diana, described in another issue as 'untarnishable, the loveliest young Englishwoman of her generation'. Loved, admired and envied for three generations, she is a person of rare qualities, her captivating warmth and quick wit enforced by great energy and iron discipline. Always the centre of attention but quite unspoilt, she is naturally bohemian and adventurous and can take on any role — hostess, mechanic, farmer, author, ambassador, mother, actress, builder. Third and youngest daughter of the Duke of Rutland, she grew up at Belvoir Castle. The Duchess brought her up along highly unusual aesthetic lines. As a child she was always dressed in black velvet, as a debutante she wore grey and beige instead of the usual white and pink. At Ascot she was noticeable among the rosy straws in a black picture hat with sheaves of gold and silver wheat, and when she appeared in a group of debutantes dressed as swans for a pageant, she was the single black swan. Against parental opposition she married Mr Duff Cooper of the Grenadier Guards, and her role as the Madonna in Max Reinhardt's spectacle *The Miracle* made her a popular heroine in two continents. During the war she ran her own farm single-handed. An entry in her diary reads, 'The Pig Family Hutchinson is in splendid fatness and should make me a nice profit . . . I spend a lot of my time asphyxiated by the smell and bent double inside the stye shovelling their dung.' She appears in *Vogue* regularly, and her changes of appearance reflect the course of fashion since 1919.

. 1919.
. With her photograph
s the Madonna, 1926.
. 1930.
. 1923.
. 1937.
. With her portrait by
Ambrose McEvoy, at
ome in Little Venice, 1963.

2 CHANEL   Curtis Moffat and Olivia Wyndham

5

Cecil Beaton

6

1 POIRET

IRENE CASTLE

Irene Castle, and Vernon, her husband, were world-famous dancing partners, their most famous dances the tango, the one-step and the Castle Walk. Vernon Castle started his career as a vaudeville contortionist called The String Bean. They came from New York to Paris, and were nearly down and out when they were offered a job in cabaret at the Café de Paris. Dining at the restaurant as guests of the management the night before the job began, they were recognized by a Russian count and persuaded to perform an impromptu dance: it became part of their act for them to rise from the tables among the audience. A year or two later they were international celebrities, and returned to New York to open a combined restaurant and dancing school, Castle House. 'Castles in the Air' was the name of the nightclub over a theatre where they performed in the evening. By the time they were appearing in a revue called 'Watch your Step' they were earning $6,000 a week, and owned a country house in Manhasset, where Vernon Castle played polo and kept sporting dogs. When he was killed at Fort Worth in Texas in 1918, the result of a plane crash, Irene Castle continued her career alone, never dancing with another partner. She was the embodiment of 'modern', with her boyish, healthy looks, her hair which she bobbed early on, and her crisp, bold movements — the direct opposite of Mary Pickford's simpering ringleted baby looks.

1. In one of her dancing costumes
   for *Miss 1917*, a New York revue.
2. 1921.
3. 1918.

Scalioni

THE DUCHESSE DE GRAMONT

Madame Vionnet said of her, 'She was a real model, tall and beautiful. When I was making a dress, I had only to ask her to come and try it on and I knew exactly where it was wrong.' Formerly the Princess Maria Ruspoli of Italy, she became a famous Paris hostess who was said to have entertained 90,000 people in her lifetime.

1
VIONNET

Steichen

3

Génia Reinberg

LANVIN

The new chemise arrives, pioneered by Lanvin, Worth and Paquin, cut loose and full, belted under the bosom. Diet and exercise are recommended for the new silhouette, which is flat front and back, with gathered pleats under the arms. The chemise is voted 'practical, being perfectly adapted to the demands of modern life . . . comfortable, graceful and economical — for the number of these simple frocks that are made in the seclusion of the sewing-room to be worn later with the air of having issued from les Grandes Maisons is one of the secrets of the age. Moreover it is smart.' For the morning, it is made in serge or bure, for the afternoon velvet, for evening satin or in Worth's tinted tulles and muslins. There's a new 'georgette' satin, satin top, cotton base. Premet's chemise is shortened in front and worn over a petticoat trimmed in fur. Gabrielle Chanel,

'known the world over for her sports frocks, is this season making evening gowns — a straight chemise of black charmeuse, embroidered with gold irises from waist to hem'. At home, a more practical version of the chemise is advertised by Goochs.

The coats are the thickest and warmest in years. 'The three

dimensions of the top-coat are fixed,' says *Vogue*, 'they are the highest and longest and fullest possible.' Jackets of suits rise from the knee to finger length. *Vogue* features the wardrobes of two stars — Florence Walton with her new suits from Dœuillet and Callot, Lina Cavalieri with her taffeta and rose faille evening dresses from Paquin. Hemlines clear the ankles, fur trims everything. Some of the best suits are in jersey — the colours are 'robin's egg blue, nile green, orchid, lilac, pale rose and oyster white'. Sweaters are like suit jackets, trimmed in fur and belted over the full ankle-length skirt.

The hat is as necessary a part of the outdoor costume as shoes, and is only taken off in private houses. Babies wear knitted caps, children felt or straw cloches, grandmothers toques and turbans. To complement your hat, it's new to wear a necklace of ruffled tulle.

Left: LUCILE Black satin at home, 1917; photograph Thomas Fall.

1916

1

Rita
Martin

LUCILE

2

LUCILE

3

20

ANDRÉ GROULT

Hoppé

THE
Arrol-Johnston
CAR

The Admiration of Everyone.

Arrol-Johnston Ltd., Makers of Cars, Dumfries.

Ira Hill

1. Gertie Millar in furs: photo Rita Martin.
2. Lucile suit.
3. Lucile's striped taffeta peg-top evening dress.
4. Fortuny dress.
5. André Groult 'sailor' in seal brown velvet.
6. Lanvin's tulle necklace.

1917

'Though Shops Have No Windows and Stocks are Underground, Paris Shows That Her Supreme Creative Qualities Remain Quite Unimpaired'

In spite of terrible pea-souper fogs, Paris produces a new spring silhouette out of the Russian ballet influence. The tonneau, or barrel skirt, often has peg top drapes and wings over the hips. At the same time couturiers are designing slim new day looks with a minimum of fabric: 'The war is responsible for so many things — for the new narrow skirts, for the colour of our frocks, for the shape of our hats, and for the texture (and price) of our gloves and shoes.'

It's a year of charity fetes and high hats, and everyone has an insatiable appetite for fur. You wrap furs round you however you can afford them, in coats or stoles, or you take a leaf out of Chanel's book and add bands of fur to jackets and hems. For evening, the Callot sisters introduce spun silver and gold tissues. Lucile's dresses and negligées show a new attention to sleeves. A gathered peplum makes the double-tiered evening dress the star of the year.

LUCILE

SPORTS

1. Snowproof Engadine skiing outfit.
2. Personal windscreen screwed onto a metal shoulder-frame, all packed away into a yellow leather case on arrival.
3. Green tweed gaiter suit.
4. Beige brocade and crepe evening dress with fur.
5. Jane Renouardt in Callot's tiered dress of cream tulle, silver and gold.

CALLOT

23

1917

1. Black-figured pale blue taffeta.
2. Black velvet dress and jacket, black satin waistcoat.

BARREL SKIRTS

DŒUILLET

The "JEANNETTE." Semi-evening or Afternoon Gown in best quality Chiffon Taffetas and Ninon de Soie, cut on most becoming lines and suitable for matron's wear. The bodice has sleeves of ninon and silk, vest of fine cream French lace, and finished at waist with handsome girdle and tassels in dull gold cord. Skirt has deep flounce of taffetas with top of ninon over dull gold insertion. In black, grey, nigger, and navy. **9** Gns.

The "GEORGETTE." Charming Afternoon Gown in good quality Georgette. Bodice embroidered in dull gold with large collar of flesh-pink Ninon de Soie, smart waistbelt of dull gold cord and metallic clasps. Skirt is finished with deep hem of Satin Meteor. In grey, saxe, navy, nigger, rose, and black. Large and medium sizes. **6½** Gns.

The "LOLETTE." Smart Afternoon or Semi-evening Gown in best quality Chiffon Taffetas. Bodice of Ninon de Soie veiled over dull gold metal lace. Skirt arranged with pleating of silk, trimmed Marabout. In nigger, brown, and black. **7½** Gns.

THESE three charming Gowns are indicative of the New Models for Spring. They are smart and distinctive without being in any way extravagant.

WRITE FOR OUR SPRING CATALOGUE

It is a guide to economy, and may be had Post Free for the asking.

Peter Robinson's Oxford Street

Peter Robinson Ltd.

24

2 DŒUILLET

THE SLIM SILHOUETTE

LANVIN

JENNY

WORTH

LEWIS

25

1918

ARNOLD

'Not since the war began have the couturiers produced so many good models as have appeared this year, models that were conceived and stitched to the accompaniment of the boom of "Big Bertha".'

Chanel's fur-trimmed jersey costumes are making her a fortune. Fur trims everything — even black satin evening dresses. Belted tunics make double tiers of skirts, but the slim silhouette is taking over from last year's tonneau.

In a year of enforced economy blouses and waistcoats are becoming popular as additions that help you ring the changes. Washable frocks are acceptable, but 'there are times when one prefers to have economy inconspicuous . . . conceal the fact that your frock is washable with a detachable panel and girdle of grosgrain ribbon'. There's a new 'transformation' dress, for instance, 'a navy blue serge coat-dress with a front of light georgette crepe and what seems to be an underskirt of the same colour. One removes the dark serge frock and — presto — one is wearing a light blue frock with the same georgette crepe front. In this way the Parisienne is dressed for all day in one frock.'

The Comtesse de Talleyrand and the Comtesse de Fitz-James wear black tailored suits with handkerchief linen blouses through which you can see their strings of pearls. The Princesse de Broglie is noticed in a plain dress of a dark brown silk with a knotted sash, brown stockings and shoes, a brown hat with a grosgrain band.

Big-brimmed hats fly with chiffon veils, not only for motoring but for 'walking in a stiff breeze', to protect the complexion. More formal hats climb tall with quills, and with plumes of paradise and ostrich. As straw gets short, Paris milliners turn to silk and ribbon. The scope of sweaters has become wider over the last two years, and firms like Poirette are making beautiful and imaginative silk sweaters, with sailor collars, interesting textures, good use of colour.

As Paris becomes colder and bleaker, and the price of coal rises to 300 francs a ton, furs become more desirable and harder to get. The status symbol of the moment is to be completely wrapped in leopardskin, but for the many who can't afford it, 'There are nine and sixty ways of trimming suits these days, and every single furry one is right.' This is the first year of the craze for monkey fur, which appears as a ragged black fringe on hats, hems, muffs, and veils.

'Sometimes the pelts employed in these fashions are easily recognised; but it is best not to inquire too closely into the origin of some of the strange skins which have been cut into strips or folded into collars to trim many of the smartest frocks. They bear such concealing names as 'Jacquerette' or 'Péruvienne', and, while many women of curious disposition would like to know why, if they restrain their curiosity they may have more pleasure in wearing their furs.'

1. American Mrs Alexander
Bache Pratt in furs, with a
fashionable Alsatian.
2. Chanel's fur-
trimmed jersey.
3. Paquin's monkey-
fringed dress and
coat.

REVILLE

2
CHANEL

3
PAQUIN

27

HATS

Lallie Charles

BRADLEY

MARIA GUY

1. Margaret Bannerman in a ribbon hat by Bradley.
2. Pewter tissue hat with jet beads and black paradise plumes. 'The effect is one of extreme elegance and unerring taste.'
3. Grey and fawn swathed crepe de chine, fawn quills.
4. Turban from Maria Guy in Russian sable and white ostrich feathers.
5. Tasselled mauve and white knitted sweater-suit.
6. Navy gabardine dress masquerading as a suit.

POIRETTE

5

6

de Meyer

DOEUILLET

1. Faith Celli in striped
ninon.
2. Dœuillet's is the
shortest new skirt.
3. Delysia looking
curious in a petalled
evening dress.
4 and 5. Both sides of
the picture — an
afternoon dress of
black charmeuse.

Gaby Deslys at Longchamp with Max Dearly, the actor: her foulard dress draped with chiffon. Famous for her glamour and her fantastic towering feather headdresses — she was called 'a human aviary' — she made no secret of her scandalous private life. Declaring 'Money is woman's only bulwark against the world', she amassed a fabulous collection of jewels from her lovers, including a rope of pearls as long as herself from King Manuel of Portugal. When she died she left her money to the poor of Marseilles.

There's racing at Longchamp, and in Paris and London the season starts up again. At home there's professional cricket, yachting at Cowes, polo, and hunt balls in spite of a lack of male partners. At the Derby the favourite, Panther, comes in fourth. Dame Nellie Melba sings, the Russian ballet dances. At Wimbledon Mlle Suzanne Lenglen defeats Mrs Lambert Chambers. In Paris the city is packed, taxis are available again, and there are flowerstalls by the river. Poiret returns from the army to open up his salon, and with it a nightclub, L'Oasis, famous for not playing jazz. There is ragtime to dance to, or the new pasa doble and women dance in swaying fringes of beads or feathers.

Summer weekends include motoring, swimming and tennis. This is *Vogue's* list of equipment for a summer weekend: travelling dress, simple suit of wool jersey tweed or homespun with a smart tailored blouse. For walking, golf, motoring, a simple sports hat, low-heeled shoes. Face veil for walking in a breeze, sailing or motoring. Extra chiffon veil. Pleated skirt with a white blouse and coloured jumper for walking. Plain straw or felt hat, heavy white silk stockings, white buckskin shoes. Dark clocked stockings with grey or tan shoes for a change, a wool or silk scarf. Day frock, sports dress. Afternoon dress in organdie or silk. Suede or kid house shoes, stockings to match, hat. Two evening dresses for a Saturday to Monday, three for a

Friday to Monday. Dinner gown of satin or chiffon with a train, a less formal dance frock.

For the first time couturier collections are shown on living models. Women aren't content to choose from a sketch or a doll any more — they want to see how the clothes will move. In October a new house emerges, Molyneux. Captain Molyneux, who served his apprenticeship at Lucile in London, shows glamorous black evening dresses and ostrich feathers.

Formal afternoon dressing and sports suits are poles apart, but Chanel, Martial et Armand and Lanvin are beginning to find a large market between the two. The silhouette becomes slimmer; Lanvin's throwback crinolines are the exception. The summer uniform is a pale garden frock, the essential accessory a parasol, and a feather fan for evening. All evening dresses are fringed for dancing, with monkey fur, ostrich, steel beads, velvet ribbons or tassels of silk.

Hats have a new width at the sides, brims of pleated tulle, tricorne shapes, veiling . . . evening headdresses are made of ostrich feathers glycerined to make them heavy and drooping. 'At the theatre a handsome Englishwoman wore her dark hair wrapped round her small shapely head. She ornamented it with a novel diamond tiara, the centre a plume of black glycerine ostrich of which the rib was encrusted with diamonds'.

Henri Manuel

MOLYNEUX

1. Fringed black satin shawl.
2. Mistinguett in a black velvet
cape lined with stripes.
3 and 5. Day and evening of
the new house, Molyneux.
4. Sports clothes — navy
blazer, cream skirt, red
sailor hat; cream blouse
and skirt for tennis.

MOLYNEUX

LUCILE

6. A new bloused look
from Paris.
7. Black satin and crepe, net
ruffles, black straw
hat trimmed with
glycerine ostrich.
8. Gertrude Lawrence in a
tricorne by Edythe Brown.
9. Lanvin's new bouffant
crinolines are the exception
to the slim silhouette.

6
LANVIN

8
EDYTHE BROWN

9
LANVIN

33

REDFERN

REVILLE

The Comtesse d'Hautpoul by the polo field.

de Givenchy

Chanel's silhouette, staying close to the lines of the uncorseted figure, begins to make the bouffant skirts of Lanvin look old-fashioned, and the follies of Poiret too theatrical. Vionnet makes dresses that are works of art, but Chanel is more commercial. Everything she does makes news — the first quilted coat, the narrow crepe de chine dress inside a cage of tulle, and the suntan which she cultivates. *Vogue* publishes three pages of holiday beach clothes, still designed to protect you from too much sun, and three more on the backs of evening dresses, which begin at the waist. The one-year-old house of Molyneux proves itself with glamorous evening looks, and sets a fashion for hats weighted with feathers, ostrich feather fans from the Folies Bergères, bandeaux and yards of pearls. The most useful and easy way to dress is in knitted jackets or jumpers and pleated skirts, pioneered by Chanel and now generally accepted.

Hats spread out with ostrich feathers or tulle petals, and for evening there are diadems or bandeaux of silver leaves or gold tissue.

1920

CHANEL   1

De Givenchy

2

De Givenchy

ELSPETH PHELPS

3

5

6

4

VIONNET

CHANEL

7

MARGAINE LACROIX   de Meyer

1 and 2. The alternative
silhouettes.
3 and 6. Chanel's tulle bell
over a slim crepe de
chine dress.
4. Brown georgette crepe and
matching lace.
5. An English version of the
crinoline by Elspeth Phelps:
pink tulle with bands of skunk.
7. The sun is still something
from which to protect yourself
— in embroidered palest flesh
crepe.

MOLYNEUX 8

LUCILE

9

10

IRETTE

ELENID

8. The bare back — here Molyneux's crystal-beaded evening dress.
9. Draped satin by Molyneux.
10. Cécile Sorel in Lucile's tea gown of lavender and silver lamé.

1921

'The very smartest women seen during the morning promenade in the Bois, those who descend from a magnificent motor-car to walk for half an hour in the sunshine, wear strictly tailored Oxford grey suits absolutely plain, but with every accessory quite perfect'

Dresses are caught in naturally at the waist, and hems grow longer. Umbrellas or parasols are an essential part of the look. Lanvin produces a bright Riviera collection of Aztec embroideries, and Vionnet 'continues to make those "simple little things" — complex enough if one tries to copy them — and has her own distinctive way of utilizing fringe'. Fringes are everywhere: there are fringe sleeves, fringe hems, fringe cloaks.

'Owing to this craze for dancing, dining in restaurants where dancing takes place either during or after dinner has become very popular, and it is in such restaurants that one sees the newest clothes.' The newest are flat-chested and hemlines are any length, long and slender or bouffant and crinolined. Skirts drip handkerchief points to the floor, and *Vogue* shows a page of flame chiffon dresses by Ospovat, who dresses Lady Diana Cooper so beautifully.

The restaurant hat is a feather cartwheel, or a new favourite, the swagged hat, with a cascade of feathers or flowers falling over one shoulder. Reboux makes swags of cock feathers or flowers and fruit scattered on a chiffon streamer, Lewis adds tassels of chenille or jet, and Molyneux makes showers of glycerined ostrich feathers. The new motoring hat is a turban with long scarf ends to wear as a veil or a float.

'Most women at the present wear a very innocent sort of corset, which becomes more of a belt and less of a corset according to the suppleness of the figure for which it is designed. With some women, this is little more than a girdle to hold the stocking supporters; others like a bone back and front and even one

REVILLE   Navy serge costume and pleated fawn crepe petticoat.

over each hip. Hardly anyone goes further than this, and the corset is cut so that it gives support without restriction. Instead of tightening her bands, the woman who thinks that her figure is too generous now seeks some means of healthful reduction, and the change is one in

which we should all rejoice. Very tight clothes never did anything to disguise avoirdupois, just misplaced it. But the absolutely uncorseted laissez-allez effect is no longer the proper one. One should have the appearance of being comfortably supported.'

Rehbinder

1

OSPOVAT

2

MADELEINE ET MADELEINE   Rehbinder

1. Ospovat's flame chiffon with the year's uneven hemline.
2. White chiffon with crystal embroidery.

1. The Dolly sisters wearing fancy dress representing Ciro Pearls in which they won first prize at the Warriors' Day Ball, Covent Garden. They were Hungarian, originally Janzieska and Roszieska Deutch, known as Jenny and Rosie Dolly. They were almost identical, with black hair cut in fringes, and appeared in cabaret and on the stage. When Gordon Selfridge saw them at the Kit-Cat club he became infatuated with Jenny, on whom it is estimated he spent two million pounds between 1924 and 1931. He gave them the run of Selfridges and, more impressively, unlimited credit at his casinos in Le Touquet and Deauville. When Jenny won £40,000 and then lost £80,000 in a night, he sent her a diamond bracelet and Rosie a rope of pearls with a note, 'I hope this will make up for your losses last night, darling!' In the end, Jenny had to sell her jewellery and her château to pay her gambling debts. As Rosie married her third husband, she remarked, 'If this marriage doesn't take I will go into a nunnery', and her husband added, 'So will I!'

RENÉE

Brissaud

1

40

MERCIE McHARDY

Arjamand

LEWIS

Génia Reinberg

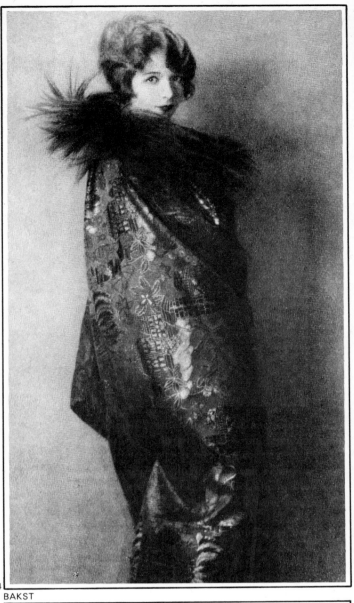

4 BAKST

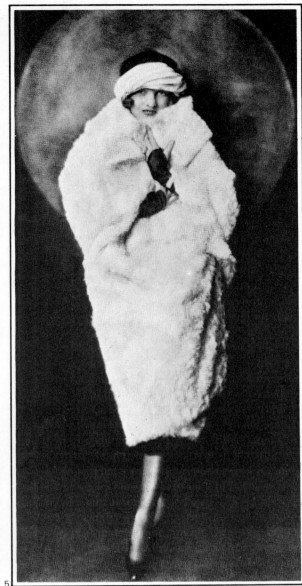

5

2. 'Mon mari — mon danseur': sketch by Brissaud, dance frock by Renée.
3. Duchess Sforza in Lewis's silver lace hat with glycerined ostrich feathers.
4. Ina Claire in a cloak of green and gold brocade designed by Bakst, with a monkey collar.
5. Leonora Hughes in a rough white caracul coat.
6. Bathing dress in crepe.
7. Summer frocks: lavender and white gingham, green-striped Japanese silk with a white silk blouse.

6

7

1922

REBOUX   Flowerpot of picot straw with cock feathers and roses: sketch by Helen Dryden.

'In their street models for the spring of 1922, the couturiers have evolved a real "Paris fashion", such as we used to have when the women in all the capitals of the world wore the same puffed sleeves at the same time'

It is the year of the peasant in Paris and London. Lanvin makes the Breton suit, short braided jacket with lots of small buttons, big white organdie collar turning down over a red satin bow, sailor hat or round straw on the head. It's a look that Chanel will take up and make her own, but this year she's selling her own version of the peasant look — black crepe de chine dresses and overblouses covered with bright Balkan embroidery. The new suits by Jean Patou and others have hiplength jackets flared or waisted over long narrow skirts, hats, mufflers and the new buckled shoe, the accessory of the year. At Molyneux, metallic brocade and monkey fur fringes on pale dresses; and everywhere, fantastic sleeves.

The year of the royal wedding brings Princess Mary's trousseau into *Vogue* item by item: 'Individual Taste Combined with Beauty of Material and Design Result in a Charming Trousseau for the Nation's Bride.' Patriotically British, it consists of designs from Reville and Handley Seymour, with hats by Millicent.

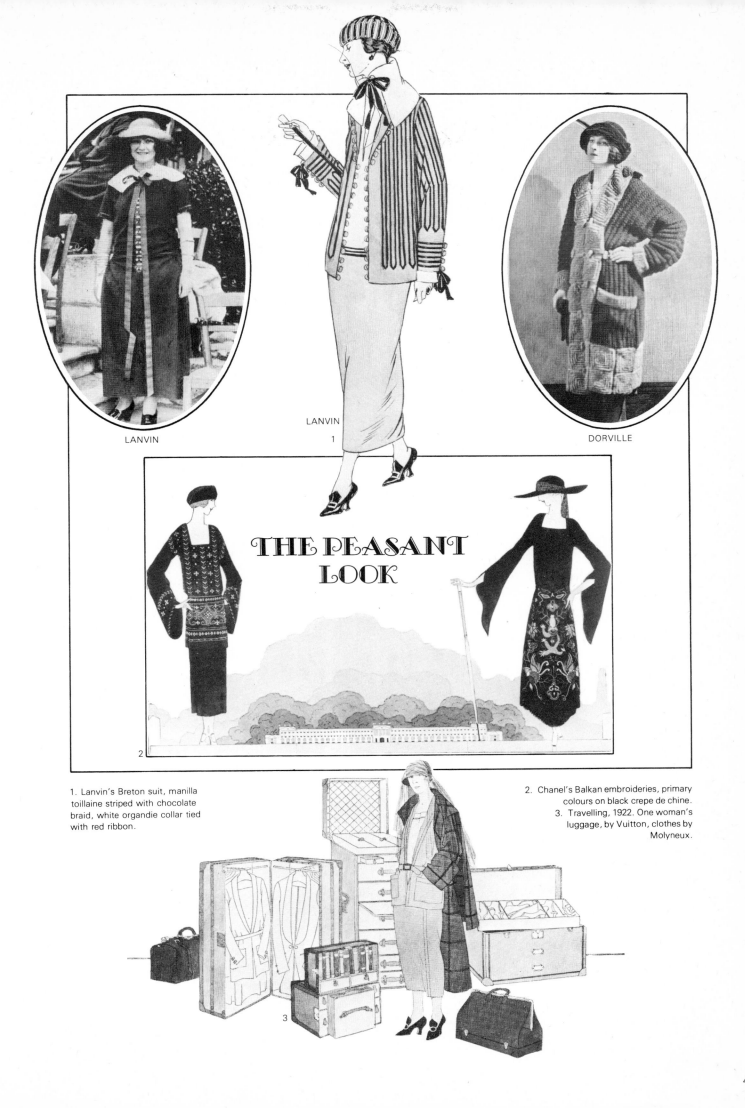

LANVIN

LANVIN
1

DORVILLE

THE PEASANT LOOK

2

1. Lanvin's Breton suit, manilla toillaine striped with chocolate braid, white organdie collar tied with red ribbon.

2. Chanel's Balkan embroideries, primary colours on black crepe de chine.
3. Travelling, 1922. One woman's luggage, by Vuitton, clothes by Molyneux.

3

1922

A E Marty

LANVIN
A E Marty

3
LUCILE

1. New suit silhouettes—jackets flared or fitted.

2. The Riviera—Lanvin's sports clothes are perfection. For golfing, blue pullover with white collar and cuffs, full white flannel skirt. Centre, scarlet cheviot suit with the new short jacket. Right, primrose wool jersey dress embroidered in checks of gold and silver thread.

3. Dolores models Lucile's shot green brocade with slashed sleeves.

4. Mme Stoisesco, poet (and the model for Proust's Mlle de Saint Loup), in evening dress.

4
Rehbinder

LANVIN   Black and white crepe.   Steichen

'Skirt lengths vary not only according to what designer creates them, and what lady wears them, but, also, according to the hour of the day when they are worn'

Chanel puts women into sweaters and pleated skirts 9-10 inches off the ground. 'The very short skirt at once suggests that the lady is dressed by Chanel who makes all her skirts short, whether for morning, afternoon or evening . . . the straight line is her medium of expression.' With cloche hats and bandeaux, a willowy flat silhouette and dropped waistlines, the look is universal: but hems are still undecided, wavering between ankle and calf. A slim figure is essential to the look, hence the emphasis on the outdoor life with sport, exercise, sunshine. Vionnet's crepe dresses are the most beautiful in Paris.

After the discovery of Tutankhamen's tomb Ancient Egypt suddenly becomes fashionable, with hieroglyphic embroideries, scarab and lotus jewellery, serpents, and stiff folds tied into the fronts of dresses. 'The concentration of fullness in front, which some call Indo-Chinese and others Egyptian, is very prominent in many collections, so that the plain flat — not to say, tight — back is everywhere in evidence.'

45

1923

PARIS
AGREES TO DISAGREE
about
THE LENGTH
of
SKIRTS

IN Paris, at the present moment, there are many opinions about skirt lengths. Not only do the couturiers disagree among themselves, but, to make matters more confusing, the ladies whom they costume hold quite as conflicting views as the couturiers who dress them. Again, skirt lengths vary not only according to what designer creates them, and what lady wears them, but, also, according to the hour of the day when they are worn. The snapshots on this page illustrate some of the vagaries of Paris skirts. Take, for instance, the tailleurs shown at the lower left. The very short skirt at once suggests that the lady is probably dressed by Chanel who makes all her skirts short, whether for morning, afternoon, or evening. The more conservative skirt worn by her companion stops above the ankle. This is the length that Jenny makes. The lady at the lower right wears her skirt a little longer, while the Marquise de Saint-Sauveur, at the upper right, shows a hem-line fully ten inches off the ground.

The Parisienne treats the length of her afternoon frocks with the same diversity of opinion as her tailleur, but, generally speaking, she wears them two inches longer. In the centre is a snapshot of Madame Meyer wearing a smart frock which completely conceals her ankles, the length approved by Poiret. In the afternoon frock at the left above, an effect of length is achieved by panels. This is the length approved by Vionnet.

In London, skirts obey the same laws that obtain in Paris, the only difference being that, for the street, the English woman wears her slightly longer than does the Parisienne. Also, the rules of length are more definite here: skirts are well above the ankle for the sports suit or severe tailleur; to the ankle for the elaborate tailleur; just below it for the afternoon frock; barely escaping the floor for the evening

MOLYNEUX

VLADIMIR

VIONNET

1. The different lengths as they're being worn in London and Paris — two inches longer in London.
2. Gladys Cooper in Molyneux's silver turban and sheath with chiffon roses. The silver cloak is embroidered with pearls and lined with rose velvet.
3. Three-piece suit by Vladimir of soft green crepe de chine and hat worn low over the eyes.
4. Vionnet's summer crepes, appliquéd and printed. *Left*, black with crimson and scarlet poppies on green stems. *Centre*, black and white appliqué. *Right*, sky, tree and water colours in a reflection print.

JENNY   DOUCET   DRECÖLL

The Egyptian Look

5
DÉSIRÉE

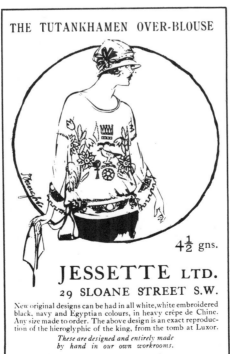

THE TUTANKHAMEN OVER-BLOUSE

4½ gns.

JESSETTE LTD.
29 SLOANE STREET S.W.

New original designs can be had in all white, white embroidered black, navy and Egyptian colours, in heavy crêpe de Chine. Any size made to order. The above design is an exact reproduction of the hieroglyphic of the king, from the tomb at Luxor.

*These are designed and entirely made
by hand in our own workrooms.*

6

Maurice Beck and Helen Macgregor

7

CHÉRUIT, PATOU   Meserole

5. Cathleen Nesbitt wears Désirée's Egyptian brocade
with a Nile green georgette underskirt.
6. 'Dashing romance lurks' in the velvet-trimmed
black taffeta modelled by Mrs Rudolph Valentino.
Formerly Natasha Rambova — and born Winifred
Shaugnessy De Wolf Hudnut, she had been a
costume designer for Nazmova. Like her husband, to
whom she had given a slave bracelet which he
always wore in public, she believed in occultist powers.
They lived in Beverly Hills in a house called 'Falcon's Lair'.
7. Cinema capes from Chéruit and Patou.

1924-1929

THE RECKLESS TWENTIES

By 1924 all the people had arrived, and the party was under full steam. It roared on until 1929, and expired with a Crash, leaving the guests bewildered and hung over. So much had happened in those six years, and ended so abruptly, that only a couple of years later the period seemed as distant as the days before the war. It is remembered as the Gay Twenties, the Roaring Twenties, but for the people who hadn't been asked to the party, nine-tenths of the population, it was a time of despair with hunger marches, dole queues and war heroes reduced to selling matches on the street. The undergraduates who rushed to man the buses and trains in the General Strike didn't know or care that the miners were striking for more work so that they could feed their families. There was a great distance between opposites which intensified the gaiety of the party-goers, the intolerance of the establishment and the misery of the working class.

Meanwhile the twenties in *Vogue* are a rich cocktail of society, the *avant-garde* and the popular jazz, Hollywood, reportage and criticism. The regular contributors included Aldous Huxley and Nancy Cunard, Clive Bell and Cecil Beaton, and called in features by Virginia Woolf, Noël Coward, Jean Cocteau, D. H. Lawrence, Evelyn Waugh, Vita Sackville-West, the Sitwells, and many more. *Vogue* extended its territory, and found an energetic style quite different from the tone of its first decade. The pages looked ten times more interesting with photographs by Steichen and Hoynin-

gen-Huene, Man Ray and Beaton, and came alive with subjects as different as Gertrude Stein – 'Certainly the union of oxygen with ostriches is not that of the taught tracer' – and the rhythms of the *Revue Nègre*:

> Skiddle up skat!
> Skiddle up skat!
> Oh, skiddle up, skiddle up,
> Skat! Skat! Skat!

Everything in the twenties was done after a cocktail, to jazz. How should a cocktail be drunk? 'Quickly, while it's still laughing at you,' replied Henry Craddock in the *Savoy Cocktail Book*. You bought the ice from the fishmonger for a shilling a lump, tied it up in a tea cloth and bashed it to bits on the floor. There was soon a cocktail shaker in every middle-class house, and *Vogue* showed designs for a private cocktail bar ... 'Planning a Gay Corner Devoted to the Shaker, the Cherry and the Row of Happy Bottles'. Before the war you drank nothing until you sat down for dinner, but now there were dry Martinis, Side-cars, Bosom Caressers, Manhattans, Between the Sheets, or gin-and-ginger-beer. Marcel Boulestin, the famous restaurateur who wrote about food for *Vogue*, remarked, 'Cocktails are the most romantic expression of modern life ... but the cocktail habit as practised in England now is a vice.'

Left: Josephine Baker at the Casino de Paris 1931, photograph Hoyningen Huene.
1. Covarrubias drawings.

Fish

1. The Sitwells, 1927
2. Florence Mills in *Dover Street to Dixie*
when it came to London in 1923.
3. John Howard Lawson's Broadway play
Processional, showing June Walker, the lead,
with part of the jazz band and the cubist
backcloth.
4. Design for a cocktail bar by Aubrey
Hammond.

In the morning, at tea time, and all night long people danced. The Prince of Wales kept a band playing for an hour and a half without a break while he one-stepped and Charlestoned with Mrs Dudley Ward. Barbara Cartland describes how Friday-to-Monday guests in the country would start dancing to the gramophone as soon as they arrived, hurry upstairs to dress, drive fifteen or twenty miles to a dance or a hunt ball and dance until five in the morning. In London you went to a *thé dansant* at the Savoy for five shillings, or twenty other places for less, and after the theatre you'd take a taxi to the Berkeley, the Mayfair or the Embassy and dance again to the music of the Savoy Orpheans, Le Roy Allwood or Ambrose. When you tired of hotels there were nightclubs, but if your favourite nightclub had just been raided and closed down, there were still bottle parties, respectable at first, random later, where there would be a Negro band and possibly a cabaret.

Jazz in the early twenties meant 'heavily punctuated, relentless rhythm, with drums, rattles, bells, whistles, hooters and twanging banjoes'. By the time Aldous Huxley wrote this description in *Antic Hay*, the saxophone and trumpet had been added: 'Sweet, sweet and piercing, the saxophone pierced into the very bowels of compassion and tenderness, pierced like a revelation from heaven . . . More ripely and roundly, with a kindly and less agonizing voluptuousness, the 'cello meditated those Mohammedan ecstasies . . . the violin admitted refreshing draughts of fresh air . . . and the piano hammered and rattled away unmindful of the sensibilities of the other instruments, banged away all the time, reminding everyone concerned, in a thoroughly business-like way, that this was a cabaret where people came to dance the fox trot.'

Round and round went the dancers all over Mayfair, usually in fancy dress, women dressed as men, men as women, everybody 'terribly serious; not a single laugh, or the palest ghost of a smile. Frantic noises and occasional cries of ecstasy come from half a dozen negro players . . . Dim lights, drowsy odours and futurist drawings on the walls and ceiling.'

The 'Original' Dixieland Jazz Band, white musicians, had opened at the Hammersmith Palais as early as 1919, and there had

2

3

been a lot of diluted jazz since, but in 1925 the real thing was seen and heard in Paris. It had already happened in New York, where socialites went into the fringes of Harlem to dance and watch, and Negroes were invited up to Park Avenue apartments to teach the Charleston and the Black Bottom. The first all-coloured show written, produced and acted by Negroes was *Shuffle Along*, on Broadway in 1923. Since then there had been *Runnin' Wild*, *Chocolate Dandies*, *Honey*, and *Dover Street to Dixie*, and there was soon to be a King Vidor film *Hallelujah*, made in Hollywood with an all-black cast. The *Revue Nègre* was the first to come to Paris, and the audiences were almost knocked out by the waves of energy and noise which engulfed them from the footlights. Josephine Baker in her frill of bananas became an overnight sensation. Nancy Cunard was ecstatic about the 'perfect delight ... of Josephine Baker, most astounding of mulatto dancers, in her necklets, bracelets, and flouncing feathered loincloths. The fuzz has been taken out of her hair, which shines like a dark blue crystal, as she yodels (the nearest one can get to expressing it) and contorts her surprising form through a maze of complicated rhythms.' Another *Vogue* writer called her 'a woman possessed, a savage intoxicated with tom-toms, a shining machine à danser, an animal, all joint and no bones ... at one moment she is the fashion artist's model, at the next Picasso's.' A year or two later, when she'd opened her own nightclub in Paris, John McMullin went to interview her. 'She has come in without a wrap, and the length of her graceful body, which is light sealskin brown, is swathed in a full blue tulle frock with a bodice of blue snakeskin ... she wears an enormous diamond ring and a very impressive diamond bracelet. Her hair, which naturally grows in tight curls, is plastered close to her head with white of egg and looks as though it were painted on her head with black shellac. As she appears at the Folies Bergères, one is struck by her great decadence of line. When, for the finale, she wears only a diamanté maillot of tulle and red gloves with diamond balls hanging from the tips of her fingers, the effect is up to the wildest imagination of Beardsley.' She went everywhere in her Voisin car, painted brown and upholstered in brown snakeskin

4

E.J. Mason

SCENE: "THE LAST JUMP," CABARET ON A SATURDAY NIGHT.

Here is Nick Fie Rastus with his "teasin' brown," getting in a word or two (I'll say he is) between dances and sips of that red ale which is the rage of Negro cabarets. Note the lady's neutral attitude, expressed by the chaste and exquisite clasping of her hands

THAT TEASIN' YALLA GAL

Seen in Paris in a cabaret or a "dancing" between the hours of 10 p.m. and 5 a.m. She gets right there each time, and don't you be making any mistake. A lady of mystery. Unescorted. Unescortable. Likely to have a greyhound at home. Impossible to tell the exact colour of her skin

KIND O' MELANCHOLY LIKE

He's jess natchely a quiet sort of fellow, dat boy is. Bin at dat table all night, sittin' down, waitin' for somebody, it seem. Don't nevah dance or sing or cut up. Nothin'. Jess sits over there, kind o' melancholy like. "You got to do bette'n dat, ole man. Ain't no time to git blue"

THE SHEIK OF DAHOMEY

Nothin'—Ah don't care whut it is—can get mah boy excited. Nothin'! And talk about havin' a way with wimmin, ain't nobody can tell him nothin' . . . He's a dressin' up fool, dat boy is, an' he sure's got luck with de high yalla ladies

Enter, The New Negro

Left, Negro types drawn by Miguel Covarrubias: captions by the negro poet Eric D. Walrond. 1. Nancy Cunard, journalist and poet. *Vogue's* Paris correspondent, 1927. She rimmed her eyes with kohl and wore African bangles to the elbows.

exactly matched to her own skin, accompanied by a maid, a chauffeur, and a white esquimau dog bearing on top of its head the red imprint of her kiss.

Josephine Baker was followed by Florence Mills and the Black-birds. If Josephine Baker was a '*machine à danser*', Florence Mills was a poignant ragamuffin, all thin wrists and legs like toothpicks. All of a sudden everything black was the rage: black and white décor, Babangi masks, heads wrapped up in turbans, bracelets up the whole arm, jazz and all Negro dances, particularly the Charleston. 'In the 18th century we made money out of Negroes. In the 20th they make money out of us,' said *Vogue*. 'The Negro is at last coming into his own. The most distinguished art critics say his sculpture is better than that of Phidias; the musicians say he composes better than Beethoven; the dance-enthusiasts add that he dances better than Nijinsky; and the cabaret and music hall proprietors admit that he pays better than anyone.' The rhythms and characters of the Negro revue were beautifully given by the Mexican caricaturist Miguel Covarrubias with captions by a Negro poet, Eric D. Walrond . . . 'Nothin' – Ah don't care whut it is – can get mah boy excited. Nothin'! And talk about havin' a way with wimmin, ain't nobody can tell him nothin' . . . He's a dressin' up fool, dat boy is, an' he sure's got luck with de high yalla ladies.'

The new Negro had entered, created by the jazz spirit of their own invention, and people had suddenly to make their minds up about 'niggers'. *Books for the Morning Room Table* reviewed Carl Van Vechten's *Nigger Heaven* about life in Harlem, and David Garnett's *The Sailor's Return*. Writing about the latter, Edwin Muir wondered whether 'relations between a sailor and a negress are a fit subject for art; whether the theme is not too fantastic to have universal significance'. *Le Village Blanc* was a controversial book by Joe Alex about a party of French ship-wrecked off Africa and captured by a tribe that had once been forced to exhibit itself in an exhibition native village in Paris. The chief turns them into an exhibition white village for the amusement of the tribe, with a bar, a café and a beauty parlour. Meanwhile Carl Einstein had written the definitive book on African sculpture *Negerplastik*, and the cubists had already absorbed Babangi masks and Dogon sculpture from the 1922 exhibition of French colonial art.

No sooner was jazz accepted as thrilling and artistic than there began to be a tendency among popular musicians to claim the credit for white culture. In 1926 *Vogue* was writing, 'How far syncopated music derives from the Negroes is doubtful, but certainly they are its best interpreters', and George Gershwin, well known for his 'Fascinatin' Rhythm' and 'Rhapsody in Blue', arrived in London to say, 'Well, sometimes I have got an inspiration from Negro spirituals. But it is doubtful if they are Negro at all. Paul Whiteman says they are mostly old English tunes.' Showing how to dance to the new tunes, old English or new American, were Maurice and Leonora Hughes, and Fred and Adèle Astaire. The Astaires drew enormous crowds in Gershwin's *Lady Be Good* in New York and London, 'Adèle squealing like a toy steam engine . . . Fred pat-a-flapping a proposal of marriage sans music', and Maurice Chevalier and Yvonne Vallée called their 1927 revue *Whitebirds* . . . 'a non-stop attaboy Charlestonized paean to the birds and the trees and the breeze – a lunatic dash past Nature at 60 miles an hour . . . if this man loves Nature, then all the nightingales will soon be drinking dry Martinis'.

Cars had a tremendous romantic appeal in the twenties, the appeal of speed, powerful machinery and status symbol rolled into one. Michael Arlen summed it up in this description of Iris Storm's car in *The Green Hat*, 'Like a huge yellow insect that had dropped to earth from a butterfly civilization, this car, gallant and suave, rested in the lowly silence of the Shepherd Market night. Open as a yacht, it wore a great shining bonnet, and flying over the crest of this great bonnet, as though in proud flight over the heads of scores of phantom horses, was that silver stork by which the gentle may be pleased to know that they have just escaped death beneath the wheels of a Hispano-Suiza car.'

In London gallery goers failed to see the point of much that was new in painting and sculpture. Clive Bell, writing in *Vogue* about Brancusi, complained, 'Within the last few months I have heard in London – in Paris, I think, that particular brand of imbecility is now known to be vulgar – the old familiar hee-haw, the fatuous comment, the time-worn joke, at the expense of one of the most serious of modern artists . . . the fools approach and read in their catalogues "L'oiseau" or "Tête d'une femme": peals of laughter. Is it possible these oafs suppose that the sculptor was trying to make a photographic likeness of a bird or a woman, and could get no nearer than this? No: people who could suppose that are not allowed out.' *Vogue* had come a long way from the 1919 review that said, 'Art cannot flourish without a wealthy and leisured class to savour it – a class which has sufficient time and energy to refine its taste and to sharpen its intellect in social encounters'. And in the popular press, 'Mr Ben Nicholson has three muddy nudes against wishy-washy backgrounds. It is obvious that the figures are not meant to be anatomically probable – one woman's ankles are three times the width of her neck; one wonders simply why he had to paint them.' Even in 1929, Epstein's Rima was daubed with tar and feathers. In *The Long Weekend* Robert Graves and Alan Hodge point out that the public were slowly being educated into seeing things in an impressionistic or post-impressionistic way by fashion sketches and advertisements. In the Underground, and in *Vogue*, you could see posters by McKnight Kauffer, and because they were not in an art gallery they were looked at without prejudice or suspicion.

Paris took the natural lead in all the arts except for films, and London followed. It was said the time lag in art fashions between France and educated England was about 12 years, and between educated England and the masses another two at least. Exhibitions held in the two cities in the mid-twenties summed up their relative positions. Wembley's Empire Exhibition was intended to enlarge the domestic market and encourage exports. Palaces of Art, Engineering and Industry jostled walled African towns, pagodas

1. Mirror-shelved library in Paris, 1928, with furniture of hardwood and snakeskin.
2. Lalique's glass dining room for the Paris Exhibition.
3. McKnight Kauffer poster, 1925.

and Indian tombs; the Great Dipper was the steepest in England. King George V's opening speech was relayed by radio and between six and seven million people heard his voice for the first time. Osbert Sitwell picked his way carefully through the sea of mud to pronounce the exhibition 'not ugly'.

In 1925 Paris opened the Decorative Arts Exhibition, the first on an international scale for over a century for which applied arts were the main reason. The exhibition gave its name to the style, which Osbert Lancaster calls 'Modernistic' and 'Functional', and Bevis Hillier defines as including Erté on one hand and the 'architectural nudism' of Le Corbusier on the other. Inspired by Cubism, the Bauhaus and Aztec art, it took its rich colours from the Russian ballet. Designs were intended for mass production in the new materials – plastics, ferro-concrete and vita-glass – and the aim was to combine art with industry. *Vogue* wrote, 'The Paris Exhibition is like a city in a dream, and the sort of dream that would give the psycho-analysts a good run for their money . . . Enormous fountains of glass play among life-size cubist dolls and cascades of music wash down from the dizzy summits of four gargantuan towers.' Instead of the simpering dummies that were usually used for fashion exhibitions, André Vigneau had made formalized wax or composition figures, Modiglianis with sculptured hair. They were silver, red, purple or natural wood colour, and showed the new clothes off beautifully, although they were found '*quelque peu troublant*'.

Poiret, who had been impressed by design education in Germany and Austria before the war, and had founded his textile and furnishing house Martine on revolutionary lines in 1922, was naturally involved in the exhibition. He made a merry-go-round of Paris figures including an apache dancer, a *modiste* and a fishwife. He designed three barges which he called 'Love', 'Organs' and 'Delights'; asked why, he answered, 'Women, always women.' 'Orgues' housed his new collection with wall hangings by Raoul Dufy, 'Délices' was a restaurant, and in 'Amours' Poiret sat playing a perfume piano, which fanned scented breezes at visitors when he pressed the notes for different scents.

The right clothes to wear for the functional pavilions and machine-turned constructions of the Art Deco exhibition were Sonia Delaunay's. A Russian who came from St Petersburg as an art student, she arrived in Paris in 1900 and married the painter Robert Delaunay. Her patchwork dresses are pure colour kaleidoscoped together into vivid geometric and abstract designs, jumbled alphabets and mosaics. They were made for golf and Bugattis, and she had cars painted to match the clothes. She shared with the vorticists and the expressionists a romantic feeling for speed, fragmentation and the influence of machines. She made coherent compositions like living paintings, and wasn't interested in the draping of cloth. Her husband said that she 'possessed colour in its atavistic state' and her clothes inspired poems – Blaise Cendrars's 'On her dress she has a body', and Tristan Tzara's

END OF BACKHAND DRIVE

4. Professor Lesieur and a pyramid of pupils, Comtesse Elie de Gaigneron, Princesse Guy de Faucigny-Lucinge and Mrs Harold Kingsland; photograph Lucien Eysserie.
5. Lady Mendl and instructor in her gardens at Antibes; photograph Lucien Eysserie.
6. Lelong tennis dress, 1928.
7. Benito's drawing of Chéruit's silver gauze dress, hand painted with lacquer-red, grey and black cubes, 1925.
8. One of Vigneau's grey wax mannequins for the Art Deco Exhibition, dressed by Lanvin and photographed by Man Ray.
9. Madame Agnès, the French milliner, in Futurist dress and earrings, 1925; photograph Steichen.

L'ange a glissé sa main
    dans la corbeille l'œil des fruits.
Il arrête les roues des autos,
    et le gyroscope vertigineux
    du cœur humain.

The woman who wore these clothes, or clothes by Vionnet, Chanel, Molyneux, Louiseboulanger or the new Schiaparelli is perfectly described in *Antic Hay*: 'fairly tall, but seemed taller than she actually was, by reason of her remarkable slenderness. Not that she looked disagreeably thin, far from it. It was a rounded slenderness. The Complete Man decided to consider her as tubular – flexible and tubular, like a section of boa constrictor . . . dressed in clothes that emphasized this serpentine slimness . . . on her head was a small, sleek black hat, that looked almost as though it were made of metal. It was trimmed on one side with a bunch of dull golden foliage.'

The serpentine slimness was an essential. If dancing and tennis weren't enough, then you took tablets and potions, slogged it out on electric camels and did physical jerks first thing in the morning. You bought rubber rollers with studs all over them, you went to Baden-Baden, or best of all you went down to the Riviera and took instruction from a dazzling 'professor' of physical fitness. *Vogue* was full of pictures of Princesses standing on their heads in pyramids, Duchesses turning cartwheels and Comtesses walking on their hands. Skirts and hair got shortest of all in 1926, and bosoms were compressed with 'flatteners'. Bathing costumes were designed with swimming in mind, and the boiling summer of 1928 put the seal on the craze for sunbathing and getting a tan. Naturally there were many criticisms of the new woman. *Vogue* warned in 1924 that 'a siren with a "stinker" between her lips does not inspire an epigram or a lyric', but in 1928 Cecil Beaton was writing in the magazine, 'Our standards are so completely changed from the old that comparison or argument is impossible. We can only say, "But we *like* no chins! Du Maurier chins are as stodgy as porridge; we *prefer* high foreheads to low ones, we *prefer* flat noses and chests and schoolboy figures to bosoms and hips like water-melons in season. We like heavy eyelids; they are considered amusing and smart. We adore make-up and the gilded lily, and why not? Small dimpled hands make us feel quite sick; we like to see the forms of bones and gristle. We flatten out hair on purpose to make it sleek and silky and to show the shape of our skulls, and it is our supreme object to have a head looking like a wet football on a neck as thin as a governess's hatpin."' English girls who looked like this were handed a giant bouquet by a member of the suite of King Amanaullah of Afghanistan who visited London in 1928. He told the *Daily News*, 'Look you, your English maidens are divinely beautiful, they are as fair as the pale moon which shines so gloriously in your western sky; their eyes are as bright as the eastern stars; and their complexion is just like the exquisite rose of Afghanistan.' That's what the reporter said he said, anyway.

The slim, brief look of twenties fashion was aided by the development of the artificial silk industry. Rayon printed well, it was light and cheap, and its production in the United States rose from eight million pounds weight in 1920 to fifty-three millions in 1925. By then everything a woman wore could be cut out of seven yards of fabric, and rayon stockings were cheap enough for almost everyone. Unlike the early art. silk stockings, these went right up the legs to the thighs, and came in sunburn colour, not just black and white.

The Art Deco exhibition had an immediate effect on design, bringing a grisly period of 'traditional' copying to an end. *Vogue* included a *House & Garden* supplement in the magazine from 1924, and showed the new decor in detail. There were flats like Mrs Viveash's 'tastefully in the movement. The furniture was upholstered in fabrics designed by Dufy – of enormous flowers, printed in grey and ochre on a white ground. There were a couple of lamp-shades by Balla. On the pale rose-stippled walls hung three portraits of herself by three different and entirely incongruous painters, a selection of the usual oranges and lemons, and a rather forbidding contemporary nude painted in two shades of green.' *Vogue* showed the later school of all-white décor, pioneered by Syrie Maugham, with white leather chairs, Kakemono pictures, white damask curtains fringed with monkey fur, and bleached Louis Quinze commodes. Mrs Maugham stripped the leaves off lilacs and peonies so that they looked like wax flowers, and hired very black Negroes to play for her parties. Rooms were thought of, not so much to be lived in, but as settings for parties. Chelsea studios were taken over by 'Bohemians', who scattered cushions on the floor, made Batik prints out of balloon silk left over from the war, and played Mahjong after dinner. Big houses were turned into flats, wood was faced in mirror glass, and everything was disguised as something else. 'Gramophones masquerade as cocktail cabinets,' said Osbert Lancaster, 'cocktail cabinets as book-cases; radios lurk in tea-caddies and bronze nudes burst asunder at the waist-line to reveal cigarette lighters.' Duncan Grant and Vanessa Bell worked together to paint furniture and panels: *Vogue* showed their work in Virginia Woolf's house in Tavistock Square and Maynard Keynes's rooms in Cambridge.

P O R T R A I T S
I N · P A S S I N G

SKETCHES *by* CECIL BEATON

1. Cecil Beaton drawings, 1927.
2. An all-white room in the style of Syrie Maugham, 1928, with cream leather chairs, cream damask curtains fringed with monkey fur, and glass-topped table.
3. A block of flats in a city of the future.
4. Amédée Ozenfant's studio house designed by Le Corbusier, 1926.
5. Mendelsohn's Einstein Tower at Potsdam, built in 1920, housing a laboratory and an observatory.
6. Maynard Keynes's rooms in King's College, Cambridge, with Duncan Grant's and Vanessa Bell's wall panels and curtains.

Fred Boissannas

E. J. Mason

Among the decoration, *Vogue* introduced the work of two architects who belonged fair and square in the machine age. Le Corbusier, who said, 'A house is a machine for living', designed rooms like operating theatres and buildings as severe as steamships. People who lived in his flats were allowed one picture, to be chosen from a picture-cupboard and changed as often as they liked. He believed that the construction should be clearly expressed in building, that kitchens and bathrooms should be given equal importance to drawing rooms and dining rooms. Eric Mendelsohn was a German architect, an expressionist whose organic buildings looked as if they were whizzing along at a hundred miles an hour, swooping round corners. He could have been the original for Otto Friedrich Silenus, the architect in Evelyn Waugh's *Decline and Fall*, who had 'first attracted Mrs Beste-Chetwynde's attention with the rejected design for a chewing-gum factory', and replaced her country house with one of ferro-concrete and aluminium.

There was to be a sad difference between these romantic Futurist ideas and the cheapened versions that would be built all over

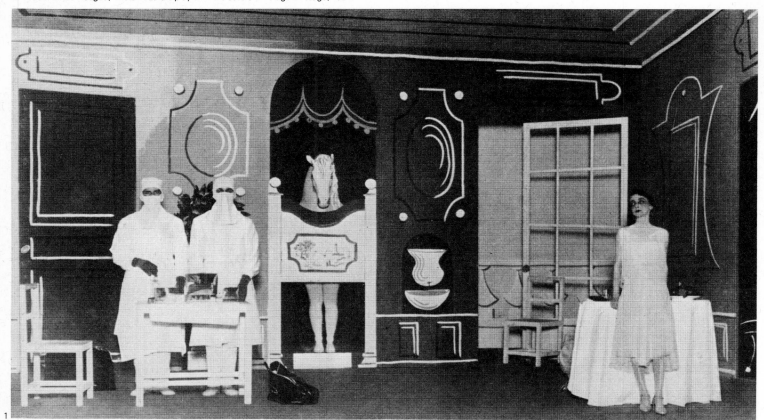

Waléry

Britain. Optimistic in 1925, *Vogue* was writing 'In the future those who work in great centres will either live in garden cities, which will encircle London and Paris, or else in tall buildings reasonably close to the business quarters. The dreary suburbs will disappear . . . it seems unlikely that most cities will increase in size. The Old World, at any rate, is greatly over-populated, and the size of urban populations depends eventually upon the size of fields upon which they depend for their food.'

The twenties gave women their freedom, sexually, through the work of Dr Marie Stopes and the setting up of birth control clinics, and politically. By the end of the decade the flapper vote had put five million more women on the electoral roll, which helped to bring in the second Labour government, fighting on unemployment. But it was not a political decade.

Ain't we got fun?
Not much money, oh! but honey!
Ain't we got fun?
There's nothing surer,
The rich get rich and the poor get – children.
In the meantime, in between time,
Ain't we got fun?

In Paris, the Cubists, Expressionists, Futurists, Dadaists and the new Surrealists were not shut off in separate boxes. They were writing and making films, putting on plays, decorating and philosophizing. Many were involved in the ballet. Picasso had painted the famous curtain for *Train bleu*, shown in 1924 with costumes by Chanel, sets by Laurens and choreography by Nijinska, Nijinsky's sister, and designed for *Parade*, *Pulcinella* and *The Three-*

Waléry

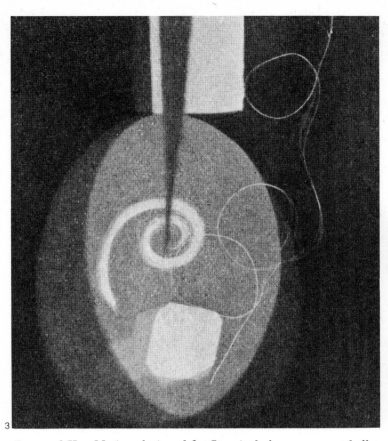

3. Two of Man Ray's 'rayographs'.
4. Cocteau drawing, 1925.
5. *Paysage animé* by Fernand
Léger, 1925.

Cornered Hat. Matisse designed for Stravinsky's new one-act ballet *Le Chant du rossignol*, Braque for *Zéphyr et Flore*, Joan Miro and Max Ernst for *Romeo and Juliet*, and Marie Laurencin had designed some brief and modern costumes for Poulenc's *Les Biches*. In *Vogue* you could see Man Ray's mechanical experiments with film, composing photographs by exposing random objects directly to sensitive paper, and the latest work of Fernand Léger, key painter of the machine age whose pictures were composed like well-constructed aeroplanes or trains, in black and white with strong poster colours. The Surrealists' conference on sex in 1927 was ignored, with its relish for bad taste. The Surrealists savoured the *frissons* 'from the seduction of nuns and women who never washed, from outré sexual positions, from homosexual eccentricity'.

Jean Cocteau was a bridge between the arts, a gifted dilettante who helped initiate *Vogue* readers into the *avant-garde* by keeping three or four steps ahead. He had his first poems published at seventeen, and went on to write novels, ballets and plays, direct films, found a group of new musicians and publish his clever, tricky drawings. His one-act surreal tragedy *Orphée* was set in the technological present. Orpheus and Eurydice, in modern dress, confronted Death the operating surgeon with his two anaesthetists complete with rubber gloves, masks and surgical trolley. It caused some excitement, and *Vogue* called it at least the most interesting play of 1926. Another provocative play was Tristan Tzara's *Mouchoir de nuages,* with the actors sitting on stage, talking and making up, while the 'real' performance went on upon a small dais in the centre. This Roumanian Dadaist poet had staged the *Grand Spectacle du désastre* in 1920, which had succeeded only too well in rousing the audience to a pitch of fury.

The real centre of experimental theatre was Berlin. German Expressionism was an attempt to put a distance between the audience and the performance, to replace naturalism with stylization, to lose the individual in the mass. Characters were not given names, they were 'The Girl', 'The Boy', 'The Mother'. Bertolt Brecht said, 'I aim at an extremely classical, cold, highly intellectual style of performance. I am not writing for the scum who want to have the cockles of their heart warmed.' The *Threepenny Opera* was performed in 1928. *Vogue* summed up the social criticism of Sternheim and Wedekind and Toller as 'dramatized Freud', and gave the parallel movement in German dancing, with Mary Wigmar leading her pupils in mass displays of gym and drill, the name 'tragic Tiller girls'. Berlin's favourite actress was Elizabeth Bergner, 'all nerves and delicacy', and Max Reinhardt, who turned crowd scenes into spectacular theatre all over Europe and America with Lady Diana Cooper's vehicle *The Miracle*, was the key figure in Expressionist theatre.

Expressionism was most successful in German films, which were acknowledged even in Hollywood as technically excellent at a fraction of the cost of American production. By 1924 they had a stronger grip on the British film market than British films themselves. The movement kicked off in 1919 with *The Cabinet of Doctor Caligari*, a nightmare fantasy set in a fairground, written by Carl Mayer and Hans Janowitz and directed by Robert Weine. Material objects took on an emotional significance by means of clever photography and disturbing prop design: angles were acute, chimneys set aslant on roofs, and shadows were painted on to jar with lighting effects. By 1926 the most successful film in Berlin was a Soviet propaganda film, *Battleship Potemkin*. The story of a mutiny and massacre in Odessa, it was called 'a marvel of mass acting and machinery in motion'. The same year *Vogue* published pictures of a new equally important film being made in Berlin, Fritz Lang's *Metropolis*, set in an underground city of the future with massed skyscrapers and terrifying machinery, and crowds surging through the maze in an attempt to escape from the flood.

That year Aldous Huxley in *Vogue* was criticizing Expressionist films for their pretentiousness and melodramatic ponderosity: 'A study of Felix the Cat would teach the German producers many valuable lessons.' He describes how Felix sings a few crotchets, seizes them and fits them together into a scooter, an easy thing to

de Meyer

At the turn of the decade there was a craze for dressing up in pageants and tableaux vivants as the Madonna, a saint or a nun, with attendant fashions for habits, drapes and wrapped heads — Paula Gellibrand's nun's-habit wedding dress, for instance. Its apogee was Lady Diana Cooper's prolonged appearance as the Madonna in *The Miracle*, for which she prepared herself by retreat into a convent.
1. Geraldine Farrar in Puccini's *Suor Angelica*, 1919.
2. Gladys Cooper in *The Betrothal*, 1921.
3. Lillah McCarthy in *Judith*, 1919.

2

3

Instead

Rita Martin

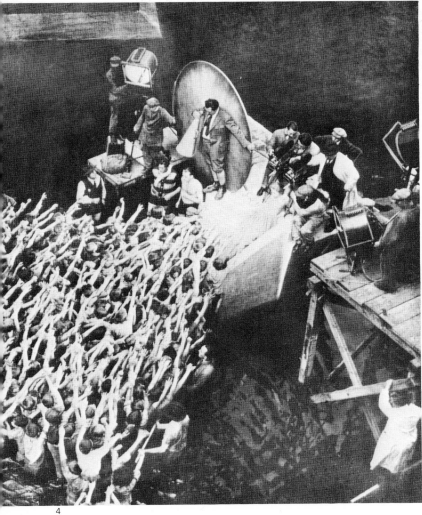

do on film, an impossible thing to do in words, and draws an analogy with the super-realist writers. 'The fact is that these "young" writers are rebelling, not against effete literary conventions, but against language itself. They are trying to make words do what they cannot do, in the nature of things. They are working in the wrong medium. The aim of the super realists is to free literature completely from logic and to give it the fantastic liberty of the dream. What they attempt to do – not very successfully – the camera achieves brilliantly.'

In England, there were three schools of writing, described by Ronald Blythe in *The Age of Illusion* as Bloomsbury, Mayfair, and the leafy Blankshire of Georgian Poetry, where few people went any more: Bloomsbury was the withdrawn and aristocratic drawing-room world of Lady Ottoline Morrell and the Woolfs, Clive and Vanessa Bell, Maynard Keynes and Lytton Strachey, with E. M. Forster on the perimeter. Mayfair, fabulously witty and irreverent, included Evelyn Waugh and Cyril Connolly. Still, for many readers, there was no writer like a dead writer and with this in mind Auden dedicated his *Poems* to Isherwood in 1930 with the words:

> Let us honour if we can
> The vertical man
> Though we value none
> But the horizontal one.

T. S. Eliot was one vertical man who was honoured and valued by contemporary writers. 'The Waste Land', written in 1922, acted as a catalyst. It had a note of gay disillusion and cynicism which they recognized as the mood of the decade:

> When lovely woman stoops to folly and
> Paces about her room again, alone,
> She smoothes her hair with automatic hand,
> And puts a record on the gramophone.

4. The children's escape from Fritz Lang's *Metropolis:* photograph of the film being made, in 1926.
5. Lady Ottoline Morrell, 1928.
6. Virginia Woolf in 1926 when she had written *Jacob's Room* and *Mrs Dalloway*. 'Try to imagine a mask that even without life, without intelligence would be beautiful. Then imagine this mask so impregnated with life and intelligence that it would seem to have been modelled by them. Imagine all this, and you will still have only a faint idea of the charm of Virginia Woolf's face, a charm that is the result of the most felicitous encounter of matter and soul in the face of a woman': Victoria Ocampo.

Cecil Beaton

Maurice Beck and Macgregor

61

Much of his work was a great deal more difficult. He said, 'genuine poetry can communicate before it is understood', and 'the poet is occupied with frontiers of consciousness beyond which words fail, though meanings still exist'. In Paris, Gertrude Stein was making connections between words as words, explained to *Vogue* readers by Edith Sitwell, who made poetry fun.

> With the flag.
> With the flag of sets.
> Sets of colour.
> Do you like flags.
> Blue flags smell sweetly.
> Blue flags in a whirl.
> The wind blows
> And the automobile goes.

'... Flags make her think of irises. Flags make her think of the wind. The wind makes her think of the speed of automobiles.'

James Joyce was more difficult than anyone. *Ulysses* had been published in 1922. Virginia Woolf wrote of 'a queasy undergraduate scratching his pimples', but T. S. Eliot said, 'How could anyone write again after achieving the immense prodigy of the last chapter?' Joyce said he had 'recorded, simultaneously, what a man says, sees, thinks and what such seeing, thinking, saying does to what you Freudians call the subconscious'.

Sexual deviation was becoming acceptable, at least by high society, due to the talent and gaiety of the homosexuals in the theatre and Mayfair, and due to the writers who put their predicament in readable form. 'And what is a "He-man?"' asked Gertrude Stein. 'Isn't it a large enough order to fill out to the dimensions of all that "a man" has meant in the past? A "He-man!"' This is how Scott Fitzgerald summed up the sexual education of the jazz age: 'We begin with the suggestion that Don Juan leads an interesting life (*Jurgen*, 1919); then we learn that there's a lot of sex around if we only knew it (*Winesburg, Ohio*, 1920), that adolescents lead very amorous lives (*This Side of Paradise*, 1920), that there are a lot of neglected Anglo-Saxon words (*Ulysses*, 1921), that older people don't always resist sudden temptations (*Cytherea*, 1922), that girls are sometimes seduced without being

1. Gertrude Lawrence, *left,* Beatrice Lillie, *right,* 1922.
2. Patrick Balfour and Cyril Connolly at home, 1927.
3. Noël Coward telephoning from his Ebury Street bedroom, 1927.

ruined (*Flaming Youth*, 1922), that even rape often turns out well (*The Sheik*, 1922), that glamorous English ladies are often promiscuous (*The Green Hat*, 1924), that in fact they devote most of their time to it (*The Vortex*, 1926), that it's a damn good thing too (*Lady Chatterley's Lover*, 1928), and finally that there are abnormal variations (*The Well of Loneliness*, 1928, and *Sodom and Gomorrah*, 1929).'

The London stage barely went further than Noël Coward's *The Vortex*, which shocked playgoers because drug-taking had never been a stage theme before. *Vogue* said, 'to excite emotions of pity or anxiety a play must contain people who rouse the sympathy of the audience by intelligence or character. The protagonists of "The Vortex" had neither, and as a result in the last act, instead of being stirred by their efforts to reform, one wished the son would continue to take drugs and the mother lovers, till they both died: a good riddance to bad rubbish.' Coward, at any rate, loved the publicity and was photographed in decadent satin pyjamas telephoning from the futurist bed of his Ebury Street flat. His *Fallen Angels* and *Sirocco* provoked 'cries of "rotter!" from the stalls, cat calls and shrieks from the gallery', but by 1927 his good lyrics and catchy tunes, light touch and perfect timing had won over audiences, and he had four shows running simultaneously. His leading lady, Gertrude Lawrence, perfectly matched the brittle, disillusioned mood of his plays. Languid and sunburnt, with a smoky voice, she gave fashion the overworked word casual, wearing a mink coat thrown over flannel trousers. She looked perfect in Molyneux's spotted pyjamas or his white satin evening dress as she leant against the balcony and sang 'Some day I'll find you'. 'She smoked cigarettes with a nuance that implied having just come out of bed and wanting to go back into it,' said Cecil Beaton. She had terrific style, and her arrival at the stage door was something worth waiting for, as she stepped out of her Hispano-Suiza with a corsage of orchids and a bevy of handsome young men with top hats and gardenias.

Bernard Shaw won the Nobel Prize for *Saint Joan* in 1924, with Sybil Thorndike in the lead. In the cast were Godfrey Winn, and Ernest Thesiger who left it for the new Cochran review. Cochran's Young Ladies were the best revue chorus of the day, and he was the leading showman and impresario of the twenties. He brought everything to London, from the Russian ballet to a cowboy rodeo, from prize fights to cabarets.

A great draw of the day was Tallulah Bankhead, who attracted in particular enormous crowds of female fans – more than any matinée idol – who choked the West End and crammed around the stage door. Her ambivalent appeal and tough wit made her an essential at smart parties, though her remarks could be killers. At a wedding she might remark, 'I've had both of them, and they were lousy', or at a first night, 'There's less in this than meets the eye.' She was a strange choice for Iris Storm in *The Green Hat*, Michael Arlen's successful novel made into a play. *Vogue* wrote, 'They take lovers as they take cocktails, and all the while use the words "clean" and "purity" as a chain-smoker uses cigarettes . . . you cannot make La Dame aux Camélias drive a Hispano-Suiza' – and you certainly would not have picked Tallulah Bankhead to play a Dame aux Camélias. A powerhouse of energy and a great show-off, she was described by Cecil Beaton as 'a wicked archangel . . . Medusa, very exotic, with a glorious skull, high pumice-stone cheekbones . . . Her cheeks are huge acid-pink peonies. Her eyelashes are built out with hot liquid paint to look like burnt matches, and her sullen, discontented rosebud of a mouth is painted the brightest scarlet, and is as shiny as Tiptree's strawberry jam.' She never stopped talking, and a friend who once took out a stopwatch and counted her words per minute calculated that she spoke

Maurice Beck and Macgregor

Maurice Beck and Macgregor

Maurice Beck and Macgregor

4. Lilian Braithwaite as Florence Lancaster in *The Vortex*, 1925.
5. Ernest Thesiger, 1925.
6. Delysia, Parisian actress and comedy star, who took the lead in Cochran revues of the early twenties, in 1925.

seventy thousand words a day – the wordage of *War and Peace* over a weekend. Emerging onto the street after lunch one day, she dropped a fifty dollar bill into the tambourine of a Salvation Army girl, and said, 'Don't bother to thank me, darling. I know what a perfectly *ghastly* season it's been for you Spanish dancers.'

Probably nothing gave so much pleasure to so many as the wireless. Everyone tuned in to the hour of dance band music in the evening, which left them whistling tunes like 'Bye Bye Blackbird', 'Valencia', or 'I Wonder Where My Baby is Tonight'. But popular music programmes were few and far between, sprinkled among chamber music and symphony concerts. John Reith, the General Manager of the British Broadcasting Company, saw that the radio was potentially as important as the printing press in terms of human enlightenment, and felt it as a religious duty to keep the B.B.C. free from commercialism and propaganda. The public re-

1

sented their diet of musical education, as the press, and *Vogue*'s music columnist Edwin Evans, were quick to point out. They called him 'the Judge of What We Ought To Want', and he bleakly replied, 'I do not pretend to give the public what it wants.' It was due to him that the announcers wore dinner jackets to read the nine o'clock news, and the public began to enjoy excellent radio plays and the best musical performances.

For sheer entertainment you went to the cinema. Everyone loved Felix the Cat, Bonzo Dog, Mickey Mouse and the slapstick comedies with Fatty Arbuckle, the nightmare acrobatics of prim, short-sighted Harold Lloyd who was always suspended by a sagging flag pole over a dizzy drop, and the surreal machine-infested world of poker-faced Buster Keaton. Every successful film was followed by its burlesque, and the melodrama of Rudolph Valentino's films were a rich inspiration to Laurel and Hardy. Charles Chaplin was still the most popular of all comedians, and *The Kid*, in which he adopts orphan Jackie Coogan, the most successful film of the twenties. Lon Chaney was Quasimodo in *The Hunchback of Notre Dame*, and it became a joke, when you saw a beetle scuttling over the floor, to shout, 'Don't kill it, it may be Lon Chaney in disguise.' Jim Tully told *Vogue* readers that Lon Chaney's father was a deaf and dumb Irish barber, that his mother was afflicted in the same way, and that he had learnt to mime by talking to them in sign language – a story that sounds as if it came from the press office. A quite different sort of film was a success in Britain when Robert Flaherty's documentary *Nanook of the North* was shown. About an Eskimo family, it showed how the camera could record domestic life without pretension or embarrassment.

2   Maurice Beck and
                                           Macgregor

1. Picnic to music, 1925, with an Amplion portable loud speaker.
2. Rudolph Valentino doing a Nijinsky, 1924.

Opposite: Vogue's early drawn covers. *Top:* Early January 1919 by George Plank. Early March 1921 by George Plank. *Bottom:* Christmas 1916 by E.M.A. Steinmetz: Late September 1918 by George Plank. *Over page: Vogue* covers of the Jazz Age by Benito. Early May and late July 1926.

VOGUE

Early January 1919

CONDÉ NAST & CO
LONDON

One Shilling & Six Pence Net

VOGUE

Early March 1921

CONDÉ NAST & CO LTD

One Shilling & Six Pence Net

1

Steichen

2

Opposite: Vogue covers. *Top:* 8 July 1931 by George Lepape. 9 December 1931 by George Lepape. *Bottom:* 11 July 1928, by Pierre Mourgue. 24 December 1930 by Benito. *Bottom:* 8 July 1931 by George Lepape. 9 December 1931 by George Lepape.

1. 'The Pola Star of the Films': Steichen's portrait of Pola Negri in 1925, when she was playing *Flower of the Night* in Hollywood.
2. First photograph in *Vogue* of Greta Garbo, with John Gilbert in the screen version of *The Green Hat*, 1928.

The two big stars of the twenties were both Paramount properties, locked in a rivalry that made good gossip. Gloria Swanson arrived in Hollywood as a flat-figured extra from Chicago with brilliantined, spit-curled hair. Her camera-proof face, rather viciously beautiful, suited the most bizarre and exaggerated of fashions. She was a symbol of movie bad taste when she secured her social position by marrying the Marquis de la Falaise de Coudray, a 'docile nobleman with a reckless taste in spats'. She returned to her house in Hollywood and installed footmen in powdered wigs and satin knee-breeches.

Her rival Pola Negri, who was able to call herself Countess Dombski, was imported by Paramount because of her success in German films. She was overschooled by her studio, never caught on with the flapper fans as Gloria Swanson had, and was never very popular in Hollywood because she made no attempt to hide her contempt of American films and culture. She had some sort of affair with Rudolph Valentino, king of movie sheikhs and lounge lizards, and staged a dramatic fainting at his funeral that provoked more laughter than sympathy. She lost box office appeal towards the end of the decade and returned to Germany where, in 1936, she was once more starring in films and was rumoured to be a girl friend of Hitler.

Elinor Glyn's *Three Weeks* was a whale of a success, both the book and the film. A story about a Ruritanian Queen who enjoys three flaming weeks with Conrad Nagel on a bed of roses, it starred Eileen Pringle. Miss Pringle was reproved by the Deaf and Dumb Society who could see that when Conrad Nagel swept her into his arms her lips were saying 'If you drop me, you —, I'll break your neck.' Clara Bow was the It Girl who invented sex appeal – *Flaming Youth* brought her 20,000 fan letters a week and made her everybody's sweetheart from 1925 to 1930. Sound came in in 1927, and by the end of 1928 the worst sound film could outdraw the best silent movie.

The greatest star of all arrived in the last years of the silent film. Greta Garbo was nineteen when she came to Hollywood in the entourage of Mauritz Stiller. Daughter of a poor labourer, she was the lather girl in a barber's shop when she had begun to play extras in a few Swedish films. She was different because she didn't give herself titles or airs, and her relationship with M.G.M. and reporters was one of icy formality. She hated publicity, and only asked to 'be alone'. On the screen her amazing beauty overwhelmed the audience. She didn't have to act, her slightest gesture conveyed more than other people's words. When her first talkie, Eugene O'Neill's *Anna Christie* arrived in 1930, her fans sat on the edges of their seats. They were dying to hear her voice, said to be guttural and thicky Swedish. They sighed with relief, then swooned with delight: her first words were 'Gif me a viskey, ginger ale on the side – and don't be stingy, baby.' When her shoulder length bob and slouch hat began to be universally copied, it signalled the end of the twenties.

By the end of the twenties fashionable restaurants could afford to spend £50,000 on redecorating, and cabarets brought in anything up to £1,000 a week. All the new restaurants and clubs were described in *Vogue*, and the people who went there. One of the smartest was the Kit-Cat where elegantly bored women looked over corsages of white orchids at cleanshaven young men with satin hair and wide shoulders: it was raided by the police the night after the Prince of Wales had dined there. Guests at Chez Victor, who

Curtis Moffat and Olivia Wyndham

crowded round the piano to hear Hutch sing 'The Man I Love', were appalled when Victor was convicted of breaking the Licensing Act and imprisoned. The Silver Slipper, with its glass floor and marvellous saxophonist, was the last big nightclub to be opened by Mrs Meyrick, who was imprisoned three times. Her clients over the years included a good cross section of twenties society, including Augustus John and Rudolph Valentino, J. B. Priestley and Sophie Tucker, Carpentier the boxer and Michael Arlen. You could find Tallulah Bankhead at Taglioni's, Epstein and his latest model at the Ham Bone in Soho, John at the Eiffel Tower, and end up at the Gargoyle eating scrambled eggs and drinking coffee by an open fire. In the dancing room was David Tennant's huge Matisse, for which Lady Latham made some Negro art curtains. As *Vogue* said, 'Everyone agrees that with Matisse you can't go wrong.'

This was the heyday of hostesses, with Elsa Maxwell for their queen. She would take over a whole nightclub or palace in any capital city and fill it with her set of international celebrities. At her parties there was a touch of the grotesque: you might have to blow a feather off a sheet or milk an artificial cow for your champagne. Mrs Corrigan was an avid party-giver who conquered London society by the extravagance of her hospitality. The most sought-after guests would find that they had won the gold cigarette cases in the tombola, and the all-star cabaret got more for their brief appearance at Mrs Corrigan's than for a week in the theatre. Finally, Mrs Corrigan would stand on her head to a drum-roll. They said, 'The only sound at night is Mrs Corrigan climbing', but they went. This was Cecil Beaton's description in *Vogue* of a typical party of the time, given by Mrs Guinness: 'people literally overflowing into the street . . . all the people one had ever known or even seen – up and down the big staircase, in the ballroom, along the corridors – "Hutch" singing in the ballroom while we all sat on the

floor – Edythe Baker playing to some of us in another room downstairs – Oliver Messel in the same room giving a ludicrously lifelike imitation of a lift-attendant describing the departments on each floor – Lady Ashley shining in a glittering short coat of silver sequins over her white dress – glimpses of the Ruthven twins – of Noël Coward looking happy and being amusing – Gladys Cooper in a Chanel rhinestone necklace that reached to the knees of her black velvet frock . . . impression after impression, before one sank and sank . . . to the supper room.'

Loelia Ponsonby, later the Duchess of Westminster, gave a different sort of party. She would ring up her friends at the last moment and ask them to come round with some food or champagne. Nine parties out of ten would be fancy dress. Evelyn Waugh in *Vile Bodies* wrote about 'Masked parties, savage parties, Victorian parties, Greek parties, Wild West parties, Russian parties, Circus parties, parties where one had to dress as someone else and almost naked parties in St John's Wood, parties in flats and studios and houses and ships and hotels and nightclubs, in windmills and swimming baths.' The swimming pool party given by Brian Howard and Elizabeth Ponsonby had a jazz band to which the guests danced in bathing suits. It caused a small scandal. The *Sunday Chronicle* wrote, 'Great astonishment and not a little indignation is being expressed in London over the revelation that in the early hours of yesterday morning a large number of society women were dancing in bathing dresses to the music of a Negro band at a "swim and dance" gathering organized by some of Mayfair's Bright Young People.' Brian Howard, down from Oxford, initiated 'Follow my Leader' through Selfridges, where a crowd of young people helpless with laughter tore about among the shoppers, jumping into lifts and climbing over the counters. Lord Bessborough and Prince Obolensky went to one of the Sutherlands'

2

Edmund Harrington

3

Cecil Beaton

4

parties as drunken waiters, taking over from house staff, finally keeling over with a crash of breaking china. Lady Diana Cooper wrote, 'there was a fancy ball at Ava Ribblesdale's last night, and all the women looked fifty per cent worse than usual – S. as Little Lord Fauntleroy quite awful, P. as a street Arab just dirty.' It was a good time for twins, and there was a pair at every party – the plain but jolly Ruthven sisters, the Ward twins and the Rowe twins, Joan and Kit Dunn, or Thelma Furness and Gloria Vanderbilt, twice the woman for being indistinguishable.

Society in the twenties was large enough to be heterogeneous and international, but small enough for the prime figures to be well known to readers of gossip columns. It was a clever, amusing, worldly set at best, greatly improved by overlapping with the theatre and the new rich. The Prince of Wales gave English society its lead, and his friends were actresses and self-made men. London's theatrical peerage included Zena Dare who had become the Hon. **Mrs Maurice Brett**, Gertie Millar (the Countess of Dudley), Rosie Boot of the Gaiety (the Marchioness of Headfort), Beatrice Lillie (Lady Peel), and Lady Inverclyde, who had been June on the stage. The well-known beauty Lady Ashley was rumoured to be the daughter of an ostler. As Sylvia Hawkes, her first job had been modelling at Reville, and she had been in the banned first London cabaret, 'Midnight Follies'. Her father-in-law, the Earl of Shaftesbury, was denying the engagement the day before the wedding, and none of the groom's family went to the marriage.

1. Iris and Viola Tree as London urchins at a 'children's party' party, 1926.
2. Mrs Gerard d'Erlanger, formerly Edythe Baker, 1929.
3. Lady Ashley, 1929.
4. Elsa Maxwell and friends at the Duc de Verdura's Palermo ball, 1929.

Cecil Beaton

Society women were the new fashion dictators. They wore couture clothes and lived by the season – Deauville in spring, the Riviera in summer, Scotland in autumn, London and Paris in the winter. Fashion had become a matter of personal style, and the embodiment of the new style was Mrs Dudley Ward, who practised the Charleston with the Prince of Wales at the Café de Paris early in the mornings. Neat as a pin, she wore natty check suits with a clove carnation and jingling bracelets, and dressed her daughters and herself to match in red gingham, with bows in the hair.

An exotic at the opposite end of the scale from Diana Cooper was Baba d'Erlanger, whose mother had brought her up to be highly unusual. As a child she had instead of a nanny a robed and turbaned mameluke, who followed her about like a page. The d'Erlangers lived in Byron's old house in Piccadilly, and gave marvellous children's parties to which Baba always wore gold. A *belle-laide* with a monkey face and scarlet lipstick, she became the Princesse Jean de Faucigny-Lucinge and set a fashion for wearing a tarbush cap and bunches of artificial fruit with a bathing suit.

The beauty of the moment was Paula Gellibrand, Baba d'Erlanger's best friend, a heavy-lidded Modigliani with a look of fatigue and sophistication. A golden blonde with enormous blue eyes, she glossed them with Vaseline, wore hats dripping with wistaria and got married in a dress as plain as a nun's habit. A *Vogue* model, she married an unusual man, the Marquis de Casa Maury, Castilian by ancestry, Cuban by nationality, English by education. He was an ace driver of a Bugatti in the Grands Prix, and the owner of the first Bermuda-rigged schooner in Europe, doing the navigating himself. When Wall Street crashed he built the Curzon cinema. He spent seven months learning the trade under assumed names, sweeping up, working the projector, selling the tickets, until he knew enough to make a great success of the Curzon.

Finally there was Mrs Reginald Fellowes, who invented the almost insulting elegance that was to be the ambition of model girls up to the 1960s. She loved making other women look silly, usually managed it by looking much less 'dressed' than they did, arriving at greater elegance with far less apparent effort. She wore the same absolutely simple dress day after day, usually with a sequin

1. Mrs Dudley Ward, 1928.
2. Paula Gellibrand, 1929.
3. Mr and Mrs Michael Arlen at Cannes, 1928.
4. Cocktail time at Antibes, 1927.

3

2

Cecil Beaton

4

dinner jacket and a green carnation. Actually the dress was probably a different one every night, since she ordered plain linen dresses in dozens. Meeting a woman in the same dress at a nightclub once, she called for a pair of scissors and snipped off her ostrich trimming. Her jewellery was remarkable: she had handcuffs of emeralds, necklets of stones brought to her from India, and conch shells made of diamonds.

So much had happened in the twenties, and so many new influences felt, that the change in fashion was bound to be radical. The people who wore the clothes overtook the designers, who were obliged by the middle twenties to conform to the uniform of short skirts, dropped waists and simplicity demanded by the lives and tastes of their public. The most important designers to emerge from the twenties were the two most involved with new movements in other fields – Chanel, whose circle included Picasso, Cocteau and Stravinsky, and the new Schiaparelli, whose friends were the Surrealists.

THE CHANGING FACE

Florence Vandamm

2

GERTRUDE LAWRENCE

She arrived on the London scene in the early twenties at the same moment as Bea Lillie, who became Lady Peel: they were photographed in *Vogue* taking tea together in 1922, when Gertrude Lawrence looks timid, demure, an entirely different creature from the alluring worldly sophisticate she became in the mid-twenties. Her first starring role was in Ivor Novello's musical *A to Z*, which ran for 433 performances. She owes much of her success to her stage partnership with Noël Coward, whose flippant, cynical, casual plays like *Bitter Sweet* and *Private Lives* provided her with roles that perfectly suited her personality. 'Her manner and charm,' says Madge Garland, 'were such that by the time anyone found out she was not a beauty, it was too late, they were bewitched.' With her curdled voice, singing 'Some day I'll find you' in a bias white satin dress by Molyneux, she won all hearts. Her permanent contribution to fashion is the full-length mink coat worn over grey flannels, or perhaps the flame-coloured pyjama pants in which she fell off the sofa fighting with Laurence Olivier in *Bitter Sweet*.

1. Steichen's portrait of 1926.
2. 1922.
3. In Molyneux's satin and fox, for *Private Lives,* 1930.

Studio Sun

LADY ASHLEY

Formerly Sylvia Hawkes, a mannequin at Reville and a chorus girl at the Winter Garden, she took part in London's first cabaret show. Said to be the daughter of an ostler, she married Lord Ashley in the teeth of his family's opposition. Lord Ashley was the first of her five husbands—Douglas Fairbanks was the second. Tall, slender, with fair hair and a mild lisp, she was a perfect English rose. Both photographs, 1932.

Cecil Beaton

MOLYNEUX   Hoyningen-Huene

BABA D'ERLANGER

Daughter of avant-garde decorator Baroness d'Erlanger
dressed in gold as a child. When she grew up, a striking
wore black paint under her eyes, brilliant red lipstick and
enamelled maroon.

MARION MOREHOUSE

Steichen, who said 'Good fashion models have the qu
a good actress', called her, 'The best fashion model I ev
She was perfect for the clothes of the twenties, and p
Steichen's formal, statuesque photographs. She later
e.e. Cummings and became a photographer herself.

Cecil Beaton

PAULA GELLIBRAND

Her look of exhausted sophistication was said to hide a perfectly simple,
straightforward nature. She attracted attention at the Ritz, wearing a hat
draped with wistaria, and became one of *Vogue's* first society models. Baroness
d'Erlanger, mother of her friend Baba, encouraged her to gloss her eyelids
with vaseline and wear simple, saintly clothes — nurses' coifs and nun's-habit
dresses. She married the Marquis de Casa Maury.

'We have been passing through the awkward age, when instead of conversing we S.O.Sed in monosyllabic slang. It might be called the "Abbreviated Period – short skirts, short shrift, short credit and short names" . . . but you ain't seen nothin' yet'

LANVIN   Steichen

Black georgette crepe dress with high neck, steel discs for decoration, and sleeves slashed with white chiffon.

'The silhouette finds a straight line the smartest distance between two points'

There's a new Labour government and opinions are mixed — about Ramsay MacDonald's mode of dress, his ability to entertain, whether there will be a season or not. The hostess at 10 Downing Street is his daughter Ishbel MacDonald. Reporters interview her to find out if she is a modern girl. 'I've never been centred in a whirlpool of jazz and I do not intend to be,' she says. Lady Diana Cooper is in America playing in Max Reinhardt's *The Miracle,* her confidence boosted by her beautiful clothes by Ospovat. Every dashing lady has her own car, and *The Green Hat* by Michael Arlen is favourite reading. The hit of the year is Shaw's *Saint Joan;* asked why he wrote the play Shaw replies, 'To save Joan of Arc from John Drinkwater.' Jackie Coogan visits London and is treated like royalty. It's the year of *Le Train Bleu,* costumes by Chanel, curtains by Picasso. Moved from the Everyman to the West End, Coward's *The Vortex,* about a nogood mother and her drug-taking son, arouses a storm of protest. Everyone who can afford it is going abroad and hostess Mrs Laura Corrigan ('the only sound at night is Mrs Corrigan climbing') has gone to India, but makes arrangements for her Grand National house party by sending back reply-paid cables.

Vogue shows maternity clothes for the first time, and couturiers announce their London and Paris showings by advertisement. The smart places to go are Oddenino's and the Café de Paris.

Narrow, boneless and elastic girdles have taken over from the corset and the line is narrow and immaculately neat. The Prince of Wales visits Paris and inspires couturiers to collections of immaculate tailored suits in men's suitings and covert cloths. Navy and black are worn for town, white with coloured scarves or cloches for the country. Hems fall between the ankle and the calf of the leg, and the cloche sits so low on the head it hides the eyebrows. The accessories of the year are suede gloves worn a bit too large, a stubby fat umbrella, and Chanel's steel beads.

For evening add to the narrow silhouette gathered panels of tulle or bunches of feathers on the hips, or a train. The back is bared, the neckline modest. Chiffon evening dresses have feather boas or scarves, or butterfly wings floating from the shoulders. Satin is used for evening for the first time — Poiret's poppy and cornflower prints make evening pyjamas that look particularly good with the brief bobbed hair. Evening shoes are brocade slippers with embroidered toes or gemmed heels, and wraps are edged all round with fur.

For day you wear a suit with a hiplength jacket buttoned low and hanging dead straight over a straight skirt — Chanel's skirt is unbuttoned to show grey crepe pantalets. Seven-eighths coats hang open over their dresses — sometimes a light tunic with an underskirt of the coat fabric, or a low-waisted dress of printed crepe. Scarves tie in 'aeroplane bows' — stiffly, like propellers.

Left: The Grand Duchess Boris of Russia in a 'perfect sports dress', 1925: photograph Steichen.

RENÉE

CHANEL

MARTIAL ET ARMAND

1. Renée satin day suit.
2. Chanel skirt unbuttoned over crepe pantalets.
3. Martial et Armand cloche and propeller scarf.
4. The shortest evening hem is Chéruit's — here black satin.
5. Louiseboulanger grey covert-cloth suit, Reboux hat.
6. Chanel's chiffon evening dresses.
7. Lady Diana Cooper, back from New York, to help canvass for her husband, models a Henri Bendel brown velours hat for *Vogue*.
8. Nicole Groult's beige toile dress, for afternoon or 'informal restaurant wear.'
9. 'The pyjama is the smartest negligée' . . . and simpler versions are being worn for the beach and informal lunches at Deauville and the Venice Lido.

CHÉRUIT

LOUISEBOULANGER

1924

6 CHANEL

7 HENRI BENDEL

8 NICOLE GROULT   Maurice Beck and Helen Macgregor

9 MOLYNEUX   MOLYNEUX   LANVIN

77

1925

DOVE

Nemtchinova of the Russian Ballet in Dove's black crepe de chine pyjamas appliquéd with vivid velvet flowers.

Maurice Beck and Macgregor

'You wanna be happy? Den watch dis kid! Ah tell de world dis sweetie sure kin make a funeral happy. Watch what she's fixin' fo' to do. Dance? She can't do nothin' else but! You show 'em sister'

Josephine Baker and the *Revuè Nègre* arrive in Paris, and black jazz, black dancing, singing and talking bowl over young society. The exhibition of Arts Décoratifs gives its name to the new applied arts out of cubism, Egyptian art, Russian Ballet and the Bauhaus. Everyone's wearing Russian boots. Nancy Cunard has her scandalous affair with Henry Crowther, and Maynard Keynes staggers the intellectual world by marrying Lydia Lopokova. Tallulah Bankhead attracts a whole generation of female fans for her performance in *Fallen Angels* and *The Green Hat*. Everyone's humming 'Tea for Two', and Fred and Adèle Astaire are dancing Gershwin's *Lady Be Good* on Broadway. John Barrymore is Hamlet, Ida Rubinstein is in *La Dame aux Camélias* in Paris, Braque has done the decor for *Zéphyr et Flore* with Serge Lifar dancing, there's *No No Nanette,* and Mrs Mayrick is out of prison to open another nightclub, the Manhattan, where you can rub shoulders with Gordon Richards the jockey, Sophie Tucker, Rudolph Valentino and Paul Whiteman. 'Artists' in Chelsea studios give 'dos' nightly, the real painters are to be found in Cassis and Cagnes, and all over London the Bright Young People are chasing policemen's helmets and actresses' shoes.

Sonia Delaunay, the painter, works with Jacques Heim and produces patchwork colour coats that personify the jazz age. This year she puts the same design on a car — a 5CV Citroën. Geometric futurist fabrics are painted at Chéruit, Lanvin, Renée and Worth, and Vionnet cuts the shapes into the structure of the dress. Patou, Lanvin and Vionnet open sports shops, and *Vogue* runs features on exercise. The straight, slim silhouette begins to move with pleats and godets, bloused bodices, swaying fringes, flying scarves and streamers, but the fullness slips back into the slim form when still. Designers are learning from Vionnet's bias cut, and jabots, winged panels ripple. For evening there are butterfly backs and straight, slim fronts, and butterfly chiffons with wings drifting from the shoulders. There's a new sweater blouse, jewelled and embroidered over a matching skirt. Skirts get shorter and shorter, with evening handkerchief points or asymmetric hems. *Vogue* does its first feature on 'The Little Black Dress'. The fabrics are kasha, printed crepes, crepe de chine, alpaca, rep, poplin, silk serge, and any fabric with a ribbed texture. At home, tea gowns are replaced by satin pyjamas in cyclamen, fuchsia, violet and jade.

Maurice Beck and Macgregor

DOVE

1. Billie Burke in the new hat, a felt cloche with a crushed crown, and the new gloves, worn a size too big.
2. Dove's tea pyjamas in cyclamen brocade and green satin with an embroidered black satin jacket, modelled by 'the famous English beauty known as "Sumurun"'.
3. Ina Claire in a typical Chanel sports suit of 1925. She was the first actress to dress naturally for the films — Chanel's were the 'real clothes' she wore during the twenties in Hollywood and on Broadway. She might wear pale beige kasha dresses for drawing-room comedies or two-piece velveteen suits out of doors.
4. New freedom in the slim silhouette.

Steichen

CHANEL

Steichen

EARLY PARIS OPENINGS:

MOLYNEUX   LELONG   PATOU

Evenings

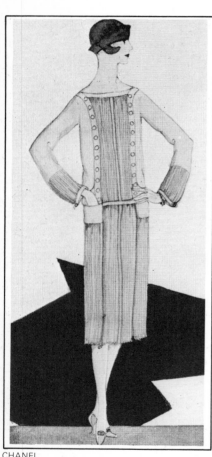

CHANEL

1. Chanel's grey crepella dress with pleated panels under the pockets, straight when still.
2. Vionnet's black velvet bias dress with crystal shoulder straps and crystal necklace embroidered on.
3. New backs for evening dresses.
4. Jean Patou's new sports department sells jersey and marocain bathing suits, which look as if you might be able to swim in them.
5. Flowered chiffon with the shortest, fullest evening skirt.
6. Lanvin's evening dress of gold brocade is embroidered with crystal and coral beads, with a bra top of peach tulle. Chéruit's cape is green and silver shot lamé with a skunk collar and green velvet lining.
7. English sports clothes — knitted suit, tweed topcoat, suede windcheater and kasha skirt
8. Isabel Jeans in Selfridge's straw hat and summer dress.

VIONNET

Douglas Pollard

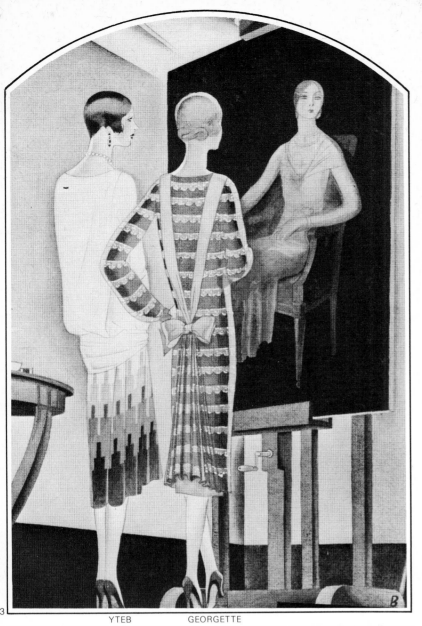

3
YTEB   GEORGETTE

5
ARTELLE   Maurice Beck and Macgregor

6
LANVIN, CHÉRUIT   Steichen

4
PATOU   Fellows

7   Benito

8   Maurice Beck and Macgregor   81

1926

A man's shop, 1926

Shortsighted old lady to mannish young woman: 'Excuse me – did you say you were going up to Trinity or Girton next term?' *Punch cartoon*

The nine-day General Strike turns London upside down. Hyde Park is a milk depot, there are troops at Whitehall, and public transport comes to a stop. Commuters walk fifteen or twenty miles to work. It's the year of the Charleston, which sweeps the country and causes the vicar of St Aidan's in Bristol to declare, 'Any lover of the beautiful will die rather than be associated with the Charleston. It is neurotic! It is rotten! It stinks! Phew, open the windows!'

Skirts are at their shortest of the twenties, and sports clothes fill the foreground of fashion. *Vogue* writes on 'The Modern Rosalind' and the unfashionable can't tell the girls from the boys. Shoulders get broader, the fit is looser, and women go to men's shops to buy themselves plaid golfing socks, cardigans, ties and cravats, sleeveless V-neck sweaters, cuff links, cigarette holders and short dressing gowns. Chanel's tweed skirts with inverted pleats are much copied, and Chéruit brings out a new navy redingote, double-breasted with brass buttons.

On the other hand the dress silhouette softens. The cut is Vionnet's, a blouson dress tying around the hips into a front bow, lifting the skirt a little in front. Coats have fur collars, neat suits have frilly jabot blouses, and with them you wear two-tone leather shoes, suede purses and gloves. Daytime colours are navy, black and white, henna. Sports clothes are beige and brown or brilliant stripes and plaids. Evening dresses are pastel lace, white crepe, and all shades of mauve from palest lavender to ecclesiastic purple. Only the evening cloak is silver and gold, and any look borrowed from the Orient or the Russian ballet belongs in the tea-gown/pyjama category — even Poiret makes sports jumpers and pleated skirts.

1
PAM   Maurice Beck and Macgregor

2
CHANEL

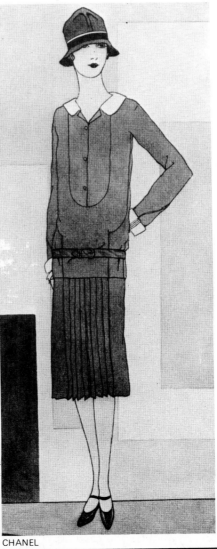

3
CHANEL

4
PATOU   Douglas Pollard

1. Three-piece travelling suit,
oatmeal angora with lynx collar and cuffs.
2. Chanel — black or purple crepella.
3. Chanel — grey-blue crepella with
collar and cuffs of white starched
linen, moiré belt.
4. Jean Patou — pleated skirt, black
jacket, white satin waistcoat.

1926

VIONNET   1   Francis

84

TALBOT

VIONNET   Sheeler

3

VIOLET NORTON   Maurice Beck and Macgregor

1. Vionnet's silver and gold dress shows her
   marvellous cutting to perfection.
2. Vionnet's new sports shop sells dresses like this
   one in natural kasha with monogram and navy
   gored crepe de chine skirt.
3. Lime green and silver wrap from Violet Norton.
4. Travel by sea — with Chanel.
5. Winter sports at St Moritz.

4
CHANEL   Steichen

5

1927

Lepape

THE SUN

'We practically live in bathing suits and coconut oil'
Méraud Guinness, 1927

Year of the Surrealist conference on sex, Lindbergh's flight, and the new phrase 'sex appeal'. The sun is god, and society congregates at Cannes, Antibes, and the Venice Lido . . . there's Nancy Cunard in a gold dress with armfuls of barbaric bangles, her eyes made up with kohl 'which on first sight makes her unrecognisable'; Mrs Reginald Fellowes in a sequin dinner jacket with a green carnation, making news by wearing the same outfit night after night; the Duchess of Peneranda with her sunburned body and bare white dresses, flashing white teeth and brilliantined black hair; the Ruthven twins, the Dunne twins, the Morgan twins, Thelma Furness and Gloria Vanderbilt; Lady Louis Mountbatten, Mrs Cole Porter, Loelia Ponsonby . . . 'there are few French in Cannes'. The waterfront is lined with boutiques, Molyneux, Chanel, Poiret, Worth, Lanvin, offering special reductions and bargains for everyone who goes in. At home Noël Coward has 4 shows running simultaneously, and Cecil Beaton and Oliver Messel launch 1927 as the year of a million parties, most of them costume balls, with Beaton's costumes and Messel's masks. There's the Kit-Cat restaurant, the Café de Paris, and the cosy Gargoyle in Dean Street. There's a saxophonist you can't miss at the Silver Slipper, and Hutch singing 'The man I love' at Chez Victor, and Ciro's, where the Prince of Wales goes immediately on his return from his Canadian tour.

Sports clothes, in other words clothes for watching sports in, are the strongest influence in fashion. Looks designed for sports graduate to country day-dressing and then arrive in town. Chanel's country tweeds have just completed the course, particularly as she's opened a London shop this year: she pins a white piqué gardenia to the neck. Her 'lingerie touches' are copied everywhere — piping, bands of contrast, ruffles and jabots. She initiates fake jewellery, to be worn everywhere, even on the beach. Worth opens a sports shop here, and sells the new jumper suit — jersey overblouse and skirt in a combination of browns. Jackets get longer, and at the end of the year the skirt begins to drop. The new fur is a flared jacket of broadtail or shaved Persian lamb. The new indoor shoes are patent, called azuré, nacré or iridescent kid.

In reaction to the informal daytime tweeds, there's a silk afternoon dress to wear from three o'clock, and evening dresses look more formal, with draped, girdled or tucked hips. The newest are in printed chiffon, with flowers of the same fabric, or in a combination of white and flesh-coloured crepe. Shoppers come up from the country to buy their clothes from Harrods, Dickins & Jones, Debenham & Freebody, Marshall & Snelgrove and Harvey Nichols, and artificial silk is called 'rayon' from now on.

By the end of the year the shingle has become curly or waved, and *Vogue* asks, 'Shall we join the Long-Haired Ladies?' The black felt cloche of spring becomes the draped skullcap of winter — a helmet shape with one wing sweeping forward onto the cheek.

Three new houses make their first appearance in *Vogue* — Norman Hartnell, Elsa Schiaparelli and Galitzine.

1
NOWITZKY

2 HARVEY NICHOLS PATOU

3
PATOU

4 PATOU   Hoyningen-Huene

1. Nowitzky bathing suits photographed on the Venice Lido.
2. Two bathing suits: Harvey Nichols's in two shades of orange jersey, Jean Patou's in black and white crepe de chine with a buttoned and monogrammed belt. The printed silk beach shoes are from Patou.
3. Patou's bare-backed bathing costume, tank top and shorts of red and white.
4. At the Bar Basque, Biarritz, in Patou jumper suits.

1
VIONNET

2

3

4
FORTUNY

Maurice Beck and Macgregor

1. Vionnet's rose and silver paillettes, matching pin and
  necklace.
2. Chanel's costume jewellery isn't meant to be mistaken for
the real thing — most of it isn't even imitation. About now,
she breaks her necklace of graduated pearls and strings them
together as she finds them — setting a fashion for irregular
beads. Here — a selection from London shops.
3. and 4. Mariano Fortuny's robes and velvets are famous, but
almost impossible to get hold of from London. Here, making
a unique appearance in British *Vogue*, his mushroom-pleat
Greek robe in soft grey-blue satin on a drawstring-neck. The
peplum hem is weighted with opalescent beads. Over
it, a richer grey-blue velvet lined with ruby poplin, the
velvet brushed with peacock and stamped with gold.
  5. Mrs Cole Porter in cloche and fake beads.
  6. New French hats, from Agnès and Marie Alphonsine.
  7. Ilka Chase, daughter of American *Vogue's* editor-in-chief,
  models Chanel's eau de nil satin.

5

6

AGNÈS

AGNÈS

MARIE ALPHONSINE

CHANEL

7

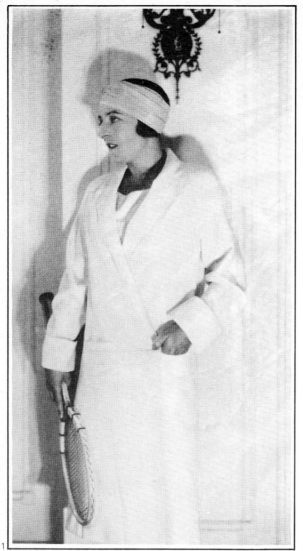

1
PATOU

2
CHANEL   Steichen

3
LOUISEBOULANGER   VIONNET   CHANEL

1. Suzanne Lenglen, 'hideously chic' in a white
bandeau, revolutionized tennis wear by
playing in a short, sleeveless, pleated dress
wrapped up here in a Patou coat.
2. Chanel—beige shaved lamb sports coat
and tweed dress.
3. Four country/town looks.
4. From Lady Paget's dress shop in Grafton
Street, a black and white silk dress matching
the lining of the coat, dots and stripes mixed.

4

Cecil Beaton

FIFINELLA   Steichen

5. Paquin's printed chiffon.
6. Garden party dress of white organdie
with an embroidered bolero.

5

PAQUIN

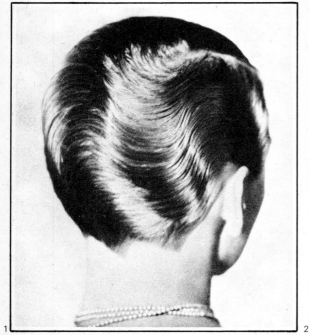

HARTNELL   Hugh Cecil

1. The waved shingle by Antoine.
2. First appearance of Norman Hartnell's name in *Vogue*, with this picture frock of pale blue taffeta with hand-painted flowers, pink chiffon bodice, orchid taffeta surplice.
3. The first Schiaparelli — and the first of her trompe l'oeil super-smart hand-knitted sweaters.
4. The hair-piece: by the end of the year women are adding to the shingle with a switch of false hair on a clasp.

'We shall be smart, but not hard; we shall gird our loins; there will be only one silhouette – the youthful one'

'To lose weight has become an obsession' and in its pursuit women go for treatments from Denglers to Brides, from Baden-Baden to Orsier, never forgetting to take their vitamins along with their cocktails — even dogs have a cocktail bar, dispensing water outside Vuitton in the Champs Elysées. As an accompaniment to drinks, the new potato crisps sell over a million packets this year. A very hot summer popularizes sunbathing at home as well as abroad — there are backless bathing suits so you can look evenly tanned in your backless evening dress. Rich smart women are flying all over the place: Lady Heath, Lady Bailey, Lady Anne Saville, Mrs Dulcibella Atkey and the redoubtable Duchess of Bedford, sixty years old before she set foot in a plane. The Dolly sisters are gambling away a fortune at Cannes, watched by a crowd six deep. *Vogue* tells you how to dress on £75 a year . . .'an evening dress from your little dressmaker, £4, three pairs of shoes, £6.10s, two hats, £3, lingerie and accessories, £2'.

Vogue gives women *carte blanche* to dress as they like — 'controlled by the permanent limitations of good taste and the current limitations of the mode'. The new 'runabout' dress is easy as any tennis dress. Waistlines begin to go up because of the fitted and moulded hipline, hems drop lower at the back, and the sweater of the year is Schiaparelli's, a *trompe l'oeil* scarf around the hips tying with a real tie on one side.

'As seen at Deauville or any other ville d'eau.'

1
CHANEL   VIONNET   PARIS TRADES   CHAMPCOMMUNAL

2 LANVIN   Hoyningen-Huene

WORTH   4   5 CHRISTABEL RUSSELL

1. Tweed ensembles.
2. Lanvin navy-blue and white bathing suit.
3. Another of Schiaparelli's trompe l'oeil sweaters, *left*;
right, Drecoll sports model in navy-blue and yellow.
4, 5 and 6. Three-piece suits: *left*, peach silk jumper with navy
bands, printed georgette skirt to match; *centre*, red crepe de chine
cardigan and skirt; *right*, clover-patterned sweater, deeply ribbed
over the hips.
7. The Marquise de Casa Maury — the beauty and model Paula
Gellibrand — with vaselined eyelids, wearing Worth's gold lamé with
pleated skirt and chiffon velvet cardigan.
8. Full tulle evening dress by Elspeth Fox-Pitt.
9. Schiaparelli's sweater (see No. 3) worn by Mrs Somerset
Maugham, *centre*, at Le Touquet.

94   3
SCHIAPARELLI, DRECOLL   Francis

WORTH

Cecil Beaton

6 FORTNUM & MASON

8 ELSPETH FOX-PITT

Bertram Park

9

SCHIAPARELLI

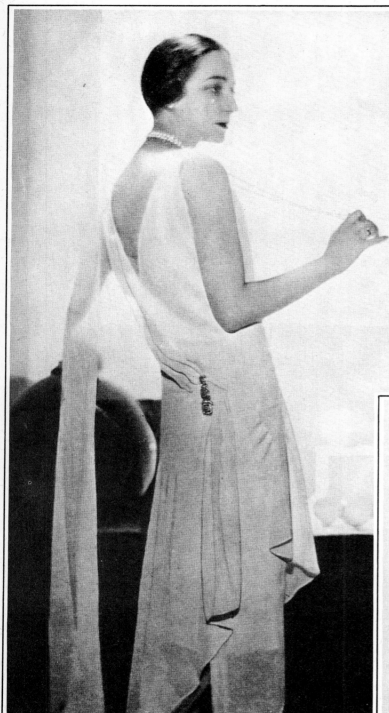

AIRY NOTHINGS
UNDERLIE
THE SUMMER MODE

PAUL CARET   Scaloni

1. Paul Caret evening dress in ivory Celanese georgette.
2. Underwear — *left*, lace-trimmed washing satin combinations with lowcut back, and *centre*, brassière and corset of pink crepe de chine with écru lace.
3. Tiers by Chanel, in black crepe.

CHANEL   Lee Erickson

Cocktails at the 500, Brian Howard in the centre   Howard and Joan Coster

'Automobiles, Movies and Bootlegging are the three biggest American industries.
After these . . . comes Beauty'   *Aldous Huxley, 1929*

There are machines to tone you, slim you and stretch you, skin nourishers, cleansers and lotions, and 'a face can cost as much in upkeep as a Rolls Royce'. This is what *Vogue's* fashion editor wears on her face: Arden's Ultra Amoretta foundation cream, powder, a little brilliantine over eyebrows and lashes — Coty's L'Origan — and Guerlain's pale lipstick. In town, Helena Rubinstein's sticky foundation called Creme Gypsy, sunburn colour, applied with a pad of cotton wool wrung out in cold water and drying to a light ochre. A little grease rouge, and two powders, first a light rachel then a deeper shade. Vaseline rubbed on the eyelid, with a blue or brown pencil line. Black mascara, brushed with a clean brush when still wet to take off excess, eyebrow pencil and a darker lipstick.

Dancing has slowed down. 'The most loved dance tunes of today are immersed in a delicious and quite artificial sentimentality, the kind of emotion that appeals only to the cynical or the sophisticated.' Two favourites of the year are 'Let's do it' and 'You're the cream in my coffee'. Rosita Forbes, the explorer, loves 'Glad Rag Doll', and Paula Gellibrand adores 'I can't give you anything but love, Baby'.

The bosom makes a gentle reappearance: most women are beginning to wear a 'combination corset', brassière and girdle in one, with a few light bones, cut to emphasize the waist. Or you can buy a bra-topped petticoat with divided legs to wear over a girdle. The day silhouette is simple, just a long jersey belted over pleats or a dress which, pure in line, has a complicated cut. Evening dresses are tiered, ruffled, bowed, butterfly-backed.

1

P. Mourgue

1. *Vogue* cover for 1 May 1929.
2. Waisted black velvet evening dress by Augustabernard.
3. Corset from Roussel.
4. Bigger one-sided hats for winter from Maria Guy, *left*, and Reboux.

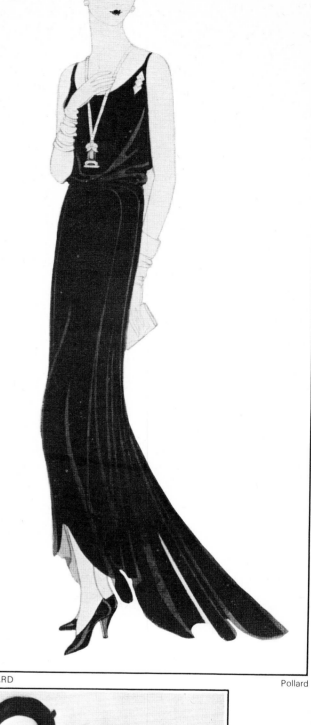

2

AUGUSTABERNARD

Pollard

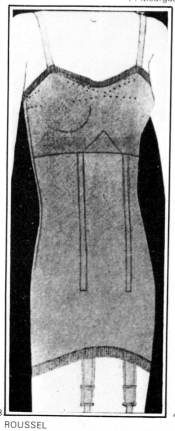

3   ROUSSEL

MARIA GUY   REBOUX

5 CHANEL

6

5. Chanel's new grège-brown jersey suit with hat, scarf, sweater and lining in red, blue and black stripes.
6. Beach trousers with big raffia hats.
7. Men's and women's jersey swimsuits.
8. Sleeveless Biarritz dress in white silk piqué with a sleeveless pale yellow jersey sweater belted in white and yellow grosgrain from Paris Trades. White folded felt hat, tan and white co-respondent shoes.

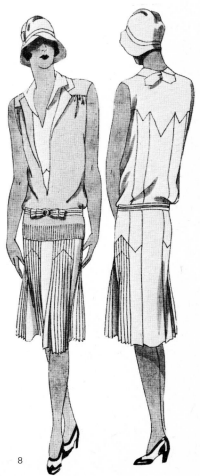

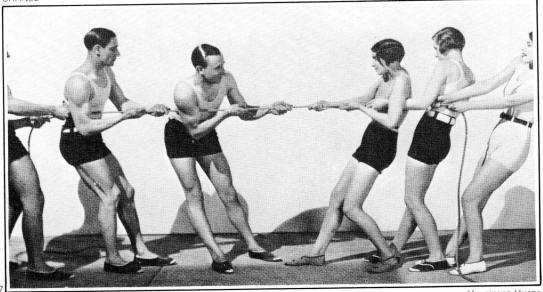

7

8

Hoyningen-Huene

1930-1939

The Threadbare Thirties

TO THE WOMEN OF BRITAIN

Your urgent duty calls you to-day, as never before, to ask in all your shopping for British goods.

Every time you buy British you are sure of getting the best quality in the world.

Every time you buy British you make work for your own fellow-countrymen.

Every time you buy British you help to improve your country's housekeeping account.

Scrutinize all advertisements.
Look at all labels.
Ask where the goods come from.

Insist, whenever you make a purchase, that you mean to

buy British
from the Empire at home and overseas

ISSUED BY THE EMPIRE MARKETING BOARD

December 1931.

The thick skin that protected the rich and secure in the twenties wore paper-thin in the thirties. Groucho Marx called the years of American Depression before the New Deal the Threadbare Thirties, but the slump was an international crisis and in Britain the unemployment figures reached three million, and feelings of anxiety and insecurity were at their highest since the middle of the war. Owing to the decline of world trade and the collapse of markets, Britain was pock-marked with Distressed Areas where almost the entire population was living on the meagre dole. A policy of national self-sufficiency was reuniting Germany and giving it identity and a sense of purpose, but Britain was divided and on the point of crisis when the National Government was formed in 1931, and politics began to invade the lives and conversation of people who had never thought politically before. Hunger marchers poured into London by the thousand instead of the hundred, and demonstrations were charged by police with batons – in Birkenhead the street fighting went on for three days. As an economy measure, the National Government had introduced reductions in unemployment pay subject to the Means Test. A man would come round, notice a new coat or find out if a boy did a paper round, and cut the allowance. Men whose families could not live on the dole as it was faced cuts and deductions of food tickets. Sympathy for them caused a rift in the Labour party, and the Left was joined by university undergraduates and dissatisfied or sensitive elements of the

middle and upper classes. University students who came out to see the hunger marchers spoke of the extraordinary sound of their feet, not marching like soldiers, but shuffling because of the flapping soles of their worn-out boots. In the twenties university students had rallied to the government in the General Strike. In the thirties they joined the marchers.

The situation was brought home to *Vogue*'s readership in other ways. Wal Hannington, organizer of the National Unemployed Workers' Movement, used the nuisance tactics exploited before the war by the Suffragettes and more recently by Gandhi's followers in India, to draw attention to the plight of the unemployed. One hundred unemployed moved right into *Vogue*'s territory when they invaded the Ritz one afternoon and asked for tea, provoking press features contrasting the lives of the unemployed with those of the Ritz tea-drinkers. Another stunt took place just before Christmas, when Oxford Street was crammed with shoppers. Unemployed men lay down head to toe, eight abreast across the road, and spread over themselves posters reading 'Work or Bread'. When the police arrived and dragged them onto the pavement, they immediately went back to their places in the road and had soon created a traffic jam that paralysed the West End.

Other facts you could not ignore were the scuffles of the Fascist party, led by Sir Oswald Mosley. Elected as Conservative member for Harrow at twenty, he had married Lord Curzon's daughter and

Left: Film star photograph, film star dress, 1932. Studio Sun's picture of an evening dress in Courtauld's Courgette, an artificial silk, in the quintessential thirties setting: a modern armchair, a bowl of white tulips.

1   Cecil Beaton   2

subsequently quarrelled with both the Conservative and Labour parties. Unfortunately for him, his wife, who kept her Socialist convictions, was half Jewish. She died and left him free to marry in 1937, with Hitler as his best man, Mrs Bryan Guinness: otherwise Diana Mitford, sister of the 'Perfect Aryan Beauty' Unity Mitford. Both wives were well known to *Vogue* readers from the society pages.

For some time after Mussolini's takeover of Italy Fascism was vaguely respected, and Rothermere for the *Daily Mail* gave it his temporary support, but as the Blackshirts were seen to be using knuckledusters on hecklers and victimizing the 'Kikes' in the East End, and as Nazism grew year by year, the papers began to speak disparagingly of the 'rule of the rubber truncheon and the castor oil bottle'. In 1935 Margot Asquith was writing in *Vogue*, 'We do not believe in mock Mussolinis, silly shirts, self-advertising up-starts. We detest dictators ... Men are tired of force and formula, they ardently desire to follow the things that make for peace.' *Vogue* had mentioned Mussolini in connection with fashion in 1933: 'À propos of an article in the Popolo d'Italia ... Mussolini gives some good advice to the Nazis, including the warning, in view of a Prussian ordinance against lipstick and rouge – "Any power whatsoever is destined to fail before fashion. If fashion says skirts are to be short, you will not succeed in lengthening them, even with the guillotine." This statement by one dictator to another, acknow-ledging a power before which both are helpless, is of peculiar interest.'

Writers were now known for their politics, not their amusing novels. Evelyn Waugh was in favour of Fascism. Stephen Spender and Cecil Day Lewis represented the Left, and in spite of the Nazi hatred of modern art, Wyndham Lewis wrote a book in praise of Hitler. George Orwell, who was wounded in the Spanish Civil War, came back to write *Homage to Catalonia*; George Barker wrote his account. Aldous Huxley was now the intellectual leader of Constructive Pacifism and had published the *Encyclopedia of Pacifism*, before leaving for America with a handful of leading writers who could see the war coming and had no wish to take part in it.

In *Vogue*, the scope of the society and gossip pages was extended to include political topics. 'Our Lives from Day to Day' took on a political flavour from the beginning of the decade. 'At Mr Wells' we began with vodka and caviare to welcome Julian Huxley back from Moscow, who spoke of communal life to as perfect a small company of famous individualists as could be gathered together in a London flat.' In the same column, an irreverent mention of Gandhi on his visit to London – 'the famous little figure ... looking very Mickey Mouse as he accepted tributes from the Ladies of India'. Asked whether he thought a dhoti sufficient garb for meeting the King, Gandhi had replied, 'The King wore enough for both of us'. On the advertising pages, readers were besought to 'Buy British', and on the fashion pages the models struck militaristic attitudes, the regimental suits that appeared in the mid-thirties giving copywriters a field day. 'Vive le Front Plisse Populaire!' ... 'Newshirts for all parties' ... 'Aux armes, Citoyennes! – the fashion cry of the moment'. Readers were told to 'March to the sound of drums by day', and shown suits with square epauletted shoulders, drummer boy frogging, gauntlet gloves and low heels, and hats with a 'forward putsch'.

One of *Vogue*'s most relevant pre-war features was a piece by Alan Stewart on finding out the real news. The silence that preceded the Abdication had brought it home to the public that the papers did not always print the whole news. Apart from what the press overlooked and chose to suppress, there were misrepresentations and actual censorship. The press continually referred to the unemployed as if they were too idle to look for work, and to the dole as though it were a comfortable wage. The facts were finally brought home by photographs of real life cases in *Picture Post*, founded on the lines of *Life* in 1938, which showed, for instance, the wife and four children of Alfred Smith waiting outside the Labour Exchange for his £2. 7s. 6d. weekly dole. Most people were in the dark about Germany's new rearmed power and the fresh European threats – just before the war angry letters to *The Times* denounced the B.B.C. for being alarmist because of its purely factual bulletins on the European situation. Alan Stewart's feature was called 'Every Woman her own Tabouis' – Geneviève Tabouis of the anti-Fascist *L'Œuvre* had a reputation for knowing what was going on behind the scenes. He said, 'If you lived in the United States, where the press is refreshingly bold and free, you wouldn't have to buy so many papers; but even in England you can discover almost all the news there is ... those who skim five dailies know much more than those who read one only. If you take *The Times*, you should also take the *Daily Worker*. The *Daily Telegraph* and the *News Chronicle* also balance one another nicely ... Unless you are Unity Mitford, it's unlikely that you will have much chance of a heart-to-heart talk with one of these Fuehrers, but it might be a good idea to have a look at the big shots of domestic politics. Go to a few political meetings, a Left Book Club Rally and persuade someone to get you into the House for a full dress Foreign Affairs debate.'

If politics were reflected only indirectly, the big scandal of the thirties happened well within *Vogue*'s scope. Mrs Simpson's name first appears in *Vogue* in 1935, obliquely mentioned in conjunction with groups including the Prince of Wales. We read that for cocktails 'hot sausages ... are out of date, back numbers. You must think up something different. The Prince of Wales has hot buttered American soda biscuits, with cod's roe, served in hot silver breakfast dishes' and, a sentence or two further down the page, 'Mrs Simpson's food is of such a high standard that the intelligent guest fasts before going to have cocktails with her ... Her hot dishes are famous.' At about this time Sir Samuel Hoare noticed Wallis Simpson for her 'sparkling jewels in very up-to-date Cartier settings'. *Vogue*'s references are so discreet that an inattentive reader might miss the point, but the two names are never far apart. 'The Prince of Wales went by boat to dine at St Tropez ... and acquired a blue and white striped sailor's pullover ... Tonight he dined at the restaurant on the quai, and when he got up to go on to another café for coffee, the entire company dining there got up and followed him, not even waiting to pay their bills ...' and in the next column, 'All the smart clothes here come from Paris and London, not St Tropez. The best-dressed women, like Mrs Ernest Simpson, for example, have Schiaparelli's "pouch" dress in silk or printed cotton' – and she was photographed for *Vogue* in Schiaparelli's white linen trouser suit. When the King died, *Vogue* came out with a blank purple cover and wrote, 'The Reign Begins ... Everything we know about the new occupant of the Throne suggests a keen, alert mind and forms the image of one who has mixed with a larger number of representative men and women than most other figures in history', and in the next issue, 'Mrs Ernest Simpson is now the best dressed woman in town.' Her immaculate, pin-neat elegance, like that of another hard-edged American contemporary, Mrs Diana Vreeland, who was to become editor of American *Vogue*, was much admired and copied in the thirties. It was a foil first for Schiaparelli's clothes, and later Mainbocher's.

Lady Furness, one of the Morgan twins who were often in *Vogue*, had introduced Mrs Simpson to the Prince of Wales and had lent her the train and feathers for the court appearance she made in spite of the rules about divorcees. In a conversation recorded by

4

5

Cecil Beaton

103

Vogue Studio

Steichen

James Laver in his anthology *Between the Wars*, when Lady Furness was leaving for a few weeks' holiday, Mrs Simpson said to her, 'Oh Thelma, the little man is going to be so lonely.' 'Well, dear,' replied Lady Furness, 'You look after him while I'm away. See that he does not get into any mischief.' On her return, she and the Simpsons were guests at Fort Belvedere: 'At dinner, I noticed that the Prince and Wallis seemed to have little private jokes. Once he picked up a piece of salad with his fingers. Wallis playfully slapped his hand. I . . . caught her eye and shook my head at her. She knew as well as everybody else that the Prince could be very friendly, but no matter how friendly, he never permitted familiarity . . . Wallis looked straight at me. That one cold, defiant stare told me the whole story. I left the Fort the following morning.' *Vogue* published honeymoon photographs of the Duke and Duchess at Schloss Wasserleonburg, one of 60 castles put at their disposal after the Abdication, and, tremendous scoop, published a portfolio of exclusive photographs by Cecil Beaton taken of them at the Chateau de Candé, the Duchess in the most elegant dresses from her Mainbocher trousseau.

Had fashion been the luxury many think it is, instead of a kind of barometer, the slump might have killed the couture – at least, for the years between the Crash and recovery. As it happened, the only Paris casualty was Augustabernard, who had just reopened in lavish new premises and who relied on a South American clientele who were all hit by the crisis at the same moment. Those houses which did not already have ready-to-wear sidelines now opened them, and even Chanel, who had one of the most expensive salons, cut her prices by half in 1932. In the first season after the Wall Street Crash, not a single American buyer came to Paris, and most of them did not return until 1933. The couture had always been prepared to wait a long time for payment, but at a time of fluctuating exchange rates this was a dangerous habit. Fortunately, all the couturiers had made so much money in the twenties that they had reserves. Their staff, who were underpaid anyway, were prepared to go on half-time, and, most important of all for the designers, the French fabric manufacturers were prepared to supply their materials on credit. A day dress took five yards of fabric in 1938, as opposed to the two yards it would have taken in the twenties. Not surprisingly, there was a vogue for economical and washable fabrics. Chanel was invited to England by Ferguson

to help promote their cottons as fashion fabrics, and in her 1931 collection she included thirty-five cotton evening dresses in piqué, lace, spotted muslin, organdie, lawn and net. These young and fresh looking dresses with their billowing skirts were the most popular evening dresses of the year with English debutantes, and with their fathers who paid the bills. Couture prices in the thirties however were not, even relatively, so very high: a plain Vionnet day dress in 1938 cost about £19, and now that it was in bad taste to look rich, there was a fashion for the 'poor' simple look. Ladies who were still fabulously rich went about in plain black dresses, furless wool coats and sweaters and slacks. *Vogue* wrote, 'It's no longer chic to be smart.' In the twenties Paris couturiers were showing four hundred outfits in a single collection. In the thirties these were whittled down to a hundred, and the showings were much better organized, with bureaux for the registration of models, a black book of cheap copyists to keep out, and press handouts to prevent misrepresentation.

It was an ill wind that made Paris less accessible to foreign clients. Now that fewer Londoners were going to Paris, London designers were given a boost and responded with new talent. Digby Morton set up his own couture business and was succeeded at Lachasse by Hardy Amies, Hartnell was prospering as the Queen's dressmaker, Molyneux and Charles Creed were to leave Paris for London at the outbreak of war. The designer Charles James, who made his reputation in America, was working in England during the early thirties and making a name for himself with the skill of his cutting and draping.

Fabrics were keeping pace with the ready-to-wear market. Artificial silk was now stronger and better made, and in 1939 the Americans began production of nylon, which they claimed to be more elastic than silk and one-and-a-half times stronger. *Vogue* drew a clothesline full of washable new clothes including a tailored linen suit, a beach dress with satinized stripes, an artificial silk jersey dress of awning stripes, and a frilled organdie and lace blouse. In shops people were asking for uncrushable fabrics like zingale, and for cottons, linens and spun rayons which were Sanforized – preshrunk. Schiaparelli matched Chanel's cottons with her own inevitably sensational experiments with Rhodophane, a glass fabric by Colcombet, and by using the nursery fabric Viyella for tailored blouses. She pioneered the use of Lightning

Fasteners – zips – used first in sports skirts and finally in evening dresses, and loved to incorporate gadget clasps and motif buttons, made for her by craftsmen like Jean Clement.

The thirties in fashion was chiefly a neck and neck race between the rivals Schiaparelli and Chanel. Schiaparelli, although her influence was limited to this single decade, was the more sensational: she dressed Salvador Dali's wife free in return for inspiration, and her fashion follies were inspired jokes – the shoe hat, the 'chest of drawers' suit, the aspirin necklace and edible cinnamon buttons, the lacquered white hair. Her lasting innovation was perfectly sober – the combination of a dress with a matching jacket – but her colours were fantastic. She would put together fuchsia purple, shocking pink and black. It was typical of Schiaparelli that, when she decided she hated the modernistic mannikins given her to dress for the Exposition Internationale des Arts et Techniques in 1937, she buried them in flowers and slung up her new collection on a clothesline.

Chanel contemptuously referred to Schiaparelli as 'that Italian artist who makes clothes' (in much the same sense as Vionnet referred to Chanel as 'that modiste'), and her own clothes of the thirties were faultlessly elegant, modern, and matchlessly chic. With Chanel No. 5 and her incredible costume jewellery – 'It does not matter if they are real,' she said, 'so long as they look like junk!' – she revolutionized Hollywood glamour by dressing Ina Claire in the simplest of white satin pyjamas or tweed suits. Unlike Schiaparelli's musical comedy military suits, Chanel's were quite effortless, the collars small, the shoulders not noticeably padded, the waist left in its natural place and not drawn in tight. Over 40 herself, she knew what made a woman look younger, and invented cardigan jackets, dashing velveteen and ciré satin cinema suits, to be worn with flattering small hats. She made hornrimmed glasses a fashion accessory, and scotched forever Dorothy Parker's overquoted remark about girls who wear glasses. Her country clothes were a revelation to tweedy Englishwomen and she was her own best advertisement. 'Chanel,' said Lesley Blanch in 1938, 'demonstrated the fact that grey flannel trousers and a hairy wool sweater are nothing if not allied to swags of pearls, wrists clogged with barbaric bracelets and a netted coiffure top-knotted with masses of geraniums and chenille plumes.'

In the twenties only two or three couturiers stood out from the

1. Cinematographic photograph by Hoyningen-Huene, a master of lighting, 1933. The evening dress by Christabel Russell.
2. Cecil Beaton's photograph of Margot Asquith, 1935. Jean Harlow, when introduced to her, said, 'Pleased to meet you, Margot', sounding the T, and Margot Asquith replied, 'The T is silent, as in Harlow.'
3. Raoul Dufy's Ascot cover for *Vogue*, 29 May 1935.

4. Benito's Surrealist drawing of Chanel's black lace and Schiaparelli's wine crepe suit with leg of mutton'sleeves.
5. Fashion photograph by Horst in Odeon style: Paquin's silver fox collared, white satin cape, 1935.
6. Salvador Dali, 1937, by Cecil Beaton.
7. Dali's sketch of his Dream House for the New York World Fair, 1939.

crowd because the look was universal. In the thirties each house had its own look, summed up by its most famous clients. Schiaparelli dressed Daisy Fellowes, the well-known fashion individualist. Molyneux was fortunate in dressing the beautiful and stylish Princess Marina, for whom he made the most flattering and well-behaved clothes that money could buy. Mainbocher, ex-editor of French *Vogue*, followed in the same tradition but his clothes acquired a harder image through his leading customer, the Duchess of Windsor. The two most sculptural of all fashion designers both began their Paris careers in the thirties: Alix, whose draped and folded silk jerseys already identify her by her later name, Madame Grès, and Balenciaga, who came to Paris at the beginning of the Spanish Civil War and had hardly time to be appreciated before the whole of Europe was at war again. Vionnet dressed Madame Martinez de Hoz, and Marcel Rochas, who is given the credit for the first padded shoulders, became famous overnight when eight ladies at a party in 1930 came face to face wearing the same Rochas dress. Charles Creed set a new standard in tailored suits for women.

By the thirties, *Vogue* had come into its fullest power over fashion. A word could make or break a collection. Couturiers would count the number of illustrations given to each house, and write off furious letters of complaint. Once the couture had recovered from the effects of the slump, it began to assume greater and greater

importance. 'Now fashion is news, fashion is big business, fashion is the intimate concern of millions,' said *Vogue*, announcing in 1938 the first ever Collections Report to be broadcast from Paris to New York and relayed from there to London almost while the clothes were still being shown, A great deal of *Vogue*'s prestige was due to the metamorphosis of photography and the talents of *Vogue*'s excellent photographers. In the hands of Steichen, Hoyningen-Huene, Horst, Man Ray and Cecil Beaton, fashion photography was real art at last, technically perfect and beautifully lit, conveying the ideal realization of the dressmaker's skill and the spirit of the times. Some of the very best fashion drawings ever done were being executed at the same time by artists including Carl Ericsson (Eric), Count René Bouet Willaumez, René Bouché and Christian Bérard, a diabetic and opium addict, a gross, shabby and much-loved figure. Raoul Dufy, Giorgio de Chirico, Pavel Tchelitchew and Salvador Dali enlivened the covers and pages of *Vogue* with their drawings and paintings.

The first Surrealist Exhibition in England was shown in 1936, ten years after the Manifesto. It was greeted with derision. J. B. Priestley gave the reactionary view of the Surrealists when he wrote, 'They stand for violence and neurotic unreason. They are truly decadent. You catch a glimpse behind them of the deepening twilight of barbarism that may soon blot out the sky, until at last

4

5

6

humanity finds itself in another long night . . . There are about too many effeminate or epicene young men, lisping and undulating. Too many young women without manners, balance, dignity . . . Too many people steadily lapsing into shaved and powdered barbarism.' Surrealism was already a familiar thing to most fashion photographers who travelled between London and Paris to work, but the exhibition made it topical and for a few years fashion illustration was dominated by Surrealism – ladies in evening dress carrying their own heads, models coiled in rope or poised by cracked mirrors, others sitting in evening dress with brooms and buckets, or on rubbish heaps. Dr M. F. Agha, Art Editor-in-Chief of *Vogue*, felt it necessary to write an explanatory dialogue: 'No one can tell me exactly what a Surrealist is. Can you?' 'A Surrealist is a man who likes to dress like a fencer, but does not fence; to wear a diving-suit, but does not dive . . . but descends to the lower depths of the subconscious . . . You know the old formula: "Man Bites Dog"? – only in this case the Dog has Paranoia, and the Man is really a couple of other guys.'

In a Surrealist film you could see, among other things, a cow sleeping in a Louis XIV salon; a man kicking a blind beggar; a burning tree, a giraffe, and a plough being thrown out of a window. At the end of the first performance of this, the producers were beaten up by the audience. Salvador Dali, who received reporters sitting on top of a desk on top of a bed with a loaf of bread on his head, drew for *Vogue* his Dream House designs for the New York World's Fair in 1939. *Vogue* wrote, 'three live mermaids . . . swim through flexible, rubberoid branches of trees, past long tendrils of typewriters. They swim past a writhing woman, chained to a piano, with the piano keys carved out of her rubberoid stomach . . . On a mammoth bed, a live woman is lying, asleep and dreaming three dreams . . . a double row of grisly, make-believe women, crowned with lobsters and girdled with eels, fades away into the distance.'

In the thirties *Vogue* began to cater for the mass fashion market. The technical improvements in fashion illustration showed the reader and the ready-to-wear manufacturers alike what to aim for, and sometimes how to cut: at first, designers had been anxious that too-accurate photography could give away their secrets. The models looked as glossy and perfect as film stars, and made women want to copy their hair and make-up. The magazine helped readers

7

directly by a concerted effort to show how to go about dressing fashionably with a limited amount of money, breaking down the given sum for essentials and accessories, leaving a margin for a beauty treatment, and adding it up neatly at the end. There was a 'Bargain of the Fortnight', and 'The Well Spent Pound', with an actual investigation into working girls' wardrobes at the end of the thirties: 'Some of the smartest girls we know turn themselves out on about £50 a year' . . . 'Business girls – they don't earn much – perhaps £5 a week. They perch on stools in snack bars for lunch. They save their pennies. That they can be well dressed is a miracle of England's ready-to-wear.' Suits for 6 gns., and dresses with coats for 8½ gns., began to appear from Fenwick and Jaeger, classic coats with 'nothing to date them' from Aquascutum and Harrods, and Vogue Patterns were devised for everything from cotton evening dresses to knitting instructions for sweaters to go under wartime uniforms. When war was finally announced *Vogue* missed an issue and then got into wartime gear with monthly, instead of fortnightly issues, to comply with government regulations. *Vogue Beauty Book* and *Vogue House and Garden Book* were incorporated, and Pattern Double Numbers stepped up. 'Our policy is to maintain the standards of civilisation . . . We dedicate our pages to the support of important industries, to the encouragement of normal activities, to the pursuit of an intelligent and useful attitude

Steichen

to everyday affairs – and a determined effort to bring as much cheer and charm into our present life as is possible.' The first stern moral judgments – 'It's your job to spend gallantly, dress decoratively, be groomed immaculately – in short, to be a sight for sore eyes' – and condemnations of open-toed sandals in the city and women slopping about in slacks – 'Slack, we think, is the word' – gave way to talk about National Service work, blackouts, all-night canteens and cocktail-bar shelters, with an ever-increasing emphasis on practical inexpensive fashion. 'Brisk Action on the Mayfair Front' was a communiqué on the war activities of the designers – Stiebel was now a river policeman, Hardy Amies in the fire brigade, Dennis Glenny in the army, and most houses were opening up mail order departments or sending fitters out to tour the country.

In direct opposition to the effects of the slump on pre-war fashion, there was the irresistible, saturating glamour of American films. If the rich looked to Paris for their new fashions, working girls and the couturiers themselves kept an eye on the movies, 'the most perfect visual medium for the exploitation of fashion and beauty that ever existed'. Formerly the most vulgar dresses and hats of the early Gloria Swanson type, seen at fashion shows, provoked

whispers among *Vogue*'s editors of 'Phew! Pretty Hollywood!' but around the late twenties films caught up with fashion. One of the first attempts to reconcile film costume with real life fashion came in 1929, when Chanel was invited to Hollywood. It was a miserable failure. Elegant, contemporary and revolutionary though they were when Chanel designed them, the clothes dated overnight when hems dropped, and films still 'in the can' were suddenly obsolete. Nevertheless, the revolution went on. Stars of great personal chic refused to be dressed like Christmas trees in films, and 'bright young playwrights pointed out that duchesses do not eat breakfast in ballgowns', as Lesley Blanch wrote. Schiaparelli, Marcel Rochas, Molyneux, Alix, Jean Patou and Lanvin all made the trip to Hollywood, but this expensive and clumsy business gradually gave way to reliance on Hollywood's own indigenous and talented designers, the best-known of whom were Adrian and Howard Greer. By 1933 the question 'Who did that look first, Hollywood or Paris?' was inextricable, and *Vogue*, seriously attempting to work it out in a feature called 'Does Hollywood Create?' came to the conclusion that fashion ideas arrive 'by a sort of spontaneous combustion', giving credit for the fashion for page-

4 Steichen

5 Steichen

1. Claudette Colbert as Cleopatra, 1934, photographed by Hoyningen-Huene. She was said to be so fastidious she washed her gold bracelets before putting them on.
2. Jean Harlow, who had just made *Hell's Angels* in 1930. *Vogue* called her 'a dazzling blonde . . . a pretty little golden vamp'.
3. Greta Garbo, photographed in 1932.
4. Tallulah Bankhead, siren in Schiaparelli's satin, 1934.
5. Norma Shearer, 'the reachable Garbo', in cape-collared ermine and black velvet, 1933.
6. Merle Oberon, an exotic beauty who married Alexander Korda, and made her name as Anne Boleyn in Korda's film starring Charles Laughton, and later in *Wuthering Heights*, playing opposite Laurence Olivier. Here, in black velvet and ermine.

6

Garbo – hollowed eye sockets and plucked eyebrows
Dietrich – plucked eyebrows and sucked-in cheeks
Joan Crawford – the bow-tie mouth
Tallulah Bankhead – a sullen expression
Mae West – the hourglass figure and an attractive bawdiness
Constance Bennett – a glazed, bandbox smartness
Jean Harlow – platinum hair
Katherine Hepburn – red curls and freckles
Vivien Leigh – gypsy colouring, a glittering combination of white skin, green eyes and dark red hair

boy hair to Garbo, feather boas to Marlene Dietrich, and accolades for a sixth sense about the fashion future to Adrian and Howard Greer, who had to design their costumes months ahead of the release date, and make clothes that would not look outdated at the end of the run, perhaps two years later.

James Laver in *Vogue* called the camera the first 'engine for imposing types of beauty' and pointed out that 'one curious result of the power of the film has been the spread of type-consciousness to classes which have previously known nothing of such conceptions'. Every important film star appeared in *Vogue* and contributed some new look or fashion:

Vogue's models were often recognizable copies of these types of beauty, and in the thirties they were photographed in cinematographic style: in statuesque bias-cut white satin evening dresses draped on sofas beside glass bowls of white tulips, and lit from one side. It was a symptom of the new acceptability of films that *Vogue* took sittings on location out to Elstree studios, and photographed behind the scenes during filming, showing such oddities as a row of girls waiting to go on in Wanger's film *Vogues of 1938* resting their arms in arm stalls, 'necessary precaution against the least wrinkle, the slightest crease'.

1. Balenciaga's beautiful neo-Victorian dress in pale blue printed moiré, not in the least obscuring the figure.
2. Bandbox smart Constance Bennett, 1933, one of the most astute film stars where money was concerned. 'If she can't take it with her,' said her sister, Joan Bennett, she won't go'.
3. Carole Lombard in a rose and silver lamé dress by the Hollywood designer Travis Banton. She married Clark Gable and was killed in a plane crash on her way to meet him.
4. The Garbo effect on her contemporaries.

Single-handed, Hollywood evolved make-up from the crude materials of the twenties into the gigantic industry it is today. In 1931 the *Sunday Express* calculated that 1,500 lipsticks were being sold in London shops for every one sold ten years previously. Cosmetics and nail enamel were now sold from all hairdressers, large stores, chemists and Woolworths, and were applied with a skill learnt from the screen and from magazines. 'Glamour is all,' said *Vogue* in 1935, and tried to pin down what it meant: 'We decided it was the quality of illusion, not just personality. After all, Hitler has personality, but you couldn't call him glamorous.' When Adrian wrote about dressing Garbo for *Camille* he said, 'She brought to the sets, with her quality of aloofness, that mystery which is a part of her and a part of the theatre's integral glamour'. Unattainable glamour, embodied in the most famous stars of the thirties, Garbo and Dietrich, was the wistful other side of the threadbare thirties.

Make-up features in *Vogue* in the twenties had been rare and tentative, but in the thirties readers were taught the techniques of the stars point by point. In 'Seven Steps to Stardom', a beauty feature in January 1938, an ordinary looking girl is transformed into a 'Glamour Girl': first, a foundation of greasepaint over the face, with a streak of darker greasepaint narrowing the jaw, then blended eye shadows hollowing the eyes. Eyebrow pencil fines the browline, powder and rouge are brushed on and off again with a soft brush, lashes are blackened with mascara and thickened with artificial eyelashes. Finally, the mouth is defined with a pencil line and filled in with lipstick or lip rouge. In this way, glamour was thoroughly analysed and its effects calculated. When *Vogue* asked George Gershwin what he noticed first about a woman, he gave an answer typical of the new attitude:

At 40 paces – her shape
At 25 paces – her ankles and shoes
At 10 paces – her face
At 8 paces – her eyes
At 5 paces – her mouth
At no paces – her conversation.

Marlene Dietrich   Juliette Compton   Anna Sten   Tallulah Bankhead

Imported together with Hollywood innovations like false finger-nails and eyelashes – which had to be applied separately with glue – there was the new slang, assimilated just as readily. *Vogue* first used the adjective 'sexy' to describe an evening dress in 1936, the year of Lesley Blanch's first article as features editor of *Vogue*. Called 'On dit – and how!', it incorporated the new American expressions and described the new tone of voice. 'Mayfair is quite "sold" on American slang, and you have only to enter any one of these drawing rooms to be engulfed in a spate of transatlanticisms, which describe "swell guys" as being "the tops" or, its equivalent, "the Camembert"; "swell gals" as being "pretty smooth"; any variety of pleasures as "easy to take"; while the finer shades of pathos and bathos are now familiar to us as "sob-stuff" or "the jerkers". "Am I right, or am I *right*?" as they would phrase it.'

Hollywood films of the thirties followed the pattern of the Depression and the New Deal. The first years of the Depression brought in Frankenstein and Dracula, followed by the realistic gangster film, Hollywood's attempt to attract an increasingly critical audience. Based on headline news stories, these ran straight into opposition from legions and clubs like the Daughters of the American Revolution, who objected that villains like Edward G. Robinson in *Little Caesar* had been turned into heroes, and who took offence at Spencer Tracy's words in *Quick Millions*: 'I'm too nervous to steal, too lazy to work . . . a man's a fool to go into legitimate business when you can clean up by applying business methods to organizing crime.' The 'confession' film, about girls who had traded on sex in the past and were trying to live it down, was almost as objectionable to moral America. In the purge that followed, film companies fell over backwards to comply with the Hays Office new Production Code. Jean Harlow's new film *Born to be Kissed* was changed in a moment of panic to *100 Per Cent Pure*, then more soberly renamed *The Girl from Missouri*. Hollywood then turned with relief to a sweeter and safer day. Films based on Dickens, Louisa May Alcott and Barrie brought to the screen Victorian life seen through a mist of nostalgia. The New Deal also brought in family films, musical spectaculars and screwball comedies.

Hoyningen-Huene

3

WARNING!
THE FASHIONS AND DESIGNS USED IN
WALTER WANGER'S VOGUES OF 1938
ARE FULLY PROTECTED BY COPYRIGHT
AND ANY ATTEMPTS TO REPRODUCE THE
EITHER PHOTOGRAPHICALLY THRU
SKETCHES OR FINISHED FABRIC
BE PROSECUTED TO THE FULL
EXTENT OF THE LAW!
NO CAMERAS ALLOWED
SKETCHING POSITIVELY PROHIB
ADMISSION
BY PASS ON

1

Neo-Victorianism was a major influence in the thirties. Victorian revivals like Dumas' *Lady of the Camellias* and Wilde's *The Importance of Being Earnest* were very popular on the stage, and so were modern plays on Victorian subjects like *The Barretts of Wimpole Street*: at one moment, three pseudo-historical plays about the Brontës were running at the same time.

The most successful of all musical, historical and costume shows was C. B. Cochran's 1932 production of Noël Coward's *Cavalcade*, a variety show that evoked the patriotism, security and sentiments of the Victorian age, and which appeared just when a great national effort was being made to overcome the Depression. A cast of 400 was brought up to the stage by six hydraulic lifts. *Vogue* wrote, 'Coming late into the darkened theatre, I was thrust into a world of 1900 . . . one of the actors stepped out in front of the curtain and announced the thrilling news that Mafeking had been relieved . . . the next scene revealed, not the stage, but the audience – a theatre of 1900 going mad over a Boer War victory; the people jumping from box to box, embracing one another; the women throwing fans into the air; the men their coats, ties and hats. The enthusiasm was infectious, and the whole theatre went mad, some people bursting into hysterical sobbing.' Coward said himself at the first night, 'In spite of the troublous times we are living in, it is still a pretty exciting thing to be English.' The British cinema also scored a major success with a historical subject, Alexander Korda's *The Private Life of Henry VIII* with Charles Laughton, followed by *Catherine the Great* with Flora Robson. There was a vogue for slashed and padded sleeves, velvet Tudor halos, shallow boaters with ribbon streamers as worn by Katherine Hepburn in *Little Women*, leg-of-mutton sleeves, and, from Norma Shearer in the film version of *Romeo and Juliet*, the Juliet bob, the Juliet cap, and the long, demure frock of full-skirted velvet with touches of white. The Victorian revival did not stop at clothes: in odd conjunction with functionalism, people were buying Victorian knick-knacks, sprigged curtains and heavy patterned wallpapers.

The movement was reinforced by Queen Elizabeth's own personal taste. With a good old-fashioned Scottish upbringing, she had conservative tastes and a love of daring finery. Dressed by Norman Hartnell, she wore velvet or furred suits, jewellery, flowers in the morning, a picture hat and a long full dress for receptions, and a crinoline for evening – 'full-skirted and décolleté in the Victorian, off-the-shoulder manner', and often in her favourite colour, powder blue. *Vogue* said, 'She is not a "fashionable" woman in the usual sense of the word. Yet her clothes superbly fulfil the two fundamental canons of good dressing. They fit her personality like a glove; and they are brilliantly suited to her way of life.' Her clothes on tour were tremendously admired and enjoyed by the public in France, America and Canada. In 1937 and 1938 every designer had fallen for the fairytale glamour of the sentimental crinoline – Patou, Molyneux, even Chanel, Vionnet and Alix.

The Duchess of Kent, Princess Marina, had lived with her father in Paris, and her sophisticated and innate elegance were Molyneux's best advertisement. *Vogue* drew a comparison between the Duchess and her great-aunt Queen Alexandra: 'There is the same classic purity of line, the same air of aloof elegance: the same charming, vague, rather wry smile: the same coiffure is topped by an identical hat . . . Women scan the papers for the Duchess' confirmation of fashion's newest trends.'

The health movement of the thirties made holiday camps popular, country resorts where campers lived in wooden huts and had their meals provided for them, spending their time walking, sunbathing, playing games and singing around the camp fire. *Vogue* went on location to take photographs round the floodlit Roe-

André Durst 2

Horst

3. 9 August 1939.

4. Princess Marina of Greece, beautiful and elegant in a dress by Molyneux, picture of 1934, the year of her marriage to the Duke of Kent. She set the seal of success on Molyneux's house by buying her trousseau there, and he continued to dress her beautifully in gentle, understated clothes — for instance, suits with fur collars and cuffs, evening dresses of bias satin with draped bateau necklines and ostrich feathers. She never adopted the padded shoulderline of the thirties, but originated many fashions of her own, such as the double pearl choker, the Edwardian hat tipped over the forehead: at George V's Jubilee she looked ravishing in a huge grey straw hat trimmed with grey ostrich feathers. It was criticized by the crowd for hiding half her face.

5. Amy Johnson, Mrs Mollison, in 1936. 'She dresses for record-breaking as if for a lunch date.' Here, on the wing of the B.A. Eagle she flew for the King's Cup.

hampton swimming club, showed playsuits and swimsuits in every summer issue, and advertised the new John Lewis country club, only 35 minutes from Paddington, where members could play tennis and croquet, go punting or swimming, and attend concerts and dances in the evening: 'The total bill for a weekend from Saturday afternoon to Sunday evening need not be more than ten shillings.' Sunbathing, nudism and hiking had all come from Germany at the time of the Weimar Republic, and all through the thirties Austria and Germany were the fashionable places for holidays abroad. Even in August 1939 *Vogue* included an advertisement for the German Railways Information Bureau: 'Germany, Land of Hospitality, offers everything you could wish for your holiday'. The result on fashion was a craze for Tyrolean peasant costume. The *Wandervogel* with his *lederhosen* was the romantic extension of the British hiker with his open-neck shirt, Borotra beret and shorts, and women took to dirndls of bright cheap cotton with a tight bodice, a bib or daisy braces, an apron and a feathered hat. 'The English have adopted the Tyrol as their own,' said *Vogue*, and described the same state of affairs in Paris, where the Princesse de Faucigny-Lucinge (Baba d'Erlanger that was) had just opened a shop selling only Tyrolean beachwear.

Open-air living had made women body-conscious and health-conscious. The slimming crazes of the twenties continued, but with the emphasis on keeping fit. Mrs Syrie Maugham, the decorator,

Schall 113

Schall

Kitrosser

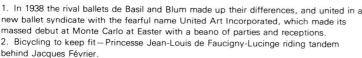

You need young stockings when Gerald tries to tango!

1. In 1938 the rival ballets de Basil and Blum made up their differences, and united in a new ballet syndicate with the fearful name United Art Incorporated, which made its massed debut at Monte Carlo at Easter with a beano of parties and receptions.
2. Bicycling to keep fit—Princesse Jean-Louis de Faucigny-Lucinge riding tandem behind Jacques Février.
3. 'Morley stockings keep the spring of youth', 1937.

was an obsessive dieter. 'Monday. Went to the first of Mrs Maugham's diet lunch parties . . . She decided to devote the first quiet spell to the interests of health and made it known to her friends that any who were feeling the effects of overeating and such a long siege of strenuous partying could come any day to lunch or dine with her on régime food.' Mrs Maugham finally went on the diet of diets. 'I starved for six weeks. Yes, literally, for six weeks I ate nothing at all . . . yet I never missed a day's work and feel better than I can ever remember.' *Vogue* profiled a New York model school in 1938, forerunner of those we know today, with 'Buddha' exercises, book-balancing for poise, lessons in dancing and make-up. People were so geared to keeping fit that the slightest excuse was enough to begin a craze for some particular exercise: when there was a French taxi strike in spring 1936, *Vogue* found 'Tout Paris on Wheels', men in dinner suits bicycling to the opera and women getting special cycling suits made up – Princesse de Faucigny-Lucinge rode tandem in a grey flannel shorts suit. The craze spread to the country, where country house stables were being filled up with secondhand bicycles for weekend guests. For those in London who would rather lose a few inches lying prone, Elizabeth Arden devised a warm paraffin Pack Treatment. The most popular way to get thin and healthy in the thirties was by dancing, and *Vogue* recommended tap lessons with Bunny Bradley, 'where Mr Cochran sends all his Young Ladies to be finished', and ballet with

Marie Rambert – together with a caution about taking it too seriously if you were already in your twenties. Zelda Fitzgerald's efforts to reach a professional standard when she was long past the ballet beginner age had contributed to her breakdown.

In 1936 Wilder Hobson wrote in *Vogue*, 'Swing is the musical fashion of the hour. Not to know the work of such swing artists as Thomas "Fats" Waller and Jack "Big Gate" Teagarden (gate meaning the ability to swing) is to confess such a dowdiness as would have been shown some years ago by someone who supposed the rumba to be one of the larger vertebrae. Judging by the heavy white-tie and Schiaparelli attendance at such New York swing saloons as the Onyx Club, swing music has penetrated the ritziest circles. It is even robust enough to appeal to Ernest Hemingway.' On liners, in the new Dorchester and the Savoy, down at the Locarno in Streatham, or even at home with the radiogram, people dressed up to the nines and danced all night to the smooth, glamorous sound of the big bands with their ranks of trumpets, clarinets and drums. The big bands, like some of the big cinemas, included crooners, tap dancers and showgirls in their performances, and teams of virtuosi would get to their feet and take the lead, playing extempore. Idols of the cinema audiences and best-loved of all the dancers in the dancing thirties – apart from the dazzling teenage Margot Fonteyn – were Fred Astaire and Ginger Rogers, one of whose most popular films was *The Castles*, about the earlier

4. Fred Astaire in May 1939, when he was making
The Castles, a film about the earlier famous
dancers, with Ginger Rogers.
5. Summer fashion for staff, 1936, from Moss Bros.
6. The Big Apple, forerunner of jitterbug.

Schenker

dancers Vernon and Irene Castle, *Vogue*'s heroine of the magazine's first decade. But whoever you were, you had to have rhythm. In the words of Irving Berlin's song, played by Jimmie Lunceford's band in 1937,

> He ain't got rhythm
> Every night he sits in the house alone.
> 'Cos he ain't got rhythm
> Every night he sits there and wears a frown.
> He attracted some attention
> When he found the fourth dimension,
> But he ain't got rhythm
> So no one's with him
> The loneliest man in town . . .

Louis Armstrong and Duke Ellington came on tour to show how swing should be played, and all the new dances came over from America. In February 1938 a forerunner of jitterbugging arrived in London, called 'The Big Apple' – a Negro euphemism for bottom. It involved lots of steps, including 'Kickin' the Mule', 'Truckin' and 'Peelin' the Apple'. Lesley Blanch, writing about it in *Vogue*, came to the sad conclusion that the British did not have rhythm. 'Nostalgic university dons and their wives, in white tennis shoes and cross garters hung with little bells, bouncing dankly through the naiveties of Parson's Wedding and Jenny Pluck Pears, cannot be considered to represent the dancing public . . . [They]

go to the Hammersmith Palais de Dance, the Astoria in the Charing Cross Road, the new Paramount in Tottenham Court Road . . . to dance to first class bands of the Henry Hall and Roy Fox kidney, for 1*s.* 6*d.* in the afternoon and 2*s.* 6*d.* in the evening . . . the Big Apple demands a complete unselfconsciousness, which is not our national forte.'

The thirties changed the style of living and entertaining. People with town houses who had kept two or three servants now had only a cook. They closed up their basements, used the breakfast room as a kitchen, added a bath on the first floor and lived more or less as if they were in a flat. Cocktail parties turned into snack dinners. 'One has a sandwich, a whisky-and-soda, and goes in for a good supper after the play. I wonder if dinner is disappearing from our social scheme of life?' wondered *Vogue* in 1932. A few years later, even grand dinner parties turned out simpler food. 'Nobody has grand food any more . . . at Lady Colefax, we ate macaroni with cream and cheese, lamb with mint sauce, potato croquettes and spinach, and apple charlotte.' Reflecting the economical mood of the times, the thirties failed to produce any sensational new ideas for house decoration other than lighting, which was much improved by indirect lights and opaque bowls set directly into the ceiling or walls, and by the introduction of 'Anglepoise' reading lamps. The photographer Hoyningen-Huene mentioned the importance of good lighting when he was asked about the new Brick Top premises he

115

1

had been asked to decorate in Paris: 'I am going to light up the cabaret so that, after midnight, it will be becoming to middle-aged people who are slightly under the influence of liquor.' Schiaparelli's London flat was furnished entirely from John Lewis – 'It is so smart, so right and so practical' – with unpainted wood tables, rush-seat stools and armchair and divan covered in an unpatterned glazed chintz at 2*s*. 11*d*. a yard. Chanel's house in Menton was also the 'essence of simplicity, without superfluous furniture. But what there is is in the most perfect of its kind: old oak tables, chests, and cupboards, and in the airy bedrooms old Italian beds.'

Some of the best parties of the thirties are described by Cecil Beaton in his 'Social Scene' column. There were mystery parties like the one at which the footmen carried in a trunk, and everyone was asked to guess who was inside. The trunk was opened and a lady stepped out in a mask, scarf, heavy gloves and high boots. Mrs Michael Arlen guessed right: it was Gaby Morlay, the French actress. There were musical parties, like the one where Serge Lifar kicked off his shoes, leapt onto the piano and performed an impromptu dance. There was a craze for Victorian games like musical chairs, blindman's buff, and bobbing for apples – in 1932 'the latter game went out of favour very quickly as none of the women would risk losing their new eyelashes'. Most popular and exciting of all were the Scavenger parties started by Mrs Marshall Field in London and immediately copied by Elsa Maxwell. Dinner guests were given a list of things to obtain, and the one who collected most between ten and midnight won. Here is Elsa Maxwell's list:

One red bicycle lamp
One cooked sausage
One live animal other than a dog
One swan from the Bois de Boulogne
One slipper worn by Mistinguette that night
One handkerchief belonging to the Baron Maurice de Rothschild

2

E. J. Mason

3

O'Doyé

One hat from Mrs Reginald Fellowes
One live Duchess
One autographed photograph of royalty signed that night
One red stocking
One *Metro* ticket
One mauve comb
Three red hairs
One pompom from a sailor's hat
The cleverest man in Paris

That night, Mistinguette came offstage to find her dressing room ransacked and all her shoes gone. The next day, they were returned tied to flowering trees and bunches of white orchids.

Elsa Maxwell gave *Vogue* her seven rules for a good party. Ruthlessness – no lame ducks, no churchmen, no financiers or diplomats. Never let guests do what they want – guests never want to do what they want. Cram them into one room, which should be too small for the number invited. Light that room brilliantly. Never show any anxiety. Try to incur some opposition so that people take sides. Keep up plenty of noise. 'I once gave a party in a room too cold and cavernous ... so I hastily procured some beehives and, successfully concealing them in the room, the ears of the guests were assailed by a pleasant buzzing during lulls in the music.'

One of the wittiest parties was given by Miss Olga Lynn, at which guests were asked to come as a well-known book or play. Lady Eleanor Smith was *Vile Bodies*, Evelyn Waugh came as Wyndham Lewis's new book which was so expensive no one could afford it, Tallulah Bankhead was *The Open Book*, and Lord Knebworth, 'who sported a photograph of a Very August Pair', was *The Good Companions*.

In summer 1938 Lady Mendl gave a huge circus party, on Gatsby proportions. The hostess, in aquamarines, diamonds and a white organdie Mainbocher, was the ringmaster in the tan-bark ring,

4   Schall

with acrobats in satin and paillettes, ponies and clowns. Guests danced on a special composition dance floor under which there were millions of tiny springs, so that it gently heaved up and down with the rhythm. Constance Spry sent three aeroplanes of roses from London to Paris for the party, and in different parts of the garden three orchestras played jazz, Cuban rumbas and Hungarian waltzes. Concealed lighting turned the garden into a dream landscape with marble statues, fountains and urns of cut flowers . . . For most of the people there, it was the last party.

1. Chanel's Riviera villa at Cap Martin, almost bare of furniture.
2. Schiaparelli's London flat, 1934, painted very pale blue and furnished from John Lewis. Here, her bare and simple dressing table with very good lighting.
3. 'Country costume at a ball in the Bois', 1931: the market gardeners' entry, Cole Porter in the cart with his wife and Princess Ilyinsky.
4. French chaperones, 1935. Three mothers appraise the débutantes.
5. Lady Mendl. As Elsie de Wolfe, the decorator, she is said to have been responsible for making America antique-conscious. She made a fortune in America, which she spent on her houses and her fantastic entertainments, bringing what Cecil Beaton calls 'the ruthlessness of a company director' to their planning and organization. She invented a cross-filing system so that her guests never had the same menu or sat next to the same people. 'When a new sandwich proved to be successful, she would dictate a memorandum that it must be photographed for *Vogue*.' She became better looking as she grew older, by dieting, facial surgery and by adopting pale blue hair, which later she allowed to grow white.

5

Nickolas
Murray

THE CHANGING FACE

THE DUCHESS OF WINDSOR

The Duchess, formerly Mrs Wallis Simpson, exemplified the crispest, neatest, hardest looks for the 30s. Even then, when every girl tried to look neat, she was described as looking strict and governessy. Never less than immaculate, she wore her hair parted in the centre, waved over the ears and pinned in a flat chignon at the back. Flattened to the head, it was brilliantined for shine, framing her clearcut features under a smart hat. She dressed first at Schiaparelli, wearing her white trouser suits in the South of France and her printed dresses in town, then turned to Mainbocher for her trousseau. He dressed her in slim crepes softened with a drape or a bow neck, in narrow bias evening dresses shined with sequins. In 1947 she was quick to adopt Christian Dior's New Look.

Man Ray

MAINBOCHER

1. 1935.
2. Honeymoon photograph at Wasserleonburg, 1937.
3. 1937

PRINCESS NATALIE PALEY

Daughter of the Grand Duke Paul of Russia, she married Lucien Lelong whose clothes helped her become one of the best dressed beauties of the 30s. In 1935 she went to Hollywood to star in *Les Folies Bergères*, and later married again becoming Mrs Jack Wilson.

2 LELONG   Steichen

3 LELONG   Hoyningen-Huene

1. In Lelong's ermine-trimmed black crepe, 1930.
2. Dressed by Lelong, 1928: grey cloth coat, fox collar, grey-beige crepe dress, grey felt hat by Maria Guy.
3. In Lelong's stripes, Maria Guy's white hat, 1931.

THE MORGAN TWINS

Dorothy Wilding

The much-publicized Morgan twins, identical except for a small scar under Thelma's chin, from roller-skating when she was a child. Thelma, Viscountess Furness, left, was an escort of the Prince of Wales, and introduced him to Mrs Ernest Simpson; Gloria married Reginald Vanderbilt. This year, 1932, marked the height of the fashion for emphasized and artificial eyelashes.

1

Hoyningen-Huene

IYA, LADY ABDY

Wife of Sir Robert Abdy, a famous Russian beauty with ash-blonde gently curling hair and a prominent upper lip, over six feet tall.

1. Her new hairstyle, 1933, with a gold Alice band.
2. White feathers, 1932.

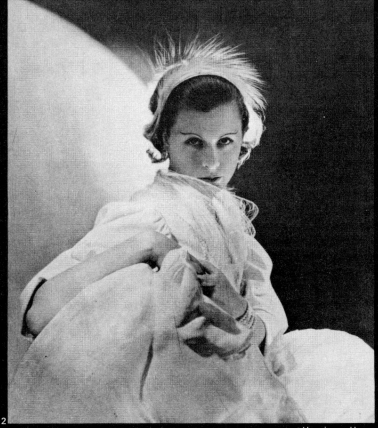

2

Hoyningen-Huene

1   SCHIAPARELLI   Cecil Beaton

MARLENE DIETRICH

Perfection of her type, Dietrich is the daughter
of a Prussian policeman, born in December
1901 — 'Just say I'm 75 and let it go at that.'
She originally wanted to be a concert violinist,
but auditioned for Reinhardt and joined his
drama school in 1921. Von Sternberg
discovered her in Berlin for Lola in *The Blue
Angel*, the film that made her famous. She
dismissed her 17 previous films before
Sternberg as 'nothing'. He said of her, 'To
exhaust her is not possible'. When she first
appeared in a man's suit and beret Paris booed
her — and later, copied her. Her other contri-
butions to women's looks: sucked-in cheeks
and plucked eyebrows.

1. The epitome of glamour in
Schiaparelli's Russian furs, 1936.
2. 1937.

2   Steichen
TRAVIS BANTON   121

1. Cock feather boa and dress by Schiaparelli, 1932.
2. In a tiered lace dress, possibly Fortuny's, 1917.
3. At the Duff Coopers' in Paquin's negligée, 1941.

SCHIAPARELLI   Hoyningen-Huene

Lachman

PAQUIN   Cecil Beaton

THE HON. MRS REGINALD FELLOWES

Daisy Fellowes, formerly Princess Jean de Broglie, daughter of the Duc Decazes, was popularly known as the best-dressed woman in the world. Half American and half French, she was known for a brilliant studied simplicity, described by Cecil Beaton as a 'scrubbed classical look, an unparalleled air of slickness, trimness and cleanness . . . she had the air of having just come off a yacht, which she very likely had'. She enjoyed undercutting fashion, making other women look foolishly overdressed. She wore the same simple dress perpetually, cut in different colours of silk for evenings, linen for day. At Ascot, she appeared hatless; for an appearance at Court, where it was the custom to wear a long white dress, she drummed up a dead relative and wore a short black dress. Just before Paris was occupied, she escaped with her husband and daughter to London, where she settled down in the basement of the Duff Coopers' Westminster house, making a dining room out of the servants' hall and a bedroom out of the cellar. In 1941 she became the first President of the new Incorporated Society of London Fashion Designers, a job for which she was uniquely suited.

JOAN CRAWFORD

Hollywood star whose prolonged career began with *Our Modern Maidens* in 1929. She gave the second half of the thirties a fashion that was almost universal — the crimson bow-tie mouth.

1. In Vionnet's white taffeta, 1938.
2. 1939.

Gertrude Lawrence's wardrobe by Molyneux for *Private Lives* sums up the day and evening looks of the year — fur-trimmed tweeds and a bias evening dress of panelled white satin. Everything she wears comes into general fashion, her beret, her tie and shirt, her open blazer, even her way of smoking a cigarette. Women use magnifying mirrors to make up their faces, with blue eyeshadow, blue or black mascara, pencilled and brilliantined plucked eyebrows. Hair is a little longer, but rolled up or curled at the back of the neck.

All skirts begin from a moulded or draped hip-yoke and flare to the calf of the leg. The best sellers are the light caped jersey dresses and the self-patterned jersey suits. Inside plain suits go the new lingerie blouses, printed chiffon with scarf necks, or silks with tucking and openwork. Dark dresses have white collars and cuffs, yokes and revers, in piqué, satin, or crepe. The new afternoon dress drops the hem nearly to the ankle, in draped wrapover crepe or chiffon, with a well-indicated waist and a full flared skirt.

For Ascot, you dress according to the weather. If it's bad, a frock of black satin with a white collar, a satin cardigan lined in white. If it's dull, a beige crepe with dipping skirt and fox-edged cape. If it's fine, a flowered chiffon to the ground with a big brimmed straw hat and gloves to the elbows.

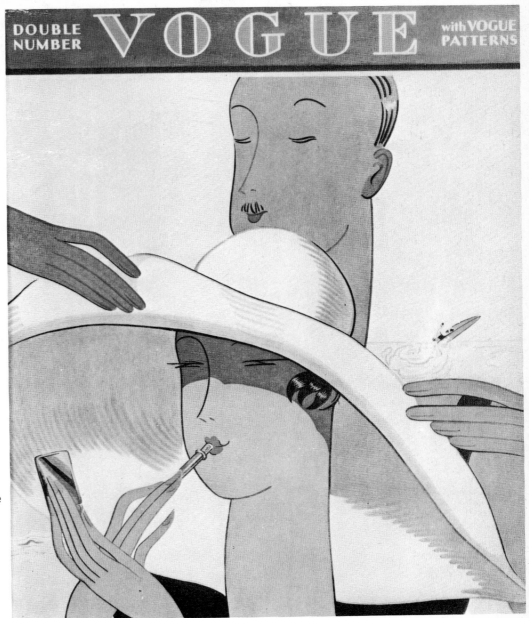

Cover, May 1930.

Left: White satin by Vionnet, 1939.

Hoyningen-Huene

1. The Maudie Littlehampton silhouette.
2. Vionnet's silk crepe afternoon dress, black and grège print, crossed and knotted at the waist.
3. Schiaparelli's black and white diagonal tweed, white shantung shirt buttoned onto the skirt.
4. Beach trousers and hand-knitted bathing suits.
5. Evening dresses by Vionnet in velvet cut to fall straight as columns when not in motion; photograph Steichen.
6. 'All smart hair is longer, but long hair is not smart.' Shoulder-length permed hair in a flat rolled chignon. Black lace dress by Chanel.
7. Motoring clothes: the biscuit tweed coat and skirt, with sleeveless woollen sweater and gaiters, cost 15½gn, together from Gamages.
8. Suit with pale top and dark skirt.

6

Steichen

8

VIONNET   Steichen

7

Howard and Joan Coster

127

1931

'Caught in the act of making up to beauty' with Pond's preparations.   Steichen

'There is more than an emphasis placed on natural feminine lines. There is exaggeration'

Clothes begin to broaden the shoulders and nip in the waist: skirts mould the hips and fall into flowing pleats. Shoes get higher heels, and late in the year the waist rises. Women are wearing their hair a little longer, but pressed close to the head to accommodate the essential new hat. The tilted mercury pierced with a quill introduces a wealth of original hats. Full length dresses or suits are worn for a formal tea, for the cinema and going out to dinner.

Fashion is swayed by two opposing influences. The financial situation is making itself felt, and *Vogue* writes about 'the new economy' and advertises *Vogue Patterns* on the cover: among the readers who send for them are Gloria Swanson and Moira Shearer. For the first time cheap washable fabrics are used for grand occasion clothes — Chanel shows a collection of 35 cotton evening dresses. Zips and the increasing sales of artificial silk make clothes cheaper. On the other hand, Hollywood sets a standard of sumptuous luxury. Women who can afford couture clothes take their lead from Paris, but the great cinema-going public copy the dresses and gowns of the screen stars. *Vogue* fills its pages with slinky cinema satins from Paris and the London shops, and takes location pictures in the Elstree studios.

A new designer opens in Paris. Mainbocher, formerly an American fashion artist and fashion editor of French *Vogue*, shows a new moulded sheath-dress and some intricately cut faille. Later, he will make his name by dressing Mrs Wallis Simpson. Lady Furness is spotted at Ciro's in a white dress, black pearls, and rings worn over her elbow-length matt black gloves. Daisy Fellowes in Paris sets a fashion for fresh flowers by wearing a daisy chain to a party, and her daughter Diana wears a Sam Browne belt of gardenias.

1

2 REVILLON   Cecil Beaton

1. White satin Court dress by Madame Hayward,
who specializes in dresses for presentation.
2. Jeanne Stuart, 'one of the blonde hopes of the
English stage', in Revillon's white satin pyjama suit.
3. Flannels and white wool shirt from Lillywhites.
4. Cinema satins. *Vogue* coins the phrase 'poured in'
to describe the fit of a sheath dress.

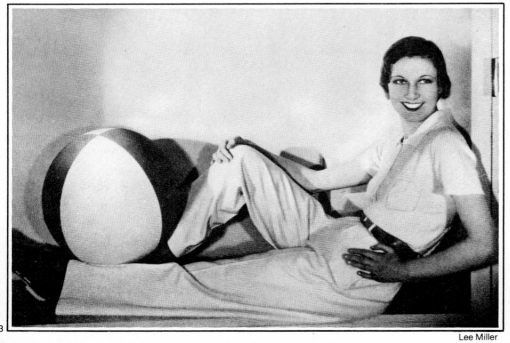

3   Lee Miller   4   HEIM   Hoyningen-Huene   129

1931

MAINBOCHER

Eric

Eric

1. *Left*, black and white coat cut like a jacket and skirt, and, *right*, black rep dress.
2. The waistline rises in the autumn. Vionnet's blouse and skirt.
3. English tweeds from the London ready to wear.
4. 'How to ruin a good dress' and wear it right, demonstrated by Bea Lillie and photographed by Steichen.
5. Draped evening dresses in chiffon, point-de-Venise and washable organdie.

HOW TO RUIN a GOOD DRESS

SHE critically surveys her new evening gown and then decides that the whole thing looks a little too plain. So she dresses it up a bit with a few long strands of imitation pearls. Her simple coiffure strikes her as unexciting, so she nips a ducky little clip in just where it shows to greatest advantage. At the last minute, her best young man sends her a massive shoulder spray, heavy with tin-foil, resplendent with changeable taffeta ribbons, and she pins that on too, pulling the décolletage regrettably askew.

Finally, someone tells her she is a *femme fatale*. She is enchanted and buys long glittering earrings, a diadem of brilliants for her hair, and giant court shoe-buckles, from under which peep coquettish wisps of tulle. To all this splendour, she adds a massive coral beaded bag, which swings from a long chain. One does not need to see to know that in due time she will produce from that bag a long chiffon handkerchief of the tie-and-die variety and a very long cigarette holder. Alone and unaided, she has ruined a good dress.

SUZANNE TALBOT   Hoyningen-Huene   CHANEL

1932-33

'A sock on your head and your chic on your sleeve'

Focus on the raised waist, emphasized by widened, heavier shoulders, means wearing a corset that pulls in the waist again — the new ones are two way stretch. The architectural V from shoulders to small fitted waist and, a mirror reflection, the flare of the skirt from the top of the hipbones, lends itself to a new fashion for stripes used on the bias. Now that zips can be set invisibly into seams, buttons are used for decoration, on revers and jabots, pockets and belts.

The big news story is Chanel's ciré satin cinema suit, but Schiaparelli's follies steal the limelight. She uses copper clamps for buttons, makes felt socks for hats that are copied everywhere, shellacs and lacquers sculptured hairdos, dusts evening hair with phosphorescent powder, and invents a short-lived, odd fashion for bustles added to backless evening dresses.

High necks and bows balance the tipped small hats or the basque berets, and the hat of hats to wear with ankle-length skirts after four o'clock is the big-brimmed sailor. Sweaters come up in the world and appear in town . . . 'the sweater has crashed even into late afternoon society'. They are brief and fitted, in everything from transparent silk to grocery string, with eyelets, rib textures and knots, puff sleeves and tied necklines. Chanel designs a ready-to-wear sweater collection for Harvey Nichols.

For evening, heavy crepes and dull satins give the flowing, folding, draping dresses their most statuesque quality yet. Boleros with puff sleeves take off to reveal bare backs, necklines in front going right up to the neck. This 'backward' movement shows up again in day clothes, with cowl-backed jackets rising behind the nape of the neck.

Hollywood's influence is at its strongest. Models wear bright lipstick like Joan Crawford's, and shadowed eyes. There is a fashion for artificial eyelashes, but it is confined to the

leisurely since they must be applied individually in a beauty salon, taking almost an hour an eye. *Vogue* reports on Garbo in man's evening dress and on the new designs by Adrian for films.

Three designers make their first appearance in *Vogue* — Teddy Tinling, Victor Stiebel and Charles James, whose influence on the ready-to-wear trade is immediately apparent.

Summer holiday fashions are set in

Saint Tropez, where clothes are beginning to be noticed for their theatricality. Madame Jeanne Duc, the modiste wife of the proprietor of l'Escale, does a line in little straw hats decorated with ribbons and fruit, Vachon (still in Saint Tropez) sells printed Provençal handkerchiefs for sunbathers to tie like boleros over their bathing suits, and Guy Baer sells original knitted sweaters.

2 AUGUSTABERNARD   Ben

Hoyningen-Huene

3 SCHIAPARELLI

1. For afternoon bridge, Rose Amado dress of green silk flecked with gold lamé and the new velvet bridge hat.
2. Augustabernard promoted the long narrow look for day and evening: here, pansy-purple crepe and blue fox boa.
3. Sports suit, grey and yellow tweed jacket, high necked blouse in silk jersey stiffened with yellow taffeta. First picture of the new Tyrolean hat.
4. Red and white spotted crepe de chine dress with a bodice cape by Mainbocher.
5. English spun silk 'washing frocks' in fashionable stripes.

1932-33

1
LANVIN   Hoyningen-Huene   2

Dorothy Wilding

5

3
CHANEL   Cecil Beaton SCHIAPARELLI   4

1. Lanvin's beautiful new idea for evening: a shell-pink satin blouse wrapped and tied around a high-waisted black satin skirt.

2. The belted 1932 suit as worn by Miss Margaret Whigham, later Duchess of Argyll. She was the first debutante to organize her own publicity. She was charming to the press, gave press conferences, and naturally had flattering press coverage and was agreed to be the beauty of the year.

3. Blue and white plaid dress in British artificial silk.

4. Schiaparelli's bustle. . . . 'that new and much-talked of padding that juts out like a shelf just below a square-cut décolletage': maroon satin jersey.

5. New notions in summer bags, 1933.

8

6. The 1933 look — Hollywood make up, sheer stockings
and high heels: advertisement for Kira silk stockings.
7. Victor Stiebel red, white and green striped chiffon for
Ascot Gold Cup Day.
8. The longer the skirt, the higher the heels: shoe
designs, 1933.
9. The cowl-backed silhouette, here in Lanvin's
astrakhan cape.

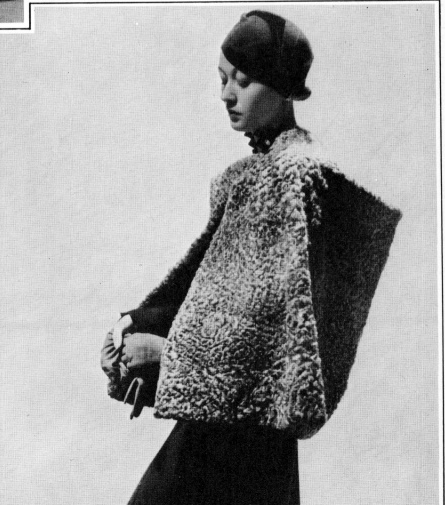

1

Cecil Beaton

CHANEL

Cecil Beaton

1. The basque beret as worn by Dietrich: *left to right*, Agnès, Rose Descat, Agnès.
2. Mrs Marshall Field in a satin cinema suit.
3. Chanel designs ready to wear sweaters for Harvey Nichols.
4. Charles James's 12gn. spring suit in marine blue facecloth. Raglan-sleeved top gathered onto a belt and the neck twisted with a spotted scarf.
5. The big-brimmed sailor, the hat sensation of 1932. Reboux hat, black crepe anklelength dress by Lanvin.

4

CHARLES JAMES

Horst

Steichen

LOUISE BOURBON

The make-up, the hat, drawn by Eric

'Your very important profile will have the windswept, fleet lines of speedboat or aeroplane'

The look is hard and smart, best seen in profile. Hair blows back and up from an uncluttered hairline, a severe hat cuts across the head at a sharp angle, the lips are a vicious red, the waist is pinched, swagger coats make triangles over thin skirts. Fewer London customers and buyers go to Paris, and in *Vogue* the names Norman Hartnell, Digby Morton, Victor Stiebel and Charles Creed appear frequently. Schiaparelli invents the bird silhouette, with a jutting tail above the bottom. Designers are making the most of man-made fibres and effects — more lamé than ever, Cellophane and anthracite ribbon weaves, paillettes and sequins . . . 'the influence upon dress of this industrial age'. Hats are one-sided, 'giant flat phonograph discs' or pancake berets, and Schiaparelli's new poke bonnet.

Princess Marina's marriage to the Duke of Kent in November gives fashion an authoritative, stylish new heroine. *Vogue* draws her Molyneux trousseau item by item.

Symptom of the passion for rambling and hiking, for sunbathing and nudism, sports clothes become briefer than ever. Bathing suits are often slashed and backless, skirts divide or shrink into shorts. In the summer we see the Tyrolean look, with feathered fishing hats, daisy braces, bibs, aprons, dirndles and tight bodices. This year *Challenge to Death* is published, a book of essays written by leading pacifists.

1934

From Spain

Horst

2   SCHIAPARELLI   MAINBOCHER

Hoyningen-Huene

— to the Tyrol

1. Holiday clothes — Schiaparelli's mantilla sunhats, slacks and bathing suit tops.
2. Schiaparelli, *left*, and Mainbocher make the new box jacket part of their autumn collections.
3. Tyrolean outfit worn by Princess Jean de Faucigny-Lucinge (Baba d'Erlanger).
4. *Left*, navy jersey dress with touches of white piqué, *right*, tailored suit of checked tie silk.

UYÈRE, JENNY

Hoyningen-Huene

1. Cellophane evening dress 'glistening like a magnificent black scarab', cape lined with black seal: by Alix, who later became Madame Grès.
2. Mainbocher's version of the sashed tunic evening dress in satin and wool.
3. One of the first two-piece bathing suits, Jacques Heim's black and white print sarong suit, with a big-brimmed hat.
4. Schiaparelli's bird silhouette in three spring suits; *left*, winged and tailed.
5. Schiaparelli's new poke bonnet: *Vogue* cover for 31 October 1934.

2 MAINBOCHER   Horst

3
JACQUES HEIM   Horst

4
SCHIAPARELLI

SCHIAPARELLI   Mourgue
5

VOGUE

SCHIAPARELLI White plaster mask with red feather eyelashes:
Vogue's Christmas cover for 1935.

'The Fashion battle cry of the moment "Aux Armes, Citoyennes!"'
. . . 'March to the sound of drums by day, dance to the music of lyres by night'

Daytime looks are severe and military, with square epauletted shoulders, frogging, plumed hats, low heels and gauntlet gloves. Schiaparelli leads the military camp with regiments of fitted suits, drummer boy jackets and a forward 'putsch' of hats. Women look 'tidy as tinkers', like Mrs Simpson in her Schiaparellis, with her meticulous grooming and attention to detail. In complete contrast to the soldierly daytime suits, evening dresses are statuesquely Greek or Indian, with Hindu jewellery — heavy carved and gemmed bracelets, rough diamonds fringed with pearls.

In 1936 King George V dies and the Prince of Wales becomes king. Mrs Simpson is still frequently mentioned, the *Queen Mary* is launched, and the *Hindenberg* crosses the Atlantic. On liners and in hotels people are dancing to swing played by the big bands. A new look is the tunic line, pulled tightly in at the waist with a stiff jutting peplum over a narrow skirt that is often of pinpleats tight as crinkled crepe. There are fabric prints of newspaper print, handwriting, radishes, buttons, pigs and matches.

Chanel's suits are gently fitted tweeds with open-neck white shirts, neither musical comedy, like Schiaparelli's, nor drab, like the London house Busvine, which has taken over Reville, with its heavy suits, box jackets, dark stockings and flat shoes.

Fresh air addiction has made women body-conscious and *Vogue's* beauty pages run separate spreads on feet, legs, hands and the figure. Cinema expertise with make-up filters through to the beauty pages, with face-shapers for accentuating the bone structure, red dots opening up the eyes, and red pencil defining the lips.

Schiaparelli's follies of the year: the white plaster mask with red feather eyelashes, black gloves with scarlet finger nails, pockets like bureau drawers, coarse hairnets anchoring pancake hats, tight blue satin trousers showing under the lifted hem of a black evening dress, and a bearskin coat from Iceland, with a wooden mask against snow glare.

'It's no longer smart to be chic,' says *Vogue.* Show the body as a superb piece of sculpture . . . the era of the dressmaker, all bits and pieces and complicated seaming, gives place to that of the mathematician and architect . . . the new London mode is neither streamlined nor sentimental. It is casual, bold, chunky and realistic. Textures rough rather than smooth: colours subtly coordinated.'

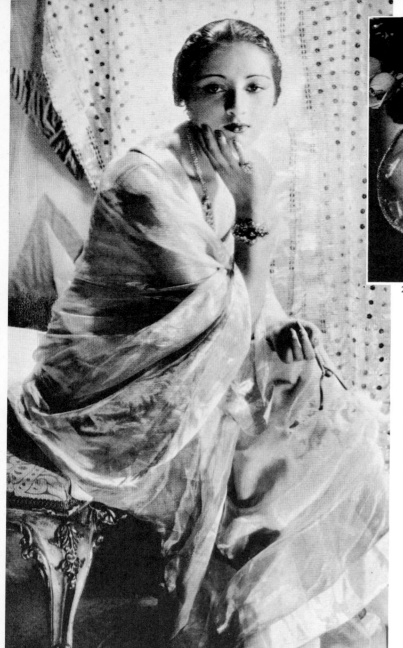

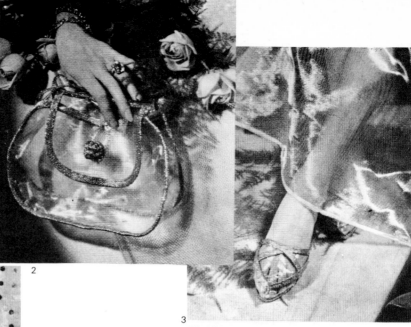

1. Princess Karam Kapurthala, a much admired Indian beauty who possibly inspired Schiaparelli's sari evening dresses.
2 and 3. Glass clothes, an invention of Schiaparelli's. A derivative of glass called Rhodophane, it is a brittle, fragile, transparent substance that has to be handled with care. Here, Talbot's bag and slipper.
4. Madame Max Ernst wearing Cartier's flexible, flat necklace and angular bangle of big yellow topazes.
5. Schiaparelli's sari dress in heavy white crepe.
6. Cellophane and accordion pleats: Vivien Leigh wears a Victor Stiebel dress, Cellophane over white taffeta.

7. Long, red, brass-
buttoned coat.
8. Cape and straight evening
dress, lassoed by 'rope,
hurtling out of oblivion,
surrealist-fashion'.
9. A cavalcade of coats and
capes.

8
SCHIAPARELLI   André Durst

9
CHARLES JAMES   Cecil Beaton

7

SCHIAPARELLI   Bérard

14

TALBOT

1

2

3. ALIX

4

VIONNET

Cecil Beaton

BATHING BREVITIES

5

Miles

1. 'The forward putsch in hats': Talbot's violet and green grosgrain turban and scarf.
2. Chanel's black velveteen cardigan suit, with a Florentine hat of beige and black velvet.
3. Alix's tunic-jacket in gold and blue brocade, with the lilt of a Bali dancer's coat.
4. Lady Brownlow in a white Vionnet afternoon dress with a bunch of white violets in her hat.
5. A shellful of Mr Cochran's Young Ladies in beach clothes.
6. Silver lamé trenchcoat, 8½gn., Fenwick.
7. Mainbocher beach outfits in white crash and checked gingham.

6

Shaw Wildman

CHRISTIAN BÉRARD 7

1937-38

'Sex appeal is the prime motif of the Paris collections . . . and sex appeal is no longer a matter of subtle appeal'

'Sequins flash like a glance from a bright eye, and kill their man at ten yards'

'This year's recipe for chic is to strip to the waist, more or less, and then shelter under a cartwheel evening hat'

Colour floods through *Vogue* — cardinal red, coronation purple, emerald green, sulphur yellow, and Schiaparelli's brand new 'Shocking Pink' mixed with plummy maroons and metallic gold. Now you dress by colour, in a 'brief, boxy reefer in shrill blue, red and white plaid, worn with a deep red blouse and skirt'. You put two handkerchiefs in the pockets of a blue car coat, one fuchsia, one emerald. At night you dance to swing in a dress of pink and cerise, with gold accessories.

The new looks are all good useful factory looks, as if the designers already had war in mind. Hair is pinned up in the 'ready-for-bath' style, hidden under headscarves, suits are broad-shouldered and skimpy-skirted, and women clump around in wedge shoes on high cork soles. Schiaparelli makes an evening headscarf of gold embroidery. Evening dresses react by returning to Winterhalter crinolines, sentimentally tight waisted and frilled, although Schiaparelli and Molyneux retain a look of modern sophistication, and Alix tends to classical drapery as she will later under the name of Mme Grès.

Hats are quite ridiculous — 'leaning towers of grosgrain toppled into hats', huge haloes and cartwheels, huge brims draped with black veiling falling to the waist, and pure fantasies like Schiaparelli's wicker basket hat filled with Cellophane butterflies and flowers. Restaurants ban hats for the evening, and *Vogue* publishes a guide to what you can get away with where.

Two new looks that will resurface in the fifties: Schiaparelli's Mexican sombrero worn with cropped dungarees or slacks, and the American shirtwaister, with a bodice as full and

PIGUET   Tail-coated cape   Horst

pouchy as a Cuban bandleader's blouse.

Fundamental fashion news is Uplift, which has arrived from the cinema. Marian Jacks and Warners make the best uplift bras, and Schiaparelli makes an uplift sequin heart brassière built into the bodice of a narrow black dress . . . evenings are all afire with a Ziegfeld glitter of sequins.

Christian Bérard suggests new make up: for a blonde, cyclamen rouge and deep blue lashes, for a brunette, brown suntan rouge, pomegranate lips.

The last word in chic is credited to Mrs Douglas Fairbanks for her short square box-jacket of sable, to Mrs Reginald Fellowes for her sapphire Mercury wing clipped to the lapel of her suit, and Vivien Leigh for her black velvet Flemish cap.

1
PAQUIN   Horst

2
MOLYNEUX

1. Merry Widow hat and
dress, audaciously cut,
filled in with not-so-modest
veiling.
2. Black velvet cartwheel
drooping an emerald
feather, narrow black
velvet dress split over
emerald satin.
3. Alix's Grecian
white jersey.
4. Velvet suit buttoned
with jewels.
5. Picture gown of
black tulle.

3

4
CHANEL   Horst

5
MOLYNEUX   Horst

147

1 CHANEL Horst

2 Rawlings

3 SCHIAPARELLI

4 Eric

1. Gold lamé evening dress and chopped jacket of pressed pleats.
2. The 'ready for the bath' look, with a ribbon: play suit by Rahvis.
3. Sequin jacket, lettuce green tweed over corduroy trousers.
4. Boxy top coats in bright colours. *Left*, Maggy Rouff, wine, violet, green and brown; *right*, Alix, navy and rust.
5. Cockleshell bag of beige calf, and a basket-ball bag carried in a net — surely inspired by Dali.

5

6
SCHIAPARELLI   Eric

7
VIONNET   Horst

8
RBW

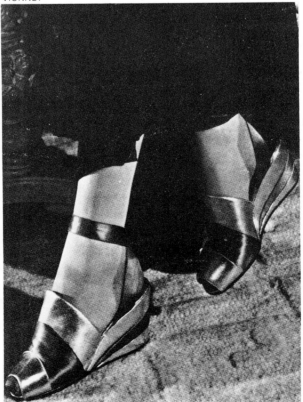

6. Shocking pink dress, scooped below the breast one side and swathed with pink mousseline.

7. Suits look as though some clever person had taken a jacket from one suit, a skirt from another, and a blouse from a third. Here, a rare Vionnet day suit.

8. The shirt-waist silhouette from America.

9. Ferragamo, the Italian shoemaker, whose shoes are made entirely by hand, designs the first wedge evening shoes in gold kid and red satin.

9
FERRAGAMO

1937-38

1. Weekend dressing — Strassner's white pullover, white wool slacks, striped blazer.
2. Schiaparelli's whole beach look — sombrero, chopped slacks, high cork sandals: *Vogue* cover, 22 June 1938.
3. 'If you haven't already started your tanning siege — try to get your first dose when you are entirely nude. It's more health-giving and it's infinitely better to get an even foundation to start with.'
4. 'Alison gets down to it — in her crinkled multi-striped cotton tub frock, 35*s*. 9*d*. Simpsons.'

VOGUE

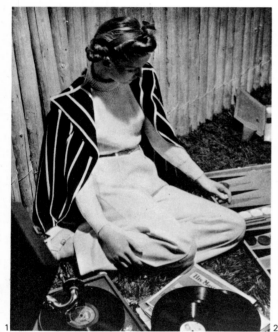

'The couturiers, every one, made the grand gesture. They caught the spirit of the moment with martial scarlet and black; they cast that nostalgic backward glance which people in troubled times bestow on a peaceful past'

'We deplore the crop of young women who take war as an excuse for letting their back hair down and parading about in slacks. Slack, we think, is the word . . . Determine, then – in this European jungle – to dress for dinner'

'Thousands of girls, trembling a bit, will go out looking for jobs this autumn. Thousands will get jobs. (Clothes will have something to do with this.) Thousands won't get jobs. (Clothes will have something to do with this, too.)'

BRAUN-SPIERER   Shoulderspan white felt Breton.

November *Vogue* is the first issue entirely produced under war conditions but from the start of the year clothes and copy are perfectly attuned to war, as though the designers knew it was coming. *Vogue* takes up its wartime attitude, 'It's your job to spend gallantly (to keep the national economy going), to dress decoratively, to be groomed immaculately – in short, to be a sight for sore eyes', and condemns slackness of appearance. There is a spread of candid camerawork showing the feet of women walking in Bond Street: 'We hope we shall be spared the sight of many little women in tailored suits running around London in open-toed sandals. Sister, watch your step.' Copy stresses economy, simplicity and practicability of the new uncrushable fabrics such as Zingal. Models are photographed on location in offices, on farms, in rainy London streets, even underwater. Leading looks are shirt dresses and simple suits with pleated skirts and 'nothing to date them', day dresses that can be worn to the office and go on, with a fur and muff, to a restaurant and dinner, and little-girl dresses — an extension of playsuits — with demure white collars and cuffs, tight waists, full short skirts, tucks, smocking and puff sleeves. Even Ascot skirts clear the turf by 17 inches.

Vogue patterns are for trousers for the volunteer owner-driver, a shirt for helping on the land, and knitting instructions for a sweater to go under uniform jackets.

The sweater has become the basis of most looks, even making the cover, worn with trousers and jewels. 'Sweaters appear, tough as you please, forever and a day, with our tweed skirts, with our golfing slacks. They appear, in highly sophisticated versions, with our town suits. Their social climb touches its peak when they appear, loaded with jewels, slashed with silk, over a grandly outsize evening skirt.'

Hair is Christy-waved and piled up on the head in curls and pompadours, or sausage-curled into a snood. Lips are painted into a bowtie shape, like Joan Crawford's, and coloured with Helena Rubinstein's 'Regimental Red' or Cyclax's 'Auxiliary Red'.

For evening, there are the Dorothy Lamour slinky crepes with plenty of uplift and a bare midriff, the draped chiffons used in contrasting panels, the simple cotton dance frocks. Fewer women now wear the crinolines that Norman Hartnell designs in powder blue and sequins for Queen Elizabeth. The London couturiers go to war and send out samples, fabric cuttings and saleswomen into the country towns. Hardy Amies joins the Fire Brigade, Victor Stiebel is a river policeman, Dennis Glenny is a soldier, and Digby Morton opens an off-the-peg department.

The clothes of 1939, the last that women invest in before the outbreak of war, will continue unchanged, like a fly in amber, throughout the war years.

1

LACHASSE

2

Siren into Suit

Digby Morton, famous tailleur, created this trouser suit in a bright tartan 'Viyella.' Beautifully warm to slip on over night-things in an emergency, with a hidey hood to cover your head. A lightning zip fastens it and military buttons trim the four patch pockets.

Viyella Thirty-six FASHION FABRICS

'Viyella' Thirty-six Fashion Fabrics—plain shades and marls, blouse checks and stripes, 5/9 a yard. Lovely new designs in novel woven effects, 6/11 a yard. All 36 inches wide.

152   3

4

BARRI

1. Uncrushable heavy cotton suit in black and white plaid, showing lacy petticoats, photographed by André de Dienes who took some of the earliest pictures of an unsophisticated Marilyn Monroe.
2. Long-sleeved playsuits.
3. The first siren suit appears in *Vogue* as an advertisement for Viyella.
4. Day-length wine jersey restaurant dress, cleverly cut and draped with a fox hat and muff.
5. 1939 accessories — sunspectacles, blazing lipstick, plenty of glamour: *Vogue* cover, 9 August.
6. Helena Rubinstein's 'pick-up' masque. More and more often in the late 1930s, husbands would come home to find their wives looking like this.
7. Milada Mladora in a Kleinert periwinkle blue rubber bathing suit with rubber roses and rubber lace frills.
8. The foundation of the look — uplift and waspwaist.

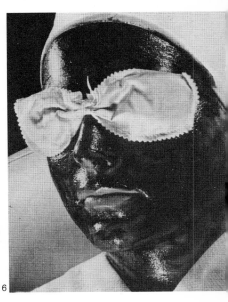

THE NIPPED-IN WAIST

DRESSES DEMAND IT·

·CORSETS CONTRIVE IT

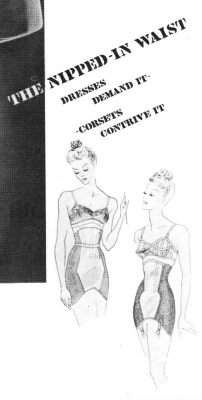

Horst

153

1939

LELONG

1. For a secretary, little-girl dress in navy wool with white touches, Harrods.
2. Silk jersey dress in panels of white and navy wrapped with a white cummerbund.
3. Half and half fur coat, leopard-skin with a black wool back: jacket, Vionnet; hat, Talbot.
4. Dorothy Lamour evening dress of white crepe with uplift, bare midriff and bolero.
5. 'Mermaid or mummy,' call this silhouette what you will, the dress clings as closely, needs a twenty-inch waist, streamline hips and bee's knees to wear it. Patou's version is in his new, deep, winter green, with gold-fringe edging the jacket, sealing the skirt.
6. Worth's tangerine dress, with a pleated skirt, white bolero jacket, easily adaptable to the ready to wear.
7. Victorian straw, set on a butter-cup yellow snood.
8. Plum felt doll hat with a 'Skye terrier' fringe of ostrich, and Émile's sausage curls.

4
MOLYNEUX

5
PATOU   André Durst

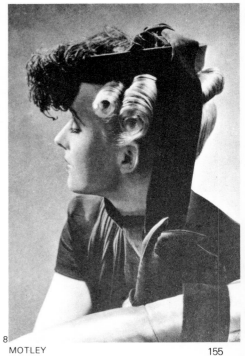

6

7
RAHVIS

8
MOTLEY

155

1940-1947

FASHION
BY GOVERNMENT ORDER

Lofman

By 1941 Londoners had settled down to a routine of chaos. Life was not only dangerous, but uncomfortable, dirty and odd. There were rabbits and chickens in backyards and on roofs, the park flower beds were full of cabbages and carrots, and habitual reserve gave way to smiles and offers of drinks. At the station, you were asked, 'Is your journey really necessary?' and a woman porter helped you with your cases. Places of entertainment were temporarily shut, and instead people went out to sleep; either in the dank and smelly municipal shelters or the muggy, convivial underground where, if you were lucky – or unlucky, some said – there might be an E.N.S.A. concert. People talked a different language, borrowed from the R.A.F., summed up by David Langdon in his cartoon of two civil servants, 'Give me a buzz on the intercom at eleven hundred hours and we'll bale out for coffee.'

Round every bombed house there spread a circle of debris, broken glass and pulverized coal which gradually settled on every surface, together with the Blitz smell of charred timber, gas and watersoaked dust. In the middle of the Blitz *Vogue* wrote, '"Come in and have a bath" rather than a drink, is the new social gesture – soap and water being a far more pleasing offer than any amount of gin.' The population was continually moving about, whether bombed out, evacuating, or snatching a weekend's leave at home.

The big hotels were crowded out. 'They are like luxury liners, their passengers signing on for an endlessly protracted, portless voyage.' They slept uneasily in the littered lounges, ate and danced in their crumpled clothes to the band – perhaps Lew Stone – while over their heads the roof spotters scanned the dark city. The problem of what to take with you, even for a night in the shelter, was a nightmare. 'All life is now lived in suitcases . . . the luggage-lugger has to decide between staggering under her all, or travelling light and free, but risking a return to nothing but demolition squads at work in the remnants of the area. "Safe as houses" now seems an obsolete phrase, and in rather poor taste, too.' It became common practice when you had dinner with friends to stay the night there. Guests camped in the basement or the bathroom, and dinner menus became a great deal simpler. 'You take what you can get, and make what you can of it, very often having to cook on an open fire, too. Onions being as scarce as peaches, even the most elegant cook can no longer baulk at hot-pots or stews as dinner-party fare.' *Vogue*'s social editor changed her milieu: 'a recent alarm found the Dorchester shelter filling up with celebrities – several ministers without portfolios or gas masks either, Lady Diana Cooper in full evening dress, Vic Oliver in serious mood, his wife Sarah Churchill sound asleep on the floor, and Leonora Corbett trying out a new

Left: 'Fashion is indestructible', perhaps Cecil Beaton's most famous fashion photograph, of a Digby Morton suit in the Temple's ruins, September 1941.

1. 'It must go on', 1942.

Here is VOGUE in spite of all!

OUTSIDE—on several nights, bombs have spattered within twenty yards. This street below our window now holds a new crater, and another length of the arcade has crashed. We were turned out temporarily for a time bomb

INSIDE—our offices have been strewn with broken glass. (See the freakishness of blast, that leaves a tumbler of water uncracked, unspilled.) Though five storeys up, our floors have been deep in soil and debris flung through the roof

BENEATH —we work on when our roof-watcher sends us down. Our editorial staff plan, lay-out, write. Our studio photograph in their wine-cellar-basement. Our fashion staff continue to comb the shops. Congestedly, unceremoniously but cheerfully, Vogue, like its fellow Londoners, is put to bed in a shelter

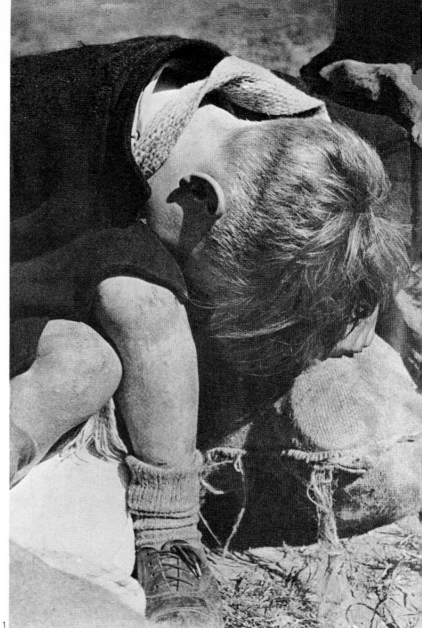

Thérèse Bonney

hairdo.' When the siren sounded in Mayfair, it often as not found the couturiers in the middle of complicated fittings. Captain Molyneux, his mouth full of pins, would ask his model, 'Do you want to go to the shelter?' and Sheila Wetton, today *Vogue*'s senior fashion editor, would obediently shake her head. At John Lewis the fittings were carried on in their shelters, while Dickens and Jones provided canteen refreshments for bomb-bound customers. 'At Grosvenor House, the new deep-shelter restaurant defies even sirens. It's left to the band to play All Clear, fitting the phrase to various tunes . . . Cinemas now flash All clear! All clear! across the screen regardless of the picture. It looked wonderful scrawled across Lillian Russell's 1880 bust, the other night.'

Vogue wrote complimentary features, 'I'm just back from town' and 'I'm just back from the country', giving the flavour of life in the summer of 1941. In town, 'Whole chunks of streets are up, choking dust turning people white . . . powdered glass tinkling about and everyone being too, too normal . . . errand *girls* instead of boys, bus conductorettes, waitresses at the Mirabelle . . . Piccadilly pretties now strut around in pseudo-sensible slacks . . . there are enormous determined cinema queues, and the Vic Wells ballet back again, and Flaganan and Allen, Oi-ing their way through the Black Vanities show, the theatrical success of the moment . . . You can hire hens by the week, they lay all over the back yard or balcony . . . in the evening nothing is fixed up ahead, and no one dreams of dressing up at night . . . Potato Bars have taken over from Milk Bars, and restaurants are full up all the time; an endless chain of meals emerging one into the next, all overlapping, women looking extra well groomed in uniform . . . Everyone's talking about

Lee Miller

1. Homeless refugee child, 1942.
2. During the war farming had to be made to pay. The number of tractors increased from 60,000 to nearly a quarter of a million. Ploughing went on by night as well as by day, the blackout being waived for the purpose, and many of the drivers were women — during the war 90,000 enrolled in the Women's Land Army.
3. The much-needed bath, 1941 — to be clean during the Blitz was a luxury.
4. January 1940.

Lee Miller

Toni Frissel

Gerald Kelly's portrait of the Queen – we all know she has the most dazzling pink and white complexion, but why leave out the white?... everywhere, the shrugging, shrilling Free French, the brightly coloured uniforms that fill the streets.' The progress of the war could be charted by the foreign uniforms in London – with the Allied troops, nearly 1½ million overseas troops were billeted in this country during the war.

In the country, 'all the big houses are commandeered ... ambulance classes, knitting bees for the Women's Institute, dressing for dinner with rigid formality, canteen stints and voluntary shifts of tractor driving and dairy work, everyone bicycling ... the difficulty of obtaining cosmetics – home-brewed lotions in the chemist's shop, car owners taking it in turns to drive into the nearest town with huge lists to do everyone's shopping for the week ... the farmer's wife sleeps under the dairy table with both her children, the vicar's wife makes for the crypt in her siren suit, the doctor's wife shares her fully equipped Anderson shelter'.

Weddings highlighted the many little austerities and restrictions of wartime life in Britain, from the rushed proposal to the ban on rice-throwing. Church bells were only to ring in case of parachute landings, there was no choir, no sugar icing for the cake, 'so enchanting tea-cosy covers have been invented to fit over plain cakes. For flowers and food, the bride takes what she can get ... the regimental flower, badge or squadron crest carried out in colour, the bouquet a mixed nosegay of any flowers in season, since the hothouses are occupied by fruit and vegetables.' The honeymoon might be a weekend in a borrowed cottage, petrol carefully saved for the purpose, or a few days in London, taking the opportunity

1. Sir Kingsley Wood, 1940.
2. 'The stuff of Vogue' — part of Cecil Beaton's waste paper hoard, 1942.
3. Lady Diana Cooper down on the farm, 1941.

Opposite: Schiaparelli dresses photographed by Horst, December 1947.
Over page, left: *Vogue*'s break-the-rules issue, June 1971: 'It is in bad taste to dress extravagantly or showily when mingling with people who are all plainly dressed.' Satin shirt and shorts by Electric Fittings, shoes by Chelsea Cobbler, hair colour by Daniel and shape by Oliver of Leonard. Photograph by Peter Knapp.
Over page, right: Photograph by Art Kane, November 1963.

Cecil Beaton

of collecting your friends together 'since no knowing, these days, when the next meeting may be'. The best presents were practical and portable, 'a portable wireless or gramophone, a portable Electrolux refrigerator that works on oil, electricity or gas . . . treasures that money can't buy – a petrol coupon, honey in the comb, home-made jam'.

The 'Lend a hand on the land' posters brought townspeople into the country to help with the digging or haymaking. They were a mixed blessing to farmers, particularly the girls who turned up in high heels and their best dresses, but there were other more reliable sources of labour – soldiers, released from barracks for the day, and prisoners-of-war, working bands of 30 or 40 Germans or Italians dressed in blue dungarees patched with green. *Vogue* wrote many features about independent people who went 'back to the land' and produced their own food, some becoming successful farmers. There was Norman Parkinson, one of *Vogue*'s first-rank photographers then and now, who had volunteered for the Navy but had been told, 'You'd be more useful to us as a photographer', and worked on a propaganda magazine repudiating the statements of Lord Haw-Haw. At the same time he ran a farm. *Vogue* sent all the clothes for their country fashion shots down on the train, and Parkinson photographed them between mucking out the pigs and collecting swill. He wrote about the farm, 'Hotels, cafés and the cinema have bins with Park's Pig Food on the lid . . . we collect the bins from the back door at four, and return for dinner by the front at eight. "Leave plenty on the side of your plate," we remind each other. "More for our pigs." ' Another Londoner running a farm was Lady Diana Cooper, who had set up a productive and profitable business with three acres, a cow and £50, and managed it single-handed until she accompanied her husband to Singapore. No Marie Antoinette, this amazingly versatile and adventurous society beauty, who had toured Europe and America as an actress, got up at 6.30 to milk the cow, feed the animals and make cheese. Another lynchpin of London society, Cecil Beaton, went down to photograph her, and was brainwashed. 'When you take into consideration the fact that their eggs replace "fixed" price fish, rare meat, or the canned foods which should be kept for emergency, fowls cannot fail to pay their way. By adding scrap to the rationed quota more fowls can be fed than have rations allotted to them.' Meanwhile Mrs John Betjeman in Berkshire was running a large vegetable and herb garden with the help of two evacuee schoolmasters, milking her goats twice a day,

driving herself about in a dogcart and riding the dawn parachute patrol on the downs.

In November 1942, *Vogue* pointed out to its readers another line of war work – welcoming the American servicemen to Britain. 'Remember, everything is twice as much fun to these American boys if there's a girl in it . . . Frankness and informality are the keynotes to strike . . . The American gullet is used to iced whisky, iced beer . . . they'll like to hear the local history and superstitions.' In the pursuit of girls, the Americans had everything their own way. They were paid at least four times the basic British pay, they drove huge flashy cars, dispensed nylons, candy and packets of Lucky Strike, and gave their girlfriends a taste of glamour at the American base dances, with lavish food and drink, and the top dance bands like Glen Miller's, here on tour. As the British service-man bitterly remarked, 'The Americans are all right, except that they are overpaid, oversexed and over here.' When they finally departed things became a little greyer and quieter. Marghanita Laski remarked in 1946 *Vogue*, you couldn't count on finding a taxi outside the American Red Cross Clubs, and the young girls in the tube weren't chewing gum any more.

The immediate effects of the war on *Vogue* had been to put up the price from 1s. to 2s. in 1940, 2s. 6d. with *Vogue Pattern Book* included, and finally 3s. in 1942; and to contract the number of pages because of the paper shortage. Maxims such as 'Waste paper is vital to the war effort' and 'Use as little paper as possible for fires' were printed at the foot of the pages. The circulation, however, increased, climbing from 52,000 in 1941 to 106,000 in 1949, and each issue was passed from hand to hand until up to twenty women had seen it. *Vogue*'s own advertisement in May 1941 said, 'Many more women are now buying *Vogue* than, on an average, used to take it in pre-war days. You've a copy in your hands – you're lucky. But every month there are countless people who miss their *Vogue* . . . The trouble is, of course, that owing to official restrictions in the supply of paper, we just can't print as many copies as we'd like to. So it's a question of first come, first served. Please, if you're one of these fortunate first, don't be dog-in-a-manger about your *Vogue*. Share it with your friends. Invite them home and give them the run of your copy. And then, when you've read it all, studied it all and planned all your outfits – pass it on to someone else.'

The Second World War, unlike the First, brought no escapist

160

Opposite: Blouse by
Albini, hat by Jean
Charles Brosseau, face by
Barbara Daly with
Maybelline make up.
Photograph by Sarah
Moon, April 1972.
1. Jacqueline Cochran,
ace airwoman, 1941.

follies, no fashion fantasies. They were impossible no less because
of the wartime spirit than the government restrictions. In a speech
to the Fashion Group of New York, Edna Woolman Chase, the
American Editor-in-Chief, said, 'When people speak to me about
this war they ask me "Isn't it going to be incredibly difficult to edit
a luxury magazine like *Vogue* in times like these? Do you think
that you can hope to survive?" My answer to that is – What kind
of a magazine do they think this is? ... Fashions would not be
fashions if they did not conform to the spirit and the needs and the
restrictions of the current times.' Naturally, as fashion exactly re-
flects the mood of the times, the fashion was for clumpy shoes,
clumsy suits, box coats and headscarves tied into turbans hiding
'a multitude of pins'. Just as even wealthy women in the Depression were dressing down in plain black dresses and furless
coats, fashionable women before clothing restrictions were dressing
in Utility-look suits or sweaters and slacks. 'It looks wrong to look
wealthy,' said *Vogue.* 'The woman well-dressed in the meaning of
today would not easily be rendered helpless or ridiculous.'

From the outset of war the magazine took what Pearson Phillips,
the journalist, has called 'a positive and optimistic line'. *Vogue*
needed to take that line as early as October 1940, when in 'No
margin for error', it discussed Sir Kingsley Wood's budget that
slapped a new Purchase Tax on clothes. 'His acts might suggest him
no friend to fashion; but *Vogue* (hopefully) detects an ally. Because
of him, designers will get together frankly, to pool their ideas and
use their limited materials to present a united fashion front. Because of him, women will buy carefully and cleverly ... by the
inescapable pressure of the Purchase Tax he will set them practising
those sound dress maxims that *Vogue* has always preached. How
often have we counselled against "the dress you buy and seldom
wear" ... If women must buy less, they will buy better.'

Clothes rationing arrived in June 1941, by which time prices had
nearly doubled in eighteen months. Coupons were distributed, and
the rationing operated by a points system, a garment costing a
number of coupon points irrespective of fabric and price. Utility
clothes, however, fulfilled government requirements and sold at
fixed prices. They were not subject to Purchase Tax. The Utility
scheme involved at first 50 per cent and later 85 per cent of all
cloth manufactured, controlling quality and price, and was reinforced by the Making of Clothes (Restrictions) Orders introduced
in 1942, which covered nearly all clothing and restricted yardage

1

My coupons too?

and style. 'Dress restrictions simply pare away superfluities,' said *Vogue*, making the best of things. 'The progress of the war has made it necessary to prohibit all superfluous material and superfluous labour . . . Fashion is undergoing a compulsory course of slimming and simplification.' Readers were reminded, 'Subtraction, not addition, is the first of fashion rules – full liberty is liberty for excess as well as excellence.' On the other hand, 'The Board of Trade has now assessed our clothing requirements at 66 coupons – and margarine coupons at that – a horrid slight. It is now said that fashion's goose is properly cooked and done in, for want of the best butter. But fashion is indestructible and will survive even margarine coupons . . . you cannot ration a sense of style.' Noël Coward's new leading lady, Judy Campbell, pointed out enthusiastically, 'Rationing is marvellous in one respect. You can make lack of money look like lack of coupons.'

Most women found the disappearance of stockings and cosmetics even harder to accept than dress restrictions. The decline and fall of the stocking was the decline and fall of women's morale. The first blow was the ban on silk stockings in 1941, when, in January, *Vogue* recommended the substitutes – cotton, rayon and the hardwearing heavy mesh – but by August even these were in such short supply that the advice became 'Discard stockings for casual wear at home and in the country substituting a plausible cream make up . . . wear sturdy stockings whenever suitable . . . wash and darn your precious rayon tenderly, taking them to the invisible menders at the first hint of a ladder.' Leg paint turned out to be thoroughly unsatisfactory, some kinds turning yellow in daylight, others rubbing off on skirts and leaving indelible marks. Worse was to come. By 1942 the Board of Trade warned that if women didn't go without stockings during the summer they would have to by winter. In a feature called 'Sock Shock', *Vogue* bravely published a picture of a woman in a smart summer afternoon dress, big hat – and ankle socks. 'Socks can contrive to look charming,' said *Vogue* brazenly. 'But we believe that it's easier to achieve a smart stockingless appearance with quite bare legs (smoothly tanned or made up) and footlets. We hope the Board will put these in production,' and meanwhile offered a knitting pattern for them. Lux advertisements, reminding the reader that Lux would one day come back on the market, ran this rhyme in 1945:

> No wonder Julia shouts hurray!
> Her sweetheart's home on leave today,
> And frequent washing in the past
> Has made his favourite stockings last.

Vogue's tone of voice had changed radically in the three years between 1939, when an editorial had rapped women over the knuckles for slopping about in town wearing open-toed sandals and slacks, and 1941: 'For the A.R.P. worker, the new, short coiffure. Long hair can be tied into a net turban which will hide under a tin hat. For the face, no make up, but a non-greasy, allpurpose cream, dusted with powder . . . Save your cosmetics for evenings out . . . That "too-good-to-be-true" look which only a personal maid can produce is absent – because the maid is absent, on munitions . . . Clothes look as if they had been taken care of, put on beautifully and then forgotten for more important things.' *Vogue*'s special issues were now devoted to Patterns and Renovations. At the beginning of the war, when there was still a pretence that fashion was changing and developing year by year, there were diagrams showing how you could alter last year's looks to this year's: later on, *Vogue* turned its attention to making the best of things. 'You can go hatless if you wear simple swept-back hair like this . . . you can go stockingless if you wear simple flat-heeled shoes like this.' Needs must, and the beauty pages, shrinking with the shrinking

supply of cosmetics, extolled the virtues of a healthy, brisk, scrubbed appearance. 'Polish yourself up: hair burnished and crisply cropped to the new length – it's a look that does not jar with uniform – with *women*'s uniform. Somehow, more and more, the eye unconsciously measures women up by this yardstick. Why does that shoulder-mane seem so out of date? Because it would look messy hanging on a uniform collar ... What's wrong with those exquisite tapered nails? They couldn't do a hand's turn without breaking. The woman who could change instantly into uniform, or munitions overalls and look charming, soignée and right, is the smart woman of today' and exhorted women to keep 'nails rosy till the day when varnish vanishes: figure kept taut by exercise and good posture, with corsets a helping, but not a decisive factor ... Wash-and-brush-up your face on occasion: because creams are rationed and soap is not.'

Prepared to make concessions over appearance in sacrificial wartime spirit, nevertheless *Vogue* was ready to take up cudgels when necessary. The line was firmly drawn in the August issue of 1942. The beauty column made the concessions. 'Today, you want to look as if you thought less about your face than about what you have to face; less about your figure than about how much you can do. You want to look as if you cared about your looks, yes, but cared more about being able to do a full day's work – whether it be in a factory, on the land, coping with a day nursery, or just managing your home single-handed as so many of us do today. You want to look beautiful, certainly – what woman in what age hasn't wanted to? ... but you want it to be a beauty that doesn't jar with the times, a beauty that's heart-lifting not heart-breaking, a beauty that's beneficent but not beglamoured, and a beauty that's responsive – not a responsibility.'

But a special feature called 'It Must Go On' inveighed against the rumour that the supply of cosmetics, already curtailed to 25 per cent of peacetime output, might be cut further. 'Cosmetics are as essential to a woman as a reasonable supply of tobacco is to a man. A welfare officer at a munitions factory said, "£1,000 worth of cosmetics, distributed among my girls, would please them more than £1,000 in cash" ... only when a woman looks her best can she feel and do her best. The supply should not be further reduced

by prejudice or puritanism – more frivolous than the cosmetics they censure.'

The war was a watershed for fashion, forcing the development of a stable ready-to-wear structure capable of prosperous large-scale production in the fifties. 'The geniuses who invented the Utility scheme had a great say in the development of the fashion industry,' said Frederick Starke, a leader in the better off-the-peg market. By controlling quantities and prices the Utility scheme forced manufacturers to choose their cloths wisely and cut economically. Standards of manufacture were improved by minimum-standard government regulations and by a public forced by coupon rationing to discriminate, and methods of manufacture were streamlined and better mechanized by the pressures of rushed uniform production. Sizing and costing were for the first time regularized and accurately worked out, and labour was reassessed. The fashion industry's workers came out of the war more secure: they were paid guaranteed wages and conditions of work were laid down. When in July 1942 the government took over extra factory space for the storage of munitions and other wartime equipment, many manufacturers had to get together to stay in business. By 1947 Frederick Starke had formed the London Model House Group, seven leading manufacturers who united to establish the prestige of British fashion abroad, and to present a united front to buyers and suppliers. In 1950 the Apparel and Fashion Industry's Association was to say, 'a revolution has taken place behind the smokescreen of wartime conditions'.

Meanwhile, London's couturiers had managed their own revolution. Early in the war *Vogue* said, 'Paris is in eclipse, making it London's opportunity to shine. Already in London are the Paris houses of Molyneux, Paquin, Worth; lending all the prestige of their Paris connection to the drive for dollars. Creed, too, is here ... In England now, every branch of the fashion trade is stirring strongly. The challenge of the times has called forth, to admiration, qualities for which we have not always been conspicuous: initiative, speed, cooperation.'

In 1942 many of the couturiers were anxiously contemplating the possible next course of action of a government that had already introduced clothes rationing and the Utility scheme. There was

just one way of proving London couture valuable to the national economy during the war, and that was export. The year before, nine couturiers had scored a success by cooperating in a special export drive, a collection for South America sent out under government auspices. *Vogue* had published a special South American edition to accompany the collection, and reproduced some of the photographs in British *Vogue*, where they looked conspicuously luxurious and glamorous among the regular diet of man-tailored tweeds and skimpy dresses. Norman Hartnell approached the managing director of Worth and other couturiers, urging a common front to the Board of Trade. Harry Yoxall, *Vogue*'s managing director, became the business head and entrepreneur of the new Incorporated Society of London Fashion Designers, aimed at developing the couture export market. The 'Inc Soc' was supported by fabric manufacturers and encouraged by the government. Early members were Norman Hartnell, Peter Russell, Worth, Angèle Delanghe, Digby Morton, Hardy Amies, Creed, Molyneux and Michael Sherard. The first president was the Hon. Mrs Reginald Fellowes, chief fashion personality of the early thirties, now camping in London in the basement of the Duff Coopers' house in Westminster.

In the spring of 1943, some well-designed, anonymous Utility clothes went into the market, the result of the Board of Trade's invitation to the couture to design basic garments subject to all the usual restrictions. Anne Scott-James had said, 'If Mayfair hasn't the skill to cut a good dress from three or four yards of material with five or six buttons it must learn – or go under'. It proved that it had, and it had turned the difficult situation to its own advantage.

For a magazine so closely concerned with Paris as *Vogue*, the blanket of silence that descended on the city during the Occupation was bound to change the character of the magazine, making it more insular but also more independent. Up to summer 1940 *Vogue* ran a regular 'Paris Sidelights' page, showing the character of the city essentially unchanged. Bettina Wilson wrote, 'Paris in the fifth month of the war is an attractive, comfortable, normal city with an intimate, almost country charm to life . . . you can enjoy such luxuries as smart hats and plentiful taxis, but nobody will look at you askance if you go hatless or ride your bicycle on fine days.

1. Fashion pages from *Album de la Mode*, 1942, the arts magazine published in Occupied Paris.
2. *Vogue* pin-up, 1943.
3. The Liberation of Paris — one of the glamorous girls in pretty clothes who provoked an envious pique in austerity Britain.

Hospitality in the home has practically become a cult – the war seems to have weakened, if not completely broken down, the impregnable barriers of French formality.' *Vogue* photographer, Arik Nepo, now a *poilu* in the French army, wrote from a barn, 'We're billeted in a barn. We tumbled in late one night, too tired to do anything but slump into the straw . . . Next morning some cut pictures out of magazines and stuck them on the walls. *Vogue*, naturally, had pride of place – being full of pretty girls, divinely dressed; what more could you want?' From the Paris Ritz *Vogue* reported, 'Mrs Reginald Fellowes and her family, Madame Schiaparelli and her daughter Gogo, Lady Mendl, the Comtesse de Montgomery and Mrs Corrigan all live on the first floor. Dropping in for a drink means visiting from one room to the next, perhaps meeting the Sacha Guitrys, Mlle Chanel, Jean Cocteau, who also have rooms there.' At Molyneux's mid-season collection there were Noël Coward, Madame la Générale Gamelin, and Mrs Fellowes – 'who knitted throughout the collection. There were four mannequins instead of 15, 30 models instead of 100, but those 30 struck clearly the informal note of the moment.' In poignant contrast to her circus ball of 1938, there were Lady Mendl's Sunday lunch parties at Versailles – 'small tables covered with oil cloth, corn beef hash to eat, and guests take away the dishes and sweep up crumbs'. The soup kitchen for out-of-work writers and musicians had a first night opening with all the familiar faces: the artistic poor paid 2 or 4 francs, according to circumstances, the wealthy visitors 20. Bettina Wilson wrote that the French were continually amazed by the fifteen-year-old look of the R.A.F. pilots on their first Paris leaves, sitting in every *boîte* and tapping their fingers and toes to the music 'to which no one is allowed to dance in Paris, except at special galas', and told the story of the Lopez-Willshaws' furniture, which had been willed to the Louvre after his death. During the first week of the war, a removals van drew into the courtyard with instructions from the curator of the Louvre to take the furniture away to a safe cellar for the duration, leaving the Lopez family sitting on the bamboo garden furniture in an empty salon.

There was grimmer news in July, when *Vogue* fashion artist Eric and his family left their home at Senlis, near Chantilly, to join a tide of refugees moving back from the German advance: as they left their house it was wrecked by a bomb. Seven months after the occupation of Paris *Vogue* received a batch of pictures relayed from New York, showing a deserted Champs Élysées, a tide of bicycles and a cycle taxi, a cross between a sidecar and push bike. 'Across the great gulf of silence – and of misunderstanding, which we still believe cannot be turned to enmity between our peoples – come pictures of a strangely subdued city.'

During the Occupation some twenty of the famous couture houses managed to stay open in Paris, with or without their chief designers. Schiaparelli and Mainbocher went to America, where Mainbocher stayed, and Molyneux, Creed, Angèle Delanghe went to London. 'One of the first things the Germans did,' said Lucien Lelong, President of the Couture Syndicate, 'was to break into the Syndicate offices and seize all documents pertaining to the French export trade.' M. Lelong successfully resisted all German efforts to remove the couture lock, stock and barrel to Berlin and Vienna. 'I told them that *la couture* was not a transportable industry, such as bricklaying.' Thanks to his negotiations, the couture houses managed to show two abbreviated collections a year. 'A few months

2

later, in 1941 to be exact, due to the lack of materials, very severe restrictions were ordered and textile cards with the point system started. We soon realised that if this regulation was applied to our great fashion houses, it would mean closing them down immediately.' M. Lelong renewed his discussions with the Germans and succeeded in obtaining exemption from point restrictions for twelve houses. 'Unfortunately, the Germans noticed at the end of six months that ninety-two houses were operating, which led to more discussions. Finally we succeeded in keeping sixty. Over a period of four years, we had fourteen official conferences with the Germans . . . at four of them they announced that *la couture* was to be entirely suppressed, and each time we avoided the catastrophe. On another occasion, they demanded that 80 per cent of our workers go into war industries; this we managed to reduce to a 5 per cent quota, which in reality never exceeded 3 per cent.' He calculated that by the Liberation, 12,000 workers had been saved from unemployment and consequent labour in German war industries.

The export market was shut, and the couture had to depend on new clients, the recently moneyed class of black-marketeers, and many German wives, together with those of the Germans' French mistresses who dared to buy their clothes there. A great deal of subterfuge went on between the couturiers to get round German regulations. Bitter rivals in peacetime, they cooperated magnificently against the common enemy. When Madame Grès and

Girls - that's all, brother

VOGUE'S

PIN-UP PRESENT

FOR THE SERVICES

Vogue, we hear, is liked and looked for in many an Army and Air Force mess, and even in the austerity of Naval wardrooms. We used to be modestly surprised. "But why?" they said. "Surrounded by men and machines, shut in by steel or canvas, we can do with all the beauty and femininity you can pack between two covers." Well, gentlemen, we give you these pages for full measure. They are girls of the Ziegfeld Follies of New York, where they've long understood the pretty power of lamé, feathers, white powder, furs, pearls and enormous hats. We hope you'll pin 'em up, with our love and thanks, and our hopes that before another Christmas comes you'll be getting beauty and femininity first-hand, at home

CHRISTINE AYRES, ZIEGFELD FOLLIES GIRL

3

Lee Miller

Balenciaga were ordered to close their houses for two weeks because they had exceeded the authorized yardage for some of their models, the rest of the couture joined forces to finish their collections so that they could show on time.

Michel de Brunhoff, editor of French *Vogue*, was unable to publish it under the Germans. 'There was no honourable way; no way without compromise and collaboration. I stalled, and found slippery answers for the Germans when they suggested, and then ordered, that our magazines reopen with German backing.' Instead, M. de Brunhoff cooperated with *Le Figaro* to produce *Album de la Mode*, a magazine of the arts, theatre and fashion, from which *Vogue* reproduced some fashion pages after the Liberation.

The Liberation of Paris appears in *Vogue* as a personal triumph. With exceptional speed, *Vogue* showed photographs of the fighting in October 1944 – fire and smoke, a priest encouraging boys at a barricade, General de Gaulle as he passed the windows of *Vogue*'s former Paris office. Lee Miller, *Vogue*'s *femme soldat*, went to check up on Picasso, 'generous and voluble as ever', Boris Kochno (Diaghilev's discovery) and Bébé Bérard ('He has only one pair of trousers and has to wear an old trench coat as a skirt to work in'), Paul Eluard and Michel de Brunhoff. Elsa Schiaparelli went back to Paris, found that food cost five to twenty times as much as it had in 1939, and resolved to give women 'clothes that they can live in, not parade in'. Cecil Beaton found Colette muffled up in bed with hot-water bottles and nine fountain pens, writing her memoirs, Gertrude Stein writing about G.I.s and Democracy, and noticed a hopeful sign: 'two actors with salmon-painted faces emerging from a jeweller's shop while a moving picture camera grinds' – the film industry had started up again. Lee Miller reported, 'There is one hairdresser in all Paris who can dry hair: "Gervais" . . . He has rigged his dryers to stove pipes which pass through a furnace heated by rubble. The air is sent by fans turned by relay teams of boys riding a stationary tandem bicycle in the basement.'

In England, life was at its drabbest and most regimented. 'The penny plain of life is three farthings,' said *Vogue*, 'and the struggle to make up the difference takes so much of women's energy.' The public reaction to the Liberation fashion photographs – 'dazzling girls in full floating skirts, tiny waist-lines, top-heavy with built up pompadour front hair-dos and waving tresses; weighted to the ground with clumsy, fancy thick-soled wedge shoes' – was one of envious pique. *Vogue* sprang to the defence of Paris. 'If it surprises you to see pretty girls in pretty dresses, to see the beautiful clothes which the fashion houses never ceased to make, reflect that the life of France and her civilian technique of resistance must necessarily have been the reverse of England's. Here, it showed patriotism to obey regulations, to do the work required of us, to take no more than our rations. There, it showed patriotism to flout regulations, to avoid work except where it would not benefit the Germans (as in the luxury trades), to black-marketeer up to the hilt.'

The Liberation allowed readers to see their first Paris collections for four years. The designs had a mixed reception here and in America, where a ban was imposed on copying the full skirts and dressmaker details from photographs in fashion magazines. There was no question of being able to copy them here. In December *Vogue* published a manifesto by Lucien Lelong, which amounted to an apology. 'It was only after the Autumn Collections were shown that I received copies of English and American dress restrictions, and I now understand why certain journalists found the Paris Collections exaggerated. However, I must explain that my colleagues and I eliminated many models prepared before the liberation – replacing them by simple suits and coats which we felt better suited the circumstances arising from France's official re-entry into the War at the side of the Allies.'

With the end of the war clothes rationing tightened. There were shortages of everything from dried eggs to soap. Even bread was rationed, and the government spent £857,000 on a meat-substitute, an oily dull fish called snoek, which the press soon discovered was a large, ferocious cousin of the barracuda, which hissed and barked when annoyed. To give it a little much-needed glamour, the government published a series of snoek recipes, including 'Snoek Piquante'. However, nothing would make the public eat it, and at the time of the Festival of Britain a mysterious quantity of tinned fish came onto the market labelled 'Selected fish food for cats and kittens'.

The patient bearing with the minor horrors of war ended with the war. Now women were resentful of the shortages and restrictions: *Vogue*'s attitude changed from 'Dress restrictions simply pare away superfluities' to 'One has only to see a collection designed for export, and the same collection toned down to comply

Lee Miller

1

2

Lee Miller

It's easy . . . it's quick . . . it's delicious

Omelette: made with dried eggs—new laid eggs with nothing but the shell and water taken away. Appetising; digestible. So simple and easy, too. For the perfect omelette, try this way:

1 Quantities for two people. Mix 4 level table-spoons dried egg, with salt and pepper, and 4 tablespoons water till smooth. Beat well. Gradually add 4 more tablespoons water, keeping mixture very smooth. Again beat well.

2 Meanwhile, heat 1 oz. cooking fat in a frying pan (use the thickest one you have) until it starts to smoke. Pan and fat must be very hot. Pour egg in quickly.

3 As it cooks, lift edges with fork, allowing liquid egg to run under, until all is set. This takes from 1 to 1½ minutes. Don't overcook it. Now add, if you want to, grated cheese, chopped vegetables, meat, bacon etc. or herbs. Or jam. Fold over omelette away from handle of the pan so that it rolls over on to a hot plate.

ISSUED BY THE MINISTRY OF FOOD

3

with austerity at home, to realize how much fashion value has been lost in the process.' In February 1946 *Vogue* invited a Cambridge economist and broadcaster, Louis Stanley, to explain why, after nine years without new curtains, linen, upholstery or pretty clothes, we still could not get hold of new goods. Stanley called his feature 'The Second Battle of Britain' and said, 'It is bad enough when such goods do not exist, but to learn that they are being produced – the best this country can make – only not for domestic consumption is a bitter pill ... Women are further exasperated by illustrations in periodicals and the national press showing exotic fashions in Paris, Brussels, New York, Stockholm, even Germany,' and went on to explain, 'We have to wipe out a deficit of £1,200,000,000 from Britain's balance of trade.' *Vogue* jettisoned the 'positive and optimistic line' on dress restrictions. 'It is unfair and economically unwise to leave our designers, one moment longer than is necessary, at such a disadvantage in relation to their competitors ... we add our voice to those which ask the Board of Trade to abolish austerity as soon as practicable ... and we hope that "as soon as practicable" will be construed with more urgency than it usually commands in Whitehall.' Marghanita Laski let fly: 'Patriotism is definitely NOT ENOUGH, and I, for one, am fed up. I'm fed up at home and I'm fed up when I go abroad. I don't like to see the foreigner pointing out a fellow-traveller (or could it be me?) and whispering, "You can see she's English – look at her clothes!"'

And yet no post-war look had evolved. James Laver, invited to make a prediction about the look to come, replied, 'Fashion has reached one of those turning points in history when everything may happen, just because anything may happen to the world. Neither in politics, nor in social life, nor in dress, nor in millinery are the lines yet laid down. We do not know yet *what* will get itself established.' One thing was certain, that the Board of Trade had created forbidden fruit and provided a violent psychological stimulus: women were eying clothes with passionate longing. When the New Look arrived, women were going to have it.

It arrived on 12 February 1947, at the freshly painted salon of a new young designer who had emerged from the ranks at Lucien Lelong. Christian Dior opened at 30 Avenue Montaigne, backed by Marcel Boussac, the textile millionaire, and at a stroke restored world confidence in Paris as fashion leader. The models swept in with fifteen, twenty-five, even eighty yards of fabric in their skirts, and spun up the aisle to the sounds of rustling petticoats and the crashing of ashtray stands. The New Look provoked extremes of delight in women, for whom each dress and suit was an orgy of all things most feminine and forbidden. Today no fashion innovation could equal the excitement of Dior's then, because it had been preceded by thirteen uninterrupted years of the square-shouldered Schiaparelli-initiated look.

Dior said, 'I designed clothes for flower-like women, with rounded shoulders, full, feminine busts, and hand-span waists above enormous, spreading skirts.' His models looked absolutely different from the women in the audience. Dior's newly-designed woman had soft neat shoulders, a wasp waist, a bosom padded for extra curve, and hips that swelled over shells of cambric or taffeta worked into the lining: the dressmaking techniques were immensely complicated, some Victorian, some newly evolved. She walked leaning backward to make the hips more prominent, and her skirt burst into pleats, sometimes stitched over the hips or blossoming out under the stiff curved peplum of her jacket. Her hem rustled around some twelve inches from the floor, from which it was divided by the sheerest of silk stockings and the highest of pointed shoes. She was delicious, and she made all other women green with envy.

Coffin

1 and 2. Gervais's human hair-dryers, Paris 1944.
3. Ministry of Food advertisement, 1944, for a dried egg omelette.
4. Christian Dior in 1947, the year of the New Look.

For *Vogue*, Dior's collection came at the end of a dull round of collections, too late to be justly dealt with in the March issue – there's a single line at the end of the Paris report, 'The season's sensation is the new house of Christian Dior – see next issue.' The April issue said, 'Christian Dior is the new name in Paris. With his first collection he not only shot into fame, but retrieved the general situation by ... "the Battle of the Marne of the couture". His ideas were fresh and put over with great authority, his clothes were beautifully made, essentially Parisian, deeply feminine. Dior uses fabric lavishly in skirts – 15 yards in a woollen day dress, 25 yards in a short taffeta evening dress' and later, 'Fashion has moved decisively. Here are the inescapable changes. Always there is something prominent about the hips: in a shelf of peplum or a ledge of tucking; in bunched pleats or a bustle. The waist is breathtaking (except in the case of greatcoats). It is caught in with curved-to-the-form leather belts or wide, wide contrasting corselets or cummerbunds. Collars are clearly either/or: tiny or whoppers. Either way they are likely to stand up. Shoulders are gently natural. Sleeves are often pushed up; sometimes bulge at the wrists.' It was many years since the copy had been able to be so definite, so exact.

Women no sooner saw the New Look, but they had to have it. Dereta was one of the first off the mark in producing a grey flannel copy, and was taken aback to see 700 of them vanish from the rails of one West End shop within a fortnight. Naturally, because of the amount of fabric needed, the New Look could only appear in non-Utility clothes, of which production was limited. Yet manufacturers caught with large stocks of Utility 'man-tailored' suits lost money hand over fist: no one wanted them.

Sir Stafford Cripps summed up outraged official reaction: fury at the thwarting of fabric restrictions. He called a meeting of the British Guild of Creative Designers and suggested that they would be helping the national effort considerably if they would cooperate in keeping the short skirt popular – and the Guild obediently agreed to try. He then called in a committee of fashion journalists and, with the help of Harold Wilson, President of the Board of Trade, tried to persuade them to ignore Paris. They pointed out that their job was to report.

Several leading Labour party ladies including Mrs Bessie Braddock took up the struggle against what seemed to them to be a negation of all that women had won for themselves in two wars, making the classic mistake of thinking of female emancipation in male terms – that a woman has to be like a man to be free. To their attacks Christian Dior simply replied, 'I brought back the neglected art of pleasing'.

The New Look was such a success the new salon could hardly manage all their clients. I. Magnin took forty toiles, and Bergdorf Goodman, Bendel, Marshall Field, Eaton, Holt Renfrew took anything up to that number, ensuring that the whole of America would be wearing Dior or Dior copies. Buyers were still in the salon at two o'clock in the morning. The Dior staff worked eighteen hours a day. The two first famous customers were the Duchess of Windsor and Eva Peron, to be followed by Lady Marriott who ordered 40 models a season, Mrs Thomas Biddle, who had each dress repeated in four colours, Mrs David Bruce and 'all those beautiful English-women, victims of the currency restrictions in England' as the *première vendeuse* Suzanne Beguin put it – Lady Beatty, the Countess of Kenmare, Lady Peek ... and from Paris Baronne Alain de Rothschild, Madame Pierre Michelin and the Brazilian-born Madame Martinez de Hoz, formerly Vionnet's favourite client.

Unknown to Sir Stafford Cripps, the press and Norman Hartnell, there was a private showing of Dior's collection to the Queen, Princess Margaret and the Duchess of Kent at the French embassy in the autumn. Princess Margaret in due course gave her seal of approval to the New Look by wearing it everywhere. The Queen and the Duchess of Kent were soon wearing the new length and line as it influenced their own designers, Hartnell and Molyneux.

Another new designer, Pierre Balmain, had opened immediately after the war. He was a contemporary of Christian Dior at Lelong – in fact, they shared a desk and had once discussed the possibility of opening a salon together. A friend of Gertrude Stein, he had won her affection by making for her and for Alice B. Toklas 'nice warm suits', and she wrote a charming small piece about him for *Vogue*. At his first collection, Gertrude Stein whispered to Miss Toklas, 'We are the only people here wearing Balmain's clothes, but we must not let anyone know for we are not great advertisements for the world of fashion.'

A feature of the war and post-war years were the enormous queues to get into anything that was on. It took the Blitz or the appalling freak winter of 1946–7 to keep them away. From 1945 to 1950, 20 million people a week were going to the cinema: as one manager said, 'You can open a can of sardines and there's a line waiting to get in.' Shakespeare enjoyed a tremendous war-time revival, embodying for the audiences patriotism, historical romance and a secure sense of tradition in one. The Old Vic was bombed and became hydra-headed, with its companies covering the entire country. London lost its position as cultural head of Britain as companies scattered, museums and galleries closed down and musicians went on tour. London's loss was England's gain, and the provincial towns were able to see the best actors and productions available. Noël Coward took his players on the road in 1942 with *Blithe Spirit*, *Present Laughter* and *This Happy Breed*

Left: Dior's New Look, 1947, drawn by Eric.

– described by *Vogue* as '*Cavalcade* through the wrong end of opera glasses'. His first film was made at Denham with co-director David Lean. *In Which We Serve* was the story of a destroyer and the men who served on her, with Coward for the Captain, Celia Johnson as his wife, and Bernard Miles, Joyce Carey, John Mills and Kay Walsh in leading roles. It was notable for its realistic treatment of the subject, even down to a single swear word, and for its absence of condescension in dealing with the lower decks.

Whether it was Noël Coward and John Mills showing a stiff upper lip or Betty Grable and Rita Hayworth showing a bit of leg, films were a marvellous escape from reality. As *Vogue* said, 'Today's woman has less time to imagine, and a good deal of her imagining is done for her in the cinema.' Hollywood was earning about 70 million dollars a year in this country when in 1947 the Chancellor of the Exchequer, at this moment Dr Hugh Dalton, slapped a customs duty of 75 per cent on the value of all imported films, the sum to be prepaid. The day after, the Motion Picture Association

1. Noël Coward's first film, *In Which We Serve,* made at Denham in 1941-42.
2. Gertrude Stein with Alice B. Toklas, *left,* 1945.

Cecil Beaton   169

John Swope

of America announced that all shipments of films were to be suspended immediately. Dr Dalton had blundered. True, he had presented the British film industry with the home market, but without the possibility of export to America; and much too soon – it was not yet ready to fill the gap. The improved standard of British wartime films – noted by *Vogue* in an optimistic feature called 'The coming heyday of British films' – was abandoned in the pressure to pour out cheap films to fill the cinemas. These were soon competing against the best American films that had been waiting for the embargo to be lifted, as it was a few months later by Harold Wilson as President of the Board of Trade. Rank lost over six million pounds in four years. By the spring of 1949, seventeen out of twenty-six British studios were idle, and on top of that there was the crushing entertainment tax. British films had ceased to be a paying production. Laurence Olivier said, 'It is wrong to say that British films don't pay – they pay very well, but they pay the wrong people.'

During the war the B.B.C.'s staff trebled in size, due to the boom in sound broadcasting, which eventually reached virtually every adult in the country. It was not just the news, preceded by the booming notes of Big Ben, that attracted listeners, it was the radio show I.T.M.A. with Tommy Handley, the Minister of Aggravation and Mysteries in the Office of Twerps, the Mayor of Foaming at the Mouth, Funf the German spy ... *Much Binding in the Marsh* ... *Bandwagon* ... and in 1941 a different kind of programme, the *Brains Trust*, with philosopher Cyril Joad and his shrill opening, 'It depends what you mean by ...', zoologist Julian Huxley, and retired naval officer A. B. Campbell, answering such questions as 'What is love?' and 'How do flies land on the ceiling?'

Elizabeth Bowen wrote about the function of the Third Programme for *Vogue*, stressing the need for drama writing on a high plane written specially for the air and commending Laurie Lee's *The Voyage of Magellan*, Louis MacNeice's *The Careerist* and Patric Dickinson's *The Wall of Troy*. 'To an extent, the programme is to create the listener: not less, the listener is to create the programme – by his response, mobility, curiosity, sensitiveness and willingness in approach to the not yet known. Third Programme is out to take long chances and risk wide shots.' She noticed with approval a new Europeanism of outlook, pointing out, 'We have an immense amount to catch up with. We need exactly the stimulus outside thought can supply.'

The museums reopened in 1945, and there were new foreign art books for sale in the book shops again. At the British Museum one of the first collections on show was the Sutton Hoo treasure, with an interesting tale behind it. Sutton Hoo's owner, Mrs Pretty, began in 1939 to have a persistent dream telling her, 'You must open the barrow by the river'. When, eventually, archaeologists broke into the mound they unearthed a huge Anglo-Saxon vessel bearing the richest series of funeral treasure ever unearthed in England – Byzantine silver dishes, enamelled flagons and jewels.

During and after the Second World War, as after the First, there was a preoccupation with the nature of the role of women, the theme appearing and reappearing in *Vogue*, sometimes in captions, sometimes in features or odd remarks. Discussing the work of Frances Hodgkins, who died in 1947, Myfanwy Evans said, 'Many women who are creative artists of any kind manage to achieve their work in spite of the fact that they also live normal (if

Cecil Beaton

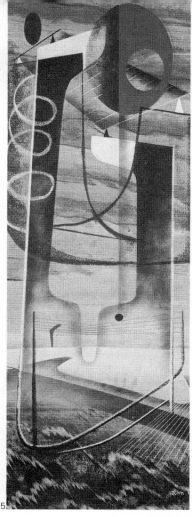

3. Frances Hodgkins painting, published in the year of her death, 1947, when she was 77.
4. Daphne du Maurier, 1946.
5. John Tunnard's illustration for Richard Busvine's feature on the future of television in 1945.

Felix Man   Coffin

nerve-wrecked) lives as women, with husband, home, children, clothes, servants and so on; it is the intensity with which they can withdraw from the world at the time that they are working that makes them into amateurs or professionals; the degree to which they can bear to be so much in the wrong as to be thoroughly selfish, at times, that makes them good or indifferent artists . . . a few take the most difficult way, and, remaining solitary, live or die by their work. Frances Hodgkins was one of these.' Anne Scott-James, reviewing *The Taming of the Shrew* at the rebuilt Old Vic, with Trevor Howard and Pat Burke, noticed, 'the Shrew was played like an honest child who grows into knowledge of guile and opportunism'. Again, Daphne du Maurier, writing in 1946 on doing nothing in the country: 'By this time I have had my bath, and am dressing, and am composing a letter to *The Times*, never published, on the subject of birth-control. The birthrate is falling, and I know why, and so do all the other women of my generation. It has nothing to do with insecurity or atom-bombs or the movies. It is because we don't *want* a lot of children, and had the women of past generations known how to limit their families they would have done so . . . Why are the churches empty? Because, with modern warfare, hellfire holds no terror for us. And was it only fear of the hereafter that made my lady in her crinoline go to church three times on a Sunday? No, it was boredom.' The feeling in the air was pinned, defined and concisely set out by Simone de Beauvoir in 'Femininity, the Trap', which appeared in *Vogue* in July 1947: the leading disciple of Jean-Paul Sartre's Existentialist philosophy, she had already published three novels and a play.

In 1947 Edith Piaf sang at the music halls and Existentialism was the new word in Paris. *Vogue* followed Sartre from the bar of the Pont Royal Hotel – 'no Bohemian café. It is like a shining Ritz bar on the left bank, and here Sartre drinks dry Martinis' – to a lecture at the Sorbonne. 'Sartre, short, broad, about thirty-eight, with thick glasses, sat at a small table and talked about the theatre. He spoke with extraordinary clearness and force, without confusion or metaphysics, or trailing ends of Existentialism, or roundhouse sentences . . . Speaking without notes and for one hour, he told these boys his theories about the theatre. His thesis is simply that the drama now must be one of situation and not of character. That life is a series of choices and the way one chooses determines one's character, not the other way around.'

Mid-way through the forties, Richard Busvine had written in *Vogue*, 'Television, as a medium of entertainment, will eventually kill sound broadcasting stone dead, just as the talkies killed silent films. This development is recognised by the experts as the natural and inevitable outcome of television progress, and they therefore await with considerable impatience official resumption of the Television Service.' It was resumed in 1946, but not looked forward to by everyone with the same enthusiasm as Richard Busvine's experts. There were growing fears that the future industrial development of England, of which television and fashion were a part, would detract from the quality of life. Would the Britain of the future be the same Britain that had been fought for? Siegfried Sassoon voiced these fears. 'Up to about 30 years ago it was still quite reasonable to say that God made the country and man made the town . . . But the process of disfigurement has been insidious, because people accept it without realising the cumulative effect. These remarks are addressed (though only theoretically, I fear) to those who live in towns, but more especially to persons responsible for urban expansion, commercial exploitation of natural resources, and other energetic operations which can make a nice neighbourhood profitable and unpleasant . . . While I write these words, the hedges of England are white with hawthorn; meadows are bright with buttercups and the golden foot of May is on the flowers. Bees rejoice in the blossoming chestnut trees; the cuckoo shouts all day at nothing . . . One might almost believe that all's well with the world. But the urban and the rural district councillors think otherwise. For them a stretch of prime pasture land is an eligible building site; a leafy lane is a valuable road-frontage; and yonder copsy hillside has already been earmarked as the location for the latest thing in sewage farms. Next comes the county council road surveyor, companioned by an official from the Ministry of Transport who doesn't know an oak from an elm. Doomed are the delightful windings of the road Plumstead Episcopi to Crabtree Canonicorum.'

DEBORAH KERR

At the beginning of her career after appearances in
films like *Major Barbara* and *Love on the Dole*, she followed up with a
triumphant stage appearance as Ellie Dunn in *Heartbreak House*. In
1943, when Cecil Beaton took this photograph, she was about to begin
work as Mary of Scotland for Gabriel Pascal. Her tranquil classic
beauty is at its best in this Molyneux black satin dress lined
with primrose crepe.

MOLYNEUX

1

1. Vivien Leigh in Molyneux star print dress
and black tweed jacket, 1941.
2. 1937, in Stiebel's magenta taffeta dress,
bordered with turquoise.
3. 1936.
4. 1941.

3

2

Rawlings

4

VIVIEN LEIGH

Vogue photographed Vivien Leigh as early as 1935, but her real fame came when she played
Scarlett O'Hara in Selznick's 3¾ hour *Gone with the Wind*, which opened in Atlanta in
December 1939, but appeared in Britain much later, delayed by wartime restrictions. Her
marriage to Laurence Olivier put the seal on her success: her name was written in lights over
three Broadway cinemas while she was playing Juliet to his Romeo on the New York stage,
and later they appeared together in *Hamlet* at the very scene of the tragedy, Kronberg Castle,
Elsinore. With her green eyes, her dark red hair, her beautiful pointed face, she looked

LORETTA YOUNG
Star in 1942 of
Bedtime Story and *The Men in Her Life*,
in a hat of spun glass and lace.

Horst

CONSTANCE BENNETT

A star of the thirties,
Constance Bennett became
the Hollywood evocation
of the forties with her
pompadour hairdo and her
beautiful surprised-looking
face. In 1926 she had married
the wealthy Philip Plant.
Four years afterwards, with a
divorce and a million-dollar
marriage settlement, she
went back to Hollywood and
stardom. As she eclipsed
Gloria Swanson at the box
office, she married Miss
Swanson's former husband
the Marquis de la Falaise.
She always showed a good
head for business, and her
sister Joan Bennett was to
say of her, 'If she can't take
it with her, she won't go.'

1. 1941, Californian elegance from
Irene: chalk-white crepe scarf and skirt,
draped bodice the colour
of tanned skin.
2. The exact wartime face —
Constance Bennett's in 1940.

IRENE   Toni Frissell

LADY LOUIS MOUNTBATTEN
Lady Louis Mountbatten was known for the height of
her heels, the brilliance of her smile and the blue of
her eyes. She dressed beautifully, whether it was in
a leather flying coat or in the faconné satins and
patterned lamés that Worth made for her
to take to Malta.

1. Painted by Salvador Dali, 1940: 'Last year
she divided her time between her Brook
Street penthouse and foreign travel. This
year between Navy Comforts Committee
work and country weekends.'
2. 1933.
3. 1943.

Horst

Clarence Bull

KATHERINE HEPBURN

Although Katherine Hepburn did much to spread the fashion for
neo-Victorian dress with Jo in *Little Women*, in private life she
has always liked trousers and no make up. She turned out to be
a superb comédienne in *Bringing up Baby*, 1938, six years after
her screen debut with John Barrymore. She was the first star
to have red curls and freckles.

Katherine Hepburn in the New York production of *The Lake*, 1934.
Opposite: Star of *The Philadelphia Story* opposite Cary Grant, 1940.

Steichen

1
MARCELLE

ADRIAN

Toni Frissell

INGRID BERGMAN

In 1941, 'the girl Hemingway would like for the star in the film version of *For Whom The Bell Tolls*'. Here in Adrian's white mousseline de soie dress with looped hems.

2 MOLYNEUX

ANN TODD

1. The forties face, in Marcelle's velvet pillbox, a cloud of spotted veiling tying under her chin: in 1944 she makes *Perfect Strangers*, a Korda production.

Lee Miller

Left: Molyneux's black mackintosh, lined in red tweed to match the dress and jacket, October 1940; photograph Cecil Beaton.

'Last year women were running households. This year they are running canteens, voluntary organizations, service units – and taking orders as well as giving them. Last year time was no object: this week, next week, sometime . . . to dine, to dance, to meet, to marry '

'This year time is of the essence of the contract. Leave is reckoned in days, hours, minutes. Dates are timed to the split second and girls no longer keep boys waiting. "Are you free next Wednesday – 4.30–8? I've special leave." "Can you lunch today?" "Can you marry me tomorrow?" '

After the occupation of Paris at the end of May, attention is turned perforce to London design, ready-to-wear and the couture who bank on the export trade. Schiaparelli's wardrobe that she takes to America is the last Paris fashion in *Vogue* for four years. Suits range from the frankly military to the rather military, and in reaction there's a brief return to evening dress. For daytime relief there are duster hats with a scarf curtain falling over the hair, and built-up shoes, solid by day but as fanciful as you can find for evening. Purchase tax and shortage of fabric oblige women to buy less and more wisely. *Vogue* helps with diagrams showing how you can alter last year's looks and bring them up to date — although nothing has really changed.

Military Alliance between the air-force blue tweed and martial cut of this suit from Debenham and Freebody; 14½ guineas

ON TOP
at the Paris
Mid-seasons

Dusters

They're sweeping Paris—
these handkerchief hats;
twisted into tight little pillboxes,
curtaining your curls.
Albouy, new milliner,
invented them

1

André Durst

2

SCHIAPARELLI

André Durst

3

BALENCIAGA

1. Fanciful duster hats by Albouy.
2. Schiaparelli's black and shocking
pink — tight-waisted black suit with
embroidered arrows, rosy pillbox.
3. Black wool jersey
dress with violet yokes, silver fox
shako and muff.
4. Mrs Max Aitken and a heap of
aluminium for the aeroplane drive of
her father-in-law Lord Beaverbrook,
the Minister of Aircraft Production.
This stunt turned into a fiasco when
treasured saucepans were left unused
because of their low aluminium
content. Jaeger marron tweed coat.
5. *Vogue* cover of April 1940,
showing the hard make up and Joan
Crawford lips of the day.

JAEGER

A deceptive jacket front gives a suit look for the coupon value of a
dress, 11 coupons, 8½gns. at Bourne & Hollingsworth.

'Your wardrobe, instead of being a three-volume novel,
will now be a short story in which every line will count'
'Il faut skimp, pour être chic'

Fashion now reaches its lowest ebb. Clothes rationing
comes into force in June. *Vogue* tries to make the best of
things but bewails the system. Utility clothes, two-thirds
of all the clothes you can buy, fulfil government
requirements and restrictions, and sell at fixed prices. The
ban on silk stockings is another blow. In January *Vogue* is
recommending the substitutes, but by August these too
are in short supply. Cosmetics disappear from the
counters, and Black Market make-up often contains a high
proportion of lead, or at least brings you out in a guilty
rash. 'Save your cosmetics for evenings out,' says *Vogue*
in November, but most women have already been make-
up-less for months.

The export drive is an essential source of income. Nine
London-based couturiers combine in a collection for South
America, sent out under government auspices. *Vogue's*
copy accompanying the pictures has a wistful note:
'Though many of the models are necessarily remote from
wartime life in England, yet still they hold much fashion
interest for us.' In another export effort backed by
government subsidy, the Cotton Board commissions
artists, including Paul Nash, Graham Sutherland and Frank
Dobson, to design new prints in co-operation with *Vogue*,
couturiers and textile experts.

Vogue publishes a feature on looking your best in
uniform with short hair, short nails and good posture, and
praises the fashionable qualities of the British Warm — 'its
pale beige colour is extremely becoming and its seven-
eighths length has great chic. It looks wonderful (and even
warmer) if lined with scarlet; but such splendour is
reserved for those of field rank . . . its capacious pockets
swallow up make-up and manicure kit without bulging.'

1
DERÉTA

WORTH   PETER RUSSELL   WORTH

2

3

Cecil Beaton

1. Déreta advertisement, camel winter coat, fifteen coupons only.
2. Forbidden luxury — a spread from *Vogue's* special South American number supporting the co-operative London collection for export.
3. Mrs Christopher Sykes pulling off her overboots in the Ritz: bicycling to Government work she wears a mustard wool suit with wrapped and buttoned skirt made by her Polish dressmaker, Mme Przeworska.
4. The standby in the silk and flax shortage is rayon crepe, here in a Molyneux dress with a yoke of fuchsia sequins and a cyclamen sash.
5. Loretta Young in a net turban from Pissot and Pavy, knotted over a handful of tulips.

4

Cecil Beaton

5 PISSOT & PAVY

1941

RAHVIS, STRASSNER

Horst

1. Rahvis's and Strassner's draped evening dresses with embroidered bands.
2. Tough coloured stockings, a necessary substitute for short-lived sheer ones: lilac, rose and apple green.
3. Uniform hair made the best of — three inches as worn in the services and in factories. For A.R.P. workers *Vogue* recommends tying long hair into a net turban which will be hidden under the tin hat, and for the face 'no make-up but a non-greasy all purpose cream dusted with powder'.
4 and 5. New cotton prints: *above*, John Armstrong's 'Fighting Dream'; *below*, Paul Nash's 'Romney Marsh'.

'Fashion is undergoing a compulsory course of slimming and simplification . . . the progress of the war has made it necessary to prohibit all superfluous material and superfluous labour '

'We are not saying that these clothes compete with the superb standard of pre-war days – but then neither does this life compare with that '

The Government gives Utility designs a much-needed boost by asking London couturiers to combine in a Utility collection for mass production. Molyneux, Hardy Amies, Digby Morton, Bianca Mosca, Peter Russell and Worth comply with Utility specifications to make topcoats, suits, afternoon dresses and cotton overalls that go anonymously into the shops in the spring of 1943. The stocking situation has become so bad that *Vogue* photographs a model in ankle socks.

Lack of every luxury forces emphasis on health, efficiency and practicality. 'Clothes look as if they had been taken care of, put on beautifully, and then forgotten for more important things. The woman well-dressed in the meaning of today would not easily be rendered helpless or ridiculous . . . that ''too good to be true'' look which only a personal maid can produce is absent – because the maid is absent, on munitions.' *Vogue* publishes a picture-strip showing you how to set your own hair, and trusts that the supply of cosmetics, already curtailed to 25 per cent of peacetime output, will not be further reduced. When the worse comes to the worst, 'there are four fundamental cosmetics you'll need, cosmetics which don't come out of jars and bottles . . . they are unrestricted, available to everybody: sleep, diet, exercise, rest for 20 minutes a day after lunch.'

The ideal wartime look: health and vigour, sleeves rolled back, socks pulled up.

Toni Frissell

1. Couturier-designed but anonymous Utility dresses commissioned by the Government: red and blue crepe.
2. Margaret Vyner shows how you can go hatless and stockingless in town, in a pale linen jumper suit from Fortnum & Mason and Pinet shoes.
3. The stocking situation has come to this: 'If we don't go without stockings this summer we shall go without stockings next winter.' The entire outfit from Fortnum & Mason, July 1942.

We can't have it both ways...

Even if we were not called to help, we could not leave men to fight this war alone. We asked for equal rights and we cannot have it both ways. It is only fair that we should face the music side by side with our men. Total war makes heavy demands on us. We must submit to routine and still keep the sparkle of unfettered days. We must take risks and show no sign of fear. We must work hard and let no weariness appear. We must remember that the slightest hint of a drooping spirit yields a point to the enemy. Never must careless grooming reflect a 'don't care' mood. Now that leisure and beauty-aids are limited, we can take pride in looking our best. Face value is more than ever high. Never should we forget that good looks and good morale are the closest of good companions.

PUT YOUR BEST FACE FORWARD.. *Yardley*

Lee Miller

It's a dream... it's HARELLA

Lee Miller

4. London couture suits in Utility tweeds, October 1942.
5. Entertaining the troops.
6. *Vogue* cover, May 1943: waistcoat, slacks and boxy jacket.

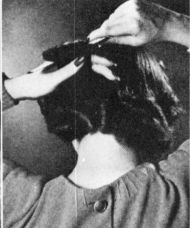

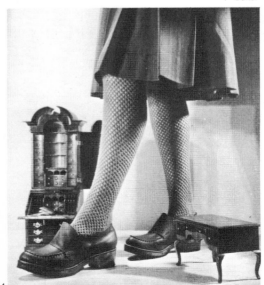

1. For limited incomes —
left, twinset 26*s*. 9*d*., skirt
25*s*. 6*d*. *right*, twinset
26*s*. 5*d*. skirt 21*s*. 1*d*.
2. How to set your own hair:
pompadour and curls, set with
Kirbigrips.
3. 'Accessories, like other
amenities, are getting scarcer,
and are too costly to be lightly
and lavishly bought.' Pancake
and huge gloves in looped
emerald green crochet.
4. Brevitt's wood-soled calf
sabots 'to eke out the nation's
shoe leather'. And to eke out
the nation's stockings, heavy
knits from a 6*d*. *Vogue*
pattern.
5. A time for doing things by
halves: 'As wardrobes wear
out and coupons contract, a
new fashion formula is
needed . . . think in half
terms for a change — a skirt
and a shirt instead of a whole
dress'. Black shirt and
plaid skirt from Harrods.

Baker

Lee Miller   HARRODS   Horst

1944

Paris Liberation fashions
'The first free demonstration of
the couture since 1940' *Lucien
Lelong*

'. . . a flagrant violation of our
imposed wartime silhouette'
*The American War Production
Board*

The Liberation of Paris in August
allows *Vogue* readers to see the first
Paris collection photographs since
1940. The autumn collections are
given a mixed reception here and in
America. The official reaction of
both countries is an angry protest
against such wastage of fabric and
labour. In spite of the recently
imposed L 85 restrictions in
America, the manufacturers are
quick to adopt the Liberation
fashions, and a ban is imposed on
copying from the photographs in
fashion magazines. In Britain, there
is no question of being able to copy
the full skirts and dressmaker
details.

Left: Molyneux's spare grey flannel suit with
rounded revers and pockets; photograph Norman
Parkinson.

189

1 MARGARET BARRY   JAYS

Norman Parkinson

2
AAGE THAARUP

SCHIAPARELLI

3

Lee Miller

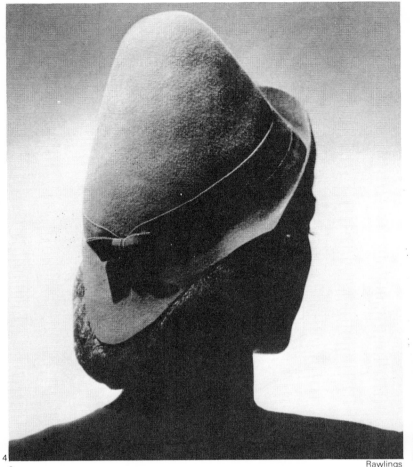

4

Rawlings

5

Joffé

6

Norman Parkinson

7

1. Norman Parkinson's photographs are a breath
of fresh air. Here, his 'change of weather' pictures,
showing the outside and inside of the 1944 wardrobe
(*left,* Margaret Barry, *right,* Jays).
2. Margot Fonteyn in the black felt Chinese hat designed
for her by Aage Thaarup.
3. Hourglass black wool coat lined in fur,
with a fur-trimmed turban.
4. Hat backward . . . hair down.
5. Hat forward . . . hair up.
6. Bicycling outfit: striped lisle shirt and divided
skirt in Moygashel spun rayon.
7. Rima advertisement.

1945-46

A 1945 silhouette: chinstrap hat, tight waist, stiff lampshade peplum, narrow longer skirt.

Joffé

'Neither in politics, nor in social life, nor in dress, nor in millinery are the lines yet laid down. We do not know yet *what* will get itself established '
James Laver, November 1946
The end of the war—and clothes rationing tightens. *Vogue*'s tone of voice, wearily patient in August 1945, 'when you read of beautiful fabrics and models being made "for export only", you would hardly be human if you did not feel a pang that they should be going out of your reach—and probably to women with fuller wardrobes than your own. But if your second thought can be "There go the means of bringing in food and raw material and the thousand things that England needs to live"—perhaps you won't feel so badly about it', acquires a sharper note by November—'these genius-thwarting austerity restrictions'. Life is to be drab for some time.

Vogue shows demobilization clothes for Servicewomen, 'You have a chance that seldom comes more than once in a lifetime—the chance of buying a completely new wardrobe', and in July 1945 publishes the first radioed

pictures and text from Moscow's Soviet State Fashion Show, in which judges pick 300 models for mass production from 1,100 shown.

In London, on 24 September 1946, the Council of Industrial Design opens the 'Britain Can Make It' exhibition at the Victoria and Albert Museum to prove that Britain can still produce the goods and to help raise the standard of design in everything from jugs and radios to dresses. The Fashion Hall is divided into three sections for inexpensive, medium-priced and couture clothes.

From Paris the news is hems lower, heels higher, waists nipped in with wired and boned corsets. Otherwise there is an air of indecision. In January *Vogue* reports 'Exaggeration of style has disappeared in Paris—austere elegance takes its place', in October 'Paris revels in femininity'. In fact, as James Laver says a month later, 'Fashion has reached one of those turning points in history when everything may happen . . . We do not know yet *what* will get itself established.'

There is a pregnant silence.

WOLSEY   Coffin

Penn

1. Yellow jersey dress with snakeskin belt.
2. 1946 straws in the wind — feathered cartwheel, deep neckline, draped longer skirt.
3. A new simplicity — white piqué dance dress from Ships, 1946.
4,5 and 6. 'Base your demobilization wardrobe on clothes like these.'

SHIPS   Blumenfeld

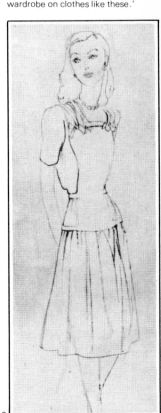

1

Eric

BALENCIAGA

2

3

Eric

194

1 and 3. Eric draws evening silhouettes in 1946, showing the indecision of line and proportion.
2. Madame Rubio, the new Paris beauty, in a red faille dress with an embroidered bodice, 1946.
4. Hartnell's swathed purple sheath, 1946.
5. Indecision in length: the American handkerchief hem and swathed waist of 1946.
6. Dinner hat, 1945.
7. The 'Britain Can Make It' exhibition, September 1946: tucked and fitted grey dinner dress by Hardy Amies; beauty iron to stimulate circulation and spread face-cream evenly, by Countess Csaky.

5

Joffé

BRITAIN CAN MAKE IT

TURN ON FOR MORE

6

7

HARDY AMIES

1. Corsets for the new nipped-in waists: 'veins of tiny wires and delicate bones make a wholly new way to let a woman look like a woman'. Here, blue grosgrain waspie used by Piguet and copied in England by Warners.
2. The first jeans in *Vogue*, July 1946 — royal blue and cropped to midcalf, from Simpsons.
3. Postwar beauty: pink-rouged cheeks, red lips, draped hair. Make up by Elizabeth Arden.
4. Forerunner of tights — pants and stockings in the same rib, 1946.
Right, Norman Parkinson's woman in white — 'wistful with the frustrations of youth, or the longing for a charm and an elegance abandoned without question during the wartime years, now hard to recover in a Utility world'? That was the longing that Dior's New Look answered.

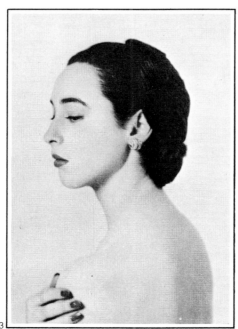

Coffin

1947

'The season's sensation is the new house of Christian Dior'

'The New Look wins – by a length!' *Commentator at Kempton Park's Easter meeting*

'Dior has saved the name of Paris' *Journalist at Dior's first collection*

'Bravo! Ravissant! Magnifique!' *Cries from the press at the collection*

'The longer skirt . . . the ridiculous whim of idle people . . . people who worry about longer skirts might do something more useful with their time' *Mrs Bessie Braddock*

'This New Look business is just completely silly' *Mrs Mabel Ridealgh, M.P.*

'There should be a law!' *Sir Stafford Cripps, President of the Board of Trade*

February 12, and to the women present at the first collection of Christian Dior, the war and its drab aftermath seems to be over at last. Dior, formerly a designer at Lucien Lelong, opens in pristine premises at 30 Avenue Montaigne, and with his New Look reinstates Paris as the authoritative leader of world fashion. At the end of the show, Englishwomen can be seen tugging their skimpy skirts down over their knees, feeling suddenly uncomfortable in their square-shouldered 'man-tailored' wartime suits.

Sir Stafford Cripps, President of the Board of Trade, sums up outraged official reaction. When the press seem reluctant to co-operate, Sir Stafford thumps the table and snorts, 'There should be a law.'

Meanwhile, in the autumn, unknown to the press, the public and Norman Hartnell, there is a special private showing of the Dior collection to the Queen, Princess Margaret and the Duchess of Kent at the French Embassy. Princess Margaret in due course gives the New Look her seal of approval by wearing it everywhere, and the Queen and the Duchess of Kent are soon wearing the new length and look as it influences their own designers, Hartnell and Molyneux. Coupons or no, the New Look has been adopted throughout the English ready-to-wear by December, and will continue as the dominant fashion look for the next ten years.

Dior's tight tussore jacket, 'padded to a teacup curve' over a long pleated black skirt.

DIOR Bérard

1. Dior's New Look sketched at Maxim's by Nobilé, April 1947.
2-6. Details from Dior's collection.
2. Shirtwaist collar and pleats.
3. Belted suit, box pleat skirt.
4. Safari hat, pleated dress.
5. Fan pleats.
6. Curved jacket, barrel skirt.

1947

1
VICTOR STIEBEL

2
HARDY AMIES

3
RAHVIS

Coffin

4 LEGROUX   Coffin

1. Moira Shearer, latest addition to Covent Garden's
premières danseuses, in Victor Stiebel's ballet-length
black taffeta with an orchid pink organdie overskirt.
2. New Look influence in April: Hardy Amies's
crossover striped cotton dress with a ballet-
length skirt.
3. Rahvis's pink faille dress with a décolletage of
sequined black lace, photographed in the bomb-
shattered ruin of a beautiful house in
Grosvenor Square.
4. White straw and black felt hat.
5. The look and style of Penelope Dudley Ward is
'A figure with that thoroughbred look . . .
cameo profile . . . smooth and intelligent forehead . . .
gentian-blue eyes'.
6. October 1947: Dior drops the hem still lower. Fan-
pleated satin dress spinning out into a full skirt.
Velvet side-beret by Sygur. Photographed by Horst
at the Paris Exhibition of Housing and Urbanism.

6 DIOR   Horst

5

The new A................................in 1954

The Fashion-conscious Fifties

Contemporary design in hats and chairs, summer 1950   Don Honeyman

Fashion was never the same after the fifties. Fundamental changes occurred thick and fast to revolutionize the industry and take it into new territories, involving bigger business than ever before. For the first time, looks and lines assumed a universal importance, making headline news in the papers all through the decade. Fashion became a new language capable of subtle interpretation, when boys and girls between 17 and 23 began to use clothes for group identification, provoking questions about fashion's role as signal, armour and decoration. For the first time in living memory, it was fashionable for men to be fashionable, a new preoccupation that cut right across society from the men about Mayfair to the Teddy Boys of the slum areas. New systems of mass production and the comparative prosperity of the late fifties made the average Englishwoman into one of the best-dressed women in the world, and the introduction of nylon made it possible for working girls in the cities to wear white and pale colours every day. Teenagers opened up a whole new category in the fashion market, and the teenage art-school designers who turned their attention to non-establishment fashion produced totally original looks, the first fashion to begin at source instead of being superimposed from abroad or adapted. These were the formative fashion years of the century – the fashion-conscious fifties.

The first ambition of the post-war years was to get back to normal. Britain was an almost bankrupt country faced with national shortages and a difficult balance of payments: austerity and rationing dragged on until 1954 in one form or another. The first sign of life had been women's appetite for the New Look, but on second sight its appeal was seen to be nostalgic, a reaction against the sexless clothes of wartime and the drudgery of home and work without a man around. Now in 1951 there was a gesture of hope and confidence in the future. The Festival of Britain was the last fling of the Labour government, a nationwide celebration of the country's contribution to civilization and a demonstration of its potential in many fields. In London the main exhibition was to be built on the blitzed South Bank site between Waterloo and Westminster bridges. The Festival Hall was the first building to be completed, a permanent fixture, and near it the Queen placed the stone for the future National Theatre. The bleak surrounding area began, under the organization of Gerald Barry and the designs of a team headed by Hugh Casson, to sprout pavilions and restaurants, constructions of cement and glass, striped awnings, flags and bunting, a Dome of Discovery with the largest unsupported roof in the world, and a towering Skylon which seems now to have been a premonition of the millions of television aerials which were to cover the country and shut down hundreds of cinemas in the course of the decade. The exhibition was bright and inviting by day, but at night it came into its own, turning into what Michael Frayn called 'a floodlit dream-world breathing music'. In *Vogue*'s eight-page Festival feature, leading off the Britannica issue, Marghanita Laski wrote, 'If all goes well ... what a country we shall live in, what a Britain we shall have! Through all our lifetimes, the man-made objects surrounding us have been devised, not to give visual pleasure, but unconsciously to assert that we are a people wealthy, provident, puritan, insular, keeping our feet firmly on the ground and not liking to make ourselves conspicuous. Suddenly on the South Bank, we discover that, no longer wealthy, we can be imaginative and experimental and ingenious, colourful, gaudy and gay.' Proving her point, *Vogue* declared, 'The most fastidious and fashion-conscious woman can dress immediately for any occasion in ready-to-wear clothes' and proved it with fashion from Jaeger, Susan Small, Dereta, and Marcus, Brenner, Rima and Mary Black.

In spite of this, *Vogue* gave the greatest emphasis all through the fifties to Paris, and for good reason. As the ready-to-wear market in America and Britain grew to giant proportions it depended more and more on Paris to act as authoritative pace-setter and to present new ideas that the public would recognize and look for in the shops. The fifties were a time of tyrannical dictatorship from Paris. Lines followed one another in quick succession: the envol line, the princess line, the tulip line, the I or H line, the A line, the trapeze line. It was a time when you couldn't be both fashionable and comfortable, unless you dressed at Chanel. You carried the weight of an enormous pyramid coat and you hobbled in pencil-slim skirts, always emphasized by photographing the model with one knee hidden behind the other. Collars turned up and bit into the chin, boned and strapless 'self-supporting' bodices made it difficult to bend, corsets pinched the waist and flattened the bust. 'Where has the waist gone?' asked *Vogue* in 1951, and answered, 'Anywhere but where you expect it.'

If you dressed in clothes from Paris or Paris copies, you wore stylized fashion with great but contrived glamour, geometric shapes, and exaggerated lines. Women obeyed Paris because of Christian Dior – no woman would forget during the fifties that a single collection had outdated everything in her wardrobe and made her self-conscious in a Utility suit. The consequence was that the fashion public were insecure, particularly about the length of their hems, and thought that every seasonal collection might bring a radical overnight change that would leave them with nothing to wear. The length of hems was headline news. Women M.P.s raged over 'short' skirts, and television news programmes quizzed women in the streets about what they thought of the new lengths.

The build up of public expectation exerted tremendous pressures on the Paris couturiers themselves. Although in fact no look could ever have the same effect as the New Look again – for first there would have to be no change for at least nine years – nevertheless the couturier trod a knife edge. Should the leading designers conflict too much in their lines, there was consternation and confusion among the buyers. Should they not change enough from the line of last season, buyers complained they were not being given a decisive lead. When Dior died of a heart attack in 1957, this public expectation was still intact. His '*Dauphin*', Yves Saint Laurent, was already signed up to a long and binding contract, and at the age of 21 found himself perched upon the multi-million franc edifice of the most influential fashion house in the world. He kept his balance with his first collection, when he launched the trapeze line – not too different from Dior's A line, but just different enough. In the salon people were trampled in the rush to embrace and congratulate him, and he had to appear like a king on the balcony

Anthony Denney

204

Henry Clarke

to wave to the cheering crowds below. 'Saint Laurent has saved France!' said the French headlines. 'The great Dior tradition will continue!' In the teeth of an unspoken agreement among the couture not to alter a hem length by more than two inches a season, Saint Laurent dropped the hem by three for his next collection. Twelve months later he bared the knees, and caused an uproar. A woman M.P. announced, 'I think it is ridiculous for a youth of 23 to try to dictate to sensible women. British women will not take any notice of this nonsense!' Radio programmes ran discussions on the likelihood of bare knees in Britain, and one newspaper headline said, 'Dior's man can do what he likes. We won't show our knees!' *Vogue* presented his collection in the kindest light, ignoring the shortest skirts and showing his new hobble hem first in its 'least exaggerated . . . utterly unalarming' form before leading up to the 'extreme trendsetter', and concluded, gallantly, 'When a new line is greeted with cries of indignation, it's a healthy sign . . . it means that the fashion world is alive and kicking.'

It was at this difficult moment in his career that the army draft, three times deferred, wrenched Saint Laurent from Dior. After two months he suffered a nervous and physical collapse, recuperated, and returned to Dior to find his assistant, the 35-year-old Marc Bohan, instated as chief designer. Saint Laurent sued and won £48,000 damages, which he used to open his own salon in 1962 with unqualified success and some of the staff from Dior.

If Dior had personified the old Paris, Chanel stood for the new. Dior's death left Chanel, who reopened in 1954, the despot of the couture. Her success was due to her overwhelming appeal directly to the wearers of her clothes. Her unalterable convictions about clothes and what they should do for women produced a phenomenon unique in the fifties – an unmistakable Paris look complete from head to toe that was flattering, easy to wear, and did not date. The envol, the princess, the tulip and all the other lines had the date stamped indelibly across them. After a year, they were finished. Chanel's was a classic line, refined again and again but never fundamentally changed. The fashionable woman's motto for the end of the decade could have been 'When in doubt, wear a Chanel'. They were as comfortable as a cardigan, you could run in them, they had real pockets where you could keep your cigarettes, and they gave a feeling of tremendous self-confidence.

In *Vogue*, the news of Chanel's return was the news of the year. In an exclusive interview before her first come-back Chanel gave Dior and the other couturiers a caustic going-over. 'A dress must function or on n'y tient pas. Elegance in clothes means being able to move freely . . . Look at today's dresses: strapless evening dresses cutting across a woman's front – nothing is uglier for a woman; boned horrors, that's what they are . . . these heavy dresses that won't pack into aeroplane luggage, ridiculous. All these boned and corseted bodices – out with them. What's the good of going back to the rigidity of the corset? No servants – no good having dresses that must be ironed by a maid each time you put them on,' and concluded the interview by saying, 'I am no longer interested in dressing a few hundred women, private clients; I shall dress thousands.' Opinion about her first collection was widely divided: she conceded nothing to the accepted stylization. *Vogue*'s cautious comment was 'At its best it has the easy livable look which is her great contribution to fashion history; at its worst it repeats the lines she made famous in the 'thirties: repeats rather than translates into contemporary terms.' By 1959 the contemporary terms had come into line with Chanel's convictions, and *Vogue*'s tone had changed completely. 'The heady idea that a woman should be more important than her clothes, which has been for almost 40 years Chanel's philosophy, has now permeated the fashion world.'

Perhaps the most unusual thing about Chanel was that she never

Norman Parkinson

1. Christian Dior, photographed by Anthony Denney at La Colle, Dior's isolated country house near Grasse, in 1957, within a year of his death.
2. Chanel told *Vogue*, 'Certain women wear a suit; certain suits wear women. In the first case the woman is bad; in the second, the suit is not good.' Here, Chanel's perfect combination: Comtesse Guy d'Arcangues, a private client, in her plaid tweed and checked silk suit.
3. The new Mayfair Edwardians, photographed in Savile Row in 1950.

minded being copied. Unlike other couturiers, who banned publication of photographs of their collections until the buyers had time to produce authentic copies from toiles, Chanel allowed pictures to be shown immediately and was happy for the streets to be full of Chanel copies even if they did not put a penny in her pocket. In this she was not unlike Mary Quant, who said, 'The whole point of fashion is to make fashionable clothes available to everyone', but she also showed a supreme confidence that quality would prevail – that the real Chanel suit would be instantly discernible from all fakes.

If Englishwomen of the fifties had never been better dressed, the men had never been so fashion-conscious either. In the prime P. G. Wodehouse years, a well-dressed man's appearance had to be remarkably inconspicuous – like Lord Emsworth, indistinguishable from his gardener – an inclination encouraged by rationing during the war when men had given up their clothing coupons to their wives and become shabbier than ever. After the war, attitudes began to change. The nostalgia which had provoked the New Look and made its success inevitable affected men's fashion too. Men-about-Mayfair began to dress in a way that owed something to Edwardian fashion, and by 1950 the look had evolved completely: curly bowlers and single-breasted coats with velvet collars and ticket pockets, trousers narrowed almost to drainpipes, and a rolled-up umbrella. The shirts they wore were striped, with the stripes running horizontally, and with stiff white collars. Suits had four-button jackets left undone over waistcoats with small lapels, some in rich velvet patterns. Recording the fashion, *Vogue* drew

1. 'She's 18, and she chooses trousers because somehow one always seems to end up sitting on the floor in her room . . .', Anthony Denney's teenager photograph. Yellow velvet pants, tapered and zipped with a cummerbund waist, flat pumps and a black jersey, blouse buttoned with jet.
2. 'The teenage thing', 1959. A 17-year-old apprentice hairdresser from Birmingham told *Vogue*, 'You can express yourself like, in clothes; you know, a nice dark red shirt with black verticals and a dark blue suit, a Perry Como and Italians; you're in there, sharp, playing it cool.'

1

Anthony Denney

2

attention to the fact that bowlers had become almost a uniform again since the recent order of the general commanding the London district that they should be worn by ex-Guards officers and Guards officers in civilian clothes. The four men *Vogue* photographed, Peter Coats, William Aykroyd, Mark Gilbey and Michael Chantry-Inchbald, were surprised to find within a year or two that they and their friends had been the inspiration for the Teddy Boys of South London, who adapted the single-breasting and velvet collars, the ticket pockets and loose fit into their own aggressively stylish look. The Teds wore plain white shirts with the collar turned up, or a bootlace tie, a silver chain round neck and wrist, a tattooed forearm and fingers, a thick draped suit and crêpe-soled brothel-creepers. Their hair was worn long and immaculately set in quiffs and sideboards, but greasy: Teddy Boys would go to a barber for 'styling', but drew the line at having it washed or dried under the dryer. For the first time the young had a fashion identity of their own.

The word 'teenager' itself was an import from America – a country where girls of six went regularly to the hairdresser and wore make-up at nine. Before the war there had been only 'girls' and 'youths'. Their independence was based on their earning capacity. A popular song was 'You gotta have something in the bank, Frank', and by 1958 the average wage was £8 a week for a boy, £6 for a girl: together just a living wage. There were jobs, shorter working hours, and somewhere to go afterwards. For the teenager in the mid-fifties there were jazz clubs, where students in 'wild-beast' sweaters jived with a girl in one hand and a bottle in the other, dance halls with a skiffle group or a rock 'n' roll band playing Bill Haley's 'Rock around the clock', clubs where juke boxes were fed by leather boys in black jeans and jackboots and studded jackets, and all day there were coffee bars, a refuge behind a bamboo grill overgrown with ivy and philodendron. Soon the West End was covered with Espressos, Wimpys, Bar-B-Ques, Moo-Cow Milk Bars and Chicken Inns.

Among the teenagers, it was the men's clothes rather than the girls' that identified their group, whether it was the Italian jacket, the fluorescent socks and the winkle-pickers of the East Enders or the shaggy sweaters, beards and sandals of the 'weekend beats'. It was a reversal of *Vogue*'s world in which women wore the conspicuous fashions and men were the decorous background. The girls from any of the groups might wear a buttoned cardigan with a string of beads and a narrow skirt, or a Sloppy Jo and tight jeans, or a tight sweater and a full skirt over layers of crackling petticoats. Towards the end of the fifties an art student look came into fashion with donkey jackets, falling-down hair, slim striped skirts, and a basket over the arm.

These were the first fashions that began in the street and worked upward into *Vogue*, and by 1959 the magazine was asking questions about the new trends. 'What does fashion represent? Decoration? Armour? A mood of society? For millions of working teenagers now, clothes like these are the biggest pastime in life: a symbol of independence, and the fraternity-mark of an age-group . . . The origins of the teenage look are urban and working class . . . and it has been taken up with alacrity by the King's Road. Contrariwise, it is itself influenced by the romantic concept of Chelsea.' By now, this look was growing out of English soil. America might have invented teenagers, but London was dressing them. As *Vogue* said, the look 'owes nothing to Paris or Savile Row; something to entertainment idols (the Tommy Steele haircut . . . the Bardot sex babe look); much to Italy, and surprisingly little to America (apart from a suggestion of the mechanized cowboy about motor cycling clothes): which may well be a symptom of a growing indifference to the American image'.

America was doing so well by the mid-fifties with her own line

in casual clothes from California – separates and co-ordinates, shirtwaisters and dirndls billowing out over drip-dry petticoats of crackle nylon, blue jeans derived from Levi Strauss's work pants for gold prospectors – that the French couture sent out a committee to study production methods, and returned surprised and impressed. More teenagers in Britain bought the 'sweater girl' bra, with its conical stiffened cups spiralled with stitching, than the copies of Dior's 'ban the bosom' corsets in 1954. In pursuit of a Jane Russell bosom girls bought a California bra – one was called the 'Hollywood Maxwell' – or shortened their shoulder straps and chanted the dormitory rhyme, 'I must, I must, achieve a bigger bust. I will, I will, make it bigger still. Hoorah, hoorah, I need a bigger bra.'

If America's influence was on the wane, it was because of a new generation of young British designers trained by the art schools into a practical knowledge of mass production, new methods of manufacture, sizing and grading, and production within limited price ranges. The Royal College of Art opened its School of Fashion Design in 1948, and its first professor of fashion was Madge Garland, a former fashion editor of *Vogue*. A long overdue acknowledgement of the kind of training needed, the school and similar departments throughout the country were quick to turn out uninhibited designs for non-establishment fashion. In 1953, the year *Vogue* started the regular 'Young Idea' feature for girls between 17 and 25, it published some ideas for skirts by the R.C.A. students: royal blue velveteen studded with silver buttons, turquoise felt slashed and slotted with velvet ribbon and tied with shoestrings, stovepipe trousers inside a double apron of glitter-scattered taffeta.

A product of art school, but not fashion school, was to give the young fashion movement its greatest impetus. Mary Quant, who failed to get her art teacher's diploma, was to be the 'major fashion force in the world outside Paris'. In 1955 she began her fashion

3. Tommy Steele, 'Buttons' in *Cinderella*, 1958. A home-grown rock idol and former seaman from Bermondsey.

4. Madge Garland, formerly *Vogue*'s fashion editor, by 1949 the first Professor of Fashion and principal of the new School of Fashion Design at the Royal College of Art. Photographed by Cecil Beaton in Bianca Mosca's blue-black brocade suit and Vernier's straw hat.

Norman Parkinson

career in the workrooms of Erik, the milliner, and in November she opened Bazaar in the King's Road, a joint venture with her future husband, Alexander Plunket-Greene. She began by buying clothes in, but could not find the kind of fashion she wanted. Within a few months she was designing her own clothes, although totally ignorant of how to set about it: she began by buying fabrics across the counter at Harrods because she didn't know that they could be obtained wholesale. She found that Bazaar was becoming a meeting place, a kind of 'nonstop cocktail party', and that the clothes were bought off the rails almost as soon as they had been put there. Her bedsitter was full of sewing women working until late at night to put dresses in the shop the next morning. A year after the Quant revolution had begun, 19-year-old John Stephen came down from Glasgow and opened his first shop for teenagers, moving it soon afterwards to Carnaby Street.

Other revolutions had provided the fabrics without which the looks of the fifties could never have taken shape. From the basic silk, wool and cotton available at the beginning of the century, there were in the fifties dozens of alternatives, most of them crease-resistant or permanently pleated, glazed, shrink-proof, water-proof, moth-proof, and washable. Synthetics had begun to appear in fashion during the thirties, with Schiaparelli's 'Rhodophane' dress, and there was a cheap rayon or 'art. silk'. By 1938 there were Lastex tops and an improved, uncrushable rayon, but it was not

until the war, which had so many beneficial effects on the fashion industry, that textile manufacturers were forced back on their resources, and made the most of them. Nylon transformed the fifties wardrobe, making the petticoats that stood up by themselves and the almost invisible 12-denier stockings, the fake furs and the permanently pleated nightdresses, the laces and the knitting yarns. In 1954 *Vogue* published a glossary of man-made fibres including acetate, Dynel, Fibrolane, Orlon, rayon and Terylene. 'Putting on clean clothes daily,' as Madge Garland pointed out in her book *Fashion*, 'once thought to be an eccentricity of the Empress Josephine, is an habitual occurrence in the life of any girl.' Washable drip-dry clothes passed into the fashion repertoire of working city girls. Thick pullovers were made for the first time in powder blues and primrose yellows with Orlon and Courtelle; foundation garments were revolutionized, nylon fabrics in great variety making possible the two-way stretch doll-size girdle of 1952. Four years later one firm, English Rose, had 90 garments in their range, an increase of 60 since 1950, a number made possible by the different kinds of synthetic fibre.

The fifties were the time when women went out to work as a matter of course. In the 1920s when Van Dongen had painted 'The Lady Wants No Children' the question had been 'Job or children?': in the fifties women were prepared to take on two jobs in order to have the best of both worlds – and this at a time when children's

Herbert Matter

1. Nylon, which arrived from America after the war, revolutionizes fashion, 1951. Here, a nylon marquisette dress by Susan Small, photographed with the vast spinning room of the British Nylon Spinners' factory in Monmouthshire.
2. 'Stocking superlatives: the sheerest — 12-denier thinness, a new low (we are used to 15), just coming off the nylon machines.' This one by Charnos.
3. The pale thick-knit sweater, now easy to wash, quick to dry and able to hold its shape in Orlon or Courtelle. This one, lemon yellow Courtelle, by Playfair.

Vernier

nurses and maids were almost impossible to find. By the end of the decade, more than half the married women of Britain were going out to work. But T. W. Higginson could still have said, as he had nearly 100 years before, 'Like Charles Lamb, who atoned for coming late to the office in the morning by going away early in the afternoon, we have, first, half educated women, and then, to restore the balance, only half paid them.' A girl might earn about three-quarters of a man's wage, doing the same job in industry, and even when she was granted equal pay, did she get equal opportunities? Out of 150 top jobs in the B.B.C., only four were held by women. One of the two women governors, Mrs Thelma Cazalet-Keir, said, 'The B.B.C. conceded equal pay for women as long ago as 1926, but what's the good of that if no women get paid at the top level?' Jacqueline Wheldon, wife of B.B.C. producer Hew Wheldon, complained about the tone of voice in which television programmes addressed women, 'that jolly welfare-worker air, and that special sort of voice, as though every woman sitting at home was a moron . . . the term they used for us in the studio, I believe, was "Mums".' The publishing of Christabel Pankhurst's memoirs, *Unshackled*, provoked in *Vogue* a spirited debate between political commentator Henry Fairlie of the *Spectator* and *Daily Mail*, and working women. Mr Fairlie wrote that women were really reluctant victors in the battle for independence, and that they were the victims of a confidence trick by an industrial society to supply a cheap new source of labour. He declared that the typewriter had re-enslaved women, 'few of whom are happy until they have had a baby', and that cosmetics, fashion, and women's magazines were

all 'drugs to keep the slaves quiet'. In reply, Jean Mann, a J.P., invited Mr Fairlie to accompany her to the factories 'and look at the "exploited". They have wages and hours fixed by the Trade Unions. Ask these women if they would prefer their pre-emancipation jobs as servants, charwomen, cleaners, washerwomen!' Dame Sybil Thorndike said, 'If we are better persons as a result of freedom how can we have lost as women?' Margaret Casson, architect, drew attention to his 'curious assumption that because women are physically constructed to bear children they are therefore mentally and emotionally bound to enjoy domesticity above every other kind of life', and Shirley Conran, fabric designer, said, 'I chose to work because I found housekeeping easy and boring and because my husband is more interested in me as a fellow worker than as a super servant. What would Mr Fairlie rather we did when our children are past the baby stage? Embroider radiator screens?' Penelope Mortimer spoke for many working women when she said, summing up, 'Thoughtlessly, often effortlessly, one somehow manages to retain the affection and attention of one's family while voting, typing, earning. Even (and this is more remarkable) while cooking, cleaning the bottoms of saucepans, and administering Syrup of Figs. Could it be that, although a woman, one is a human being?'

In Anita Loos's 'Decline and Fall of Blondes', written for *Vogue* in 1951, she expressed her point with a difference. 'Any time we

209

girls have to go to work the result, historically, is that we do things better than the opposite sex. I mean gentlemen will go to all the trouble of keeping office hours and holding Board Meetings and getting Mr Gallup to make a poll, and sending their Public Relations agents to Washington, in order to reach a decision which any blonde could reach while she was refurbishing her lipstick.'

The new word of the fifties was 'media'. Television had brought the meaning home to 26 million people by 1959, Aldous Huxley's 'television fodder', most of whom had been initiated by the televizing of the Coronation and had gone out to sign hire purchase agreements afterwards. The opening up of this enormous exploitable market came with Commercial Television in 1955, 'a national disaster', according to the Labour Party. So much was talked about 'subliminal' advertising that people began to doubt their own powers of resistance. In 1958 *Vogue* was writing, 'Having got ourselves thoroughly fussed about subliminal advertising and motivational research – the profitable quarrying of the depth-boys – we might return to ground level and look at the not so deep ideas employed upon our consciousness. The latest thought in cereal packages, expected here from America, is a celluloid gramophone record that can be cut out of the side of the package. Our sample performed, piercingly, "Goofy's Space-Trip to the Moon". "There's a big future for this little gimmick," say the instigators. "Birthday cards that sing Happy Birthday, aspirins with lullaby jingles!"'

In the new wave of commercialism, *Vogue*'s editorial policy moved closer to the fashion industry introducing an annual advertising award for good design, a colour range to help sell the new seasonal ranges in the shops, *Vogue* endorsements for featured fashions, and an attempt to catch the attention of specific markets and perform a reader's service in the introduction of Mrs Exeter in 1949 and Young Idea in 1953. After a pilot in 1945, *Vogue* initiated an annual talent contest from 1951, with a first prize of £50 and the offer of a job. This competition still operates today, and is the single way that a would-be journalist without contacts can walk straight into a job. Early winners included Cynthia Judah, Penelope Gilliatt, Anne Sharpley, Anne Scott-James, Isabel Quigly, Jill Butterfield and Edward Lucie-Smith. In 1952 the model competition began: 'Don't think, because no whistled tributes are forthcoming from corner boys, that you can't be a model.' In case of discouragement from family, *Vogue* added, 'You can reassure your father, your husband or your son, on one point: modelling is terribly respectable. Whatever you do, you will always be exemplarily clothed, and excessively chaperoned – by photographer, photographer's assistant, fashion editor (*stickler* for form), fashion editor's secretary, and studio girl.'

The technical age increased *Vogue*'s scope in several directions. On the features pages you might find a photograph of the new German Mopetta, a car no bigger than a big shopping basket, or a photograph of a pink daffodil or a blue-tinted mauve rose . . . 'no garden need now be without a yellow peony if you can spell Mlokosewitschii'. A picture of an experimental British Railways carriage, complete with reclining tweed seats, double glazed windows and thermostatic fan heating, might be paired with a new plastic greenhouse which allowed more ultra-violet light than did glass, or details of the new transatlantic telephone cable and what it might do for readers' calls to Australia.

There were new fashion photographs taken with telephoto lens, and unforgettable pictures by photographers of the calibre of Irving Penn and Norman Parkinson, whose perfected technique allowed them to realize inner fantasies. Penn's (usually 'lifts' from American *Vogue*) are of superb quality, to which end he will fly a planeload of electronic equipment across the ocean to the particular room he wants to work in, or smash to pieces an imperfect camera

Irving Penn

Norman Parkinson

rather than have it adjusted. Unlike Penn, Norman Parkinson prefers to work out of doors, and says, 'A studio is like an operating theatre. You go there to get part of yourself removed.' Taking a picture, he sets out like a water diviner – which he is – alive to every conjunction of ingredients that can produce magic. First day in a foreign country with a dress to photograph, he will tell the driver, 'Take the first right and the second left, the first right, the second left, until I tell you to stop', until 'the picture arrives'.

First of the 'send up' photographers, Antony Armstrong-Jones's pictures are outrageous moments caught by the camera when no one should have been looking – a girl teeters and falls into a river, fully dressed, a woman knocks over a couple of glasses as she rushes to embrace a man, the tide creeps up to cover the knees of a girl who has fallen asleep on a deckchair.

1. Vogue Pattern, photographed by Irving Penn, 1949.
2. The fashionable woman's image and how it changed between 1949 and 1957: Norman Parkinson's postwar heroine (*opposite*) was beautifully groomed and perfectly self-assured, Antony Armstrong-Jones's girl of the late fifties (*below*) was younger, less controlled, and supposedly unaware of the camera.
3. Twinset and pearls fashion, 1951. The caption read, 'The scene: a village pub. The theme: poise, dignity, the respect of person for person and class for class. The girl, quiet in dress and manners, waits while her husband gets drinks. The man, dropped in after work, takes his pint from a pewter mug, plays shove ha'penny on a well-made "slate" on an oak trestle table, has unselfconsciously pinned a rose in his coat.'
4. By 1957, *Vogue* was using cars as image-projectors. Here, a scampi belt Riley 2.6, with golf clubs, poodle and alpaca pile coat.

3

Norman Parkinson

Antony Armstrong-Jones

4

Norman Parkinson

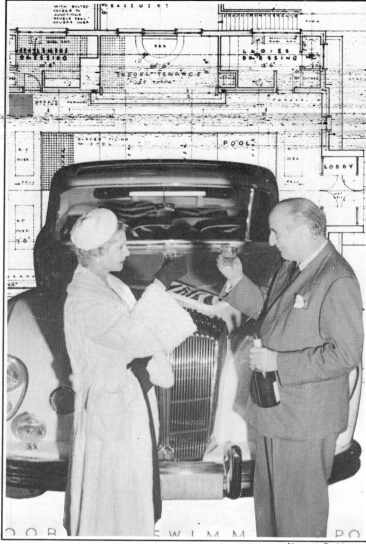

1. The fabulous Lady Docker in white ermine, with her gold-plated zebra-upholstered Daimler, and the plans for her heated indoor swimming pool convertible to an open-air one for summer. Accompanied by Sir Bernard.
2. New film star Montgomery Clift, 1952. He made his name in *A Place in the Sun*.
3. Tony Richardson and John Osborne, photographed by Penn in 1959 when Richardson's *Othello* with Paul Robeson was due to start at Stratford, and Osborne's *World of Paul Slickey* at Bournemouth: the film of *Look Back in Anger* was soon to have its premlère. *Vogue* said, 'Two of the most vivid, relaxed and serious talents in the theatre, they retain their humour and liberty despite the best efforts of the press.'
4. Dylan Thomas, poet, broadcaster and script-writer, photographed by John Deakin in Laugharne graveyard, where he was buried in 1953. In 1950, at the time of the photograph, he had just published *Death and Entrances*. In *Vogue* John Davenport described him as a genius and a 'pirate who drank our drinks and borrowed our money and kissed our girls'.

Norman Parkinson

Irving Penn

Common to the photographers who found their feet in the fifties was the independence and assurance of the model, who seemed to own the clothes and be carrying on her own life regardless of the camera, unless she faced it with a disconcerting awareness.

Vogue opened out into new territory with its features pages, edited by Siriol Hugh Jones then by Penelope Gilliatt, who was to marry John Osborne. Maria Callas faced James Dean across the pages; Gina Lollobrigida, 'the new Italian bombshell', jostled Joan Littlewood, 'a forthright genius with a band of idealists who toured the country in a lorry, clinging to the belief that the theatre is a popular art'; Satyajit Ray with his 'rapt fidelity, his realism and silence' lined up with Lady Docker and her new gold-plated, zebra-upholstered Daimler. *Vogue* was there to hear Liberace pronounce, 'It is good when fans get behind the life of a star who's a good clean citizen with a fine family life', and there to overhear Mike Todd telling a henchman, 'Now what about these cinemas? Save a lot of time if I had them both. Call 'em Liz's First House and Liz's Palace.' *Look Back in Anger* was described as 'the play that gave tongue to a generation scarcely speaking to its elders', the film *Gigi* as having produced the feeling that you were being sold something subliminally – 'M.G.M. good evenings start with Colette'. Penelope Gilliatt was quick to feel the tinge of 'Ealing-tight-little-island humour' in Alec Guinness's *The Horse's Mouth*. She asked Sidney Nolan what he thought of the performance. 'Very good,' he said. 'People usually play artists as though they were mad.' 'But, Sidney,' said his wife, 'this man was completely nutty.' 'Don't be silly,' said Sidney. 'He behaved just like I do.'

Norman Parkinson

The new writers' disillusionment with British politics and cant, system of privilege and genteel complacency, gave the old order a rough time from 1954, when Kingsley Amis published *Lucky Jim*. Osborne's *Look Back in Anger* at the Royal Court, with Alan Bates and Mary Ure, shocked people into self-awareness and marked a turning point in the decade, but it was in *The Entertainer* that he parodied most cruelly the decline of England through the deterioration of a seedy music hall performer. Reviewing John Braine's *Room at the Top* in its filmed version directed by Jack Clayton, the story of an anti-hero's climb through the British class system, Penelope Gilliatt wrote admiringly of what was dubbed 'kitchen-sink realism': 'Casually the camera-work states what a Northern town is like: cobbled streets, smudged views of chimneys, women cooking at ranges, wet slaps of washing to be dodged by children playing in the street. I know that remarking on this must sound like applauding a dress for being sufficiently in touch with reality to have a zip, but it is notable in our cinema.'

The anti-hero, who behaves disgracefully, but whose side we're on anyway, was not only a figure of British novels and plays but also of the new Hollywood films, which now produced the 'masculine brute rebellion'. Siriol Hugh Jones wrote, 'In the broad shoulders, the slouch, the regional accents and the beautiful broad peasant features of Richard Burton, the inescapable animal bulk of Marlon Brando, the neurotic-baker-boy puzzlement of Montgomery Cliff, the sulking pout of Farley Granger – there lies glamour, there lies the heroic touch, the dream of 1952.' The heroine, whatever nationality, often had a new childishness – there was more than a hint of the schoolgirl in Audrey Hepburn, of the baby in Marilyn Monroe and Brigitte Bardot.

The beginning of the men's hair cult was first noticed in Siriol Hugh Jones's feature 'Crew-cuts and Rough Diamonds', 1952, in which she said, 'I think the changing order of heroes is identified most easily along the hair-line . . . "pre-war hair" was well-cut and cared for, often even innocent of evil communications with brilliantine and other base messes. The post-war look is that of the crew-cut and its dire derivatives.'

It was not particularly surprising that the popular hero should have changed so much in a decade that had become insecure as quickly as it became self-aware. Bertrand Russell spoke of 'a fated and predetermined march towards disaster'. Sir Julian Huxley saw over-population as the gravest threat to man's future at a time when babies were being born 100 a minute to increase the world's population by nearly fifty millions a year. Meanwhile, hideous dormitory suburbs and bleak, boring new towns spread out to ruin the countryside in place of the glittering cities that had been visualized in the twenties. Not even the material prosperity of the late fifties could gloss over the disasters of Suez and Hungary, Korea, mistrust of politics and feelings of panic about the future that culminated in the Aldermaston marches and the demonstrations of civil disobedience. Television was at least the main factor in the new awareness, bringing the facts and the action of world affairs into the private lives of 26 million British viewers by 1959; no wonder the public was more involved and more anxious than it had ever been before.

THE CHANGING FACE

In the 1950s models became stars. Their names were well known, they could earn enormous salaries, and they were accorded film star status. Designers talked of models being their inspiration — there was Alla, the beautiful Eurasian girl at Dior, Bettina at Jacques Fath, Bronwen Pugh — later Lady Astor — at Balmain.

FIONA CAMPBELL-WALTER

Fiona Campbell-Walter, one of the great beauties of the time, was *Vogue*'s star British model, superbly photogenic, suitably haughty for the 1950s, and equally convincing in a mackintosh or tiara. She had the perfect proportions for a model, being 5 ft 8 ins tall with a 23 in waist, had long streamlined eyes and delicate features together with tawny hair which she lightened at the temples to widen her brow, and grew long enough to wear up or down. On her marriage to Baron Thyssen she gave up modelling.

AUDREY HEPBURN

Audrey Hepburn, real name Edda Hepburn van Heemstra, is a Belgian-born star actress of Irish-Dutch parentage. In 1952, when Norman Parkinson took this photograph, she was playing *Gigi* on Broadway, with 'fabulous personal success': her film *Secret People* was showing in England, and she had a Paramount contract waiting. In 1954, after *Roman Holiday* and *Sabrina Fair*, *Vogue* called her, 'Today's wonder-girl . . . She has so captured the public imagination and the mood of the time that she has established a new standard of beauty, and every other face now approximates to the 'Hepburn look'. Cecil Beaton said in *Vogue*, 'her appearance succeeds because it embodies the spirit of today . . . it took the rubble of Belgium, an English accent and an American success to launch the striking personality that best exemplifies our new Zeitgeist. Nobody ever looked like her before World War II . . . now thousands of imitations have appeared. The woods are full of emaciated young ladies with rat-nibbled hair and moon-pale faces.' She was 25, and she wore a 'monkey fur' fringe, highwayman coats, clergyman cassocks, and students pants, overalls and scarves, often with felt ballet pumps. She wore no powder, only a smudge of black greasepaint above and below her eyes. Cecil Beaton analysed her features, ' . . . character rather than prettiness; the bridge of the nose seems almost too narrow to carry its length, which flares into a globular tip with nostrils startlingly like a duck's bill. Her mouth is wide, with a cleft under the lower lip too deep for classical beauty, the delicate chin appears even smaller by contrast with the exaggerated width of her jaw bones . . . she owes a large debt to the ballet for her bearing and abandon in movement.' Through the years she has been a kind of barometer of fashion, looking each year as though she had been born for that minute in time.

Norman Parkinson

Cecil Beaton

BRIGITTE BARDOT

1. Brigitte Bardot, photographed by William Klein in 1959, three years after *And God Created Woman*. *Vogue* called her, 'the sensuous idol, a potent mixture of the sexy and the babyish, a seething milky bosom below a childish pout'. The phrase 'sex kitten' was coined to describe her. She reinforced her international success in 1965 with *Viva Maria*, and is still in demand today at forty years old.

LAUREN BACALL

2. Lauren Bacall told *Vogue* about her make up, 'For my peculiar face I look best when I look as though I'm not wearing any' and about clothes 'nothing itsy-bitsy—you shouldn't have to do too much to them, just wear them'.

BARBARA GOALEN

3. Barbara Goalen, Coffin's favourite model, appeared continually in *Vogue* from 1950, and could make the simplest cotton dress look expensive and smart. She personified the air of aloof sophistication that meant elegance throughout the decade, and looked perfect in stylized clothes that were extremely difficult to wear well. She is now Mrs Nigel Campbell.

2

Rutledge

3

137

William Klein

Vernier

Milton Greene

MARILYN MONROE

The first and last pictures to appear in *Vogue*. Olivier, Monroe, Rattigan, (*top*) were photographed in 1956 as they began work on the unhappy production *The Sleeping Prince:* Olivier told Monroe, 'Be sexy', which incapacitated her for weeks.

Bert Stern took the revealing last magazine pictures of her (*opposite*). News of her death came just as 15 September *Vogue* was going to press with this photograph, and *Vogue* said, 'The waste seems almost unbearable if out of her death comes nothing of insight into her special problems: no step towards a knowledge that might save, for the living, others as beautiful and tormented.'

GRACE KELLY

'Her composed, in-bred prettiness is rapidly revising Hollywood's idea of what's box-office. Public demand, since *Mogambo* and *Rear Window*, has landed her parts in *The Bridges at Toko-Ri*, *The Country Girl* and *Green Fire'*. 1955.

ANITA EKBERG

'In the colossal film version of *War and Peace*, just shown, she plays the Princess Elena Kouraguine, an invention of Tolstoy's that anticipated central heating. "Lissen", she said primly when we met her. "I am not an Iceberg. I am hot-blooded. I wear nothing under this." Our photographer, who takes snuff, has never taken it faster.' 1956.

Norman Parkinson

VOGUE

The Black and
White Idea

London Season

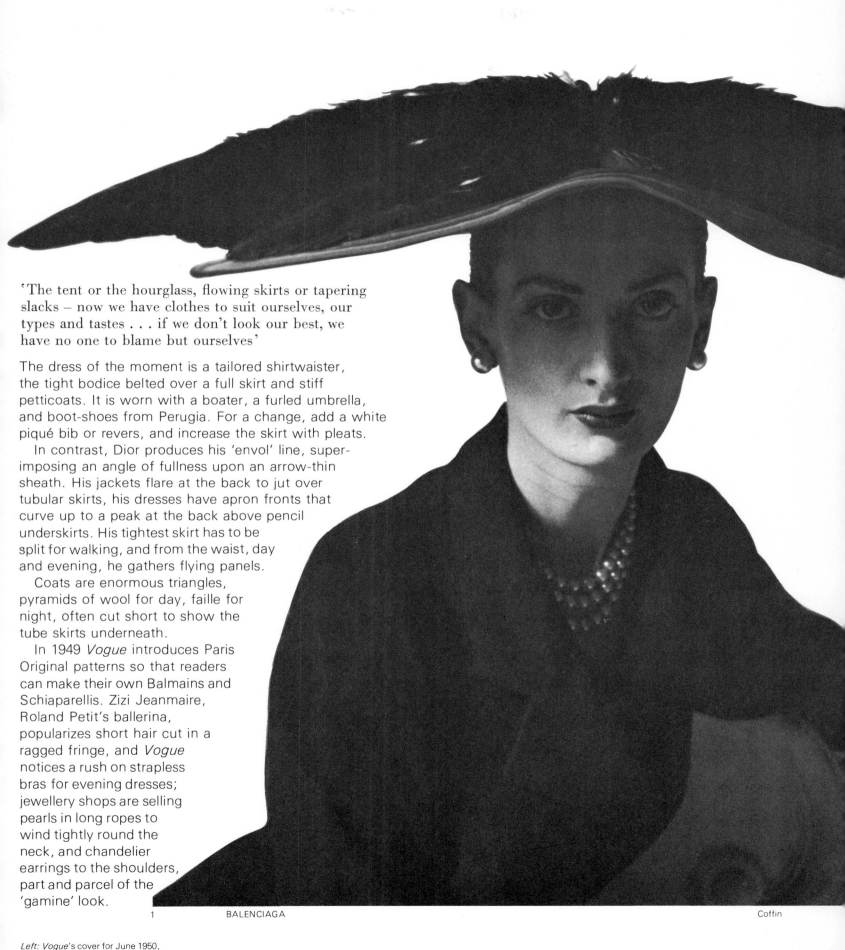

'The tent or the hourglass, flowing skirts or tapering slacks – now we have clothes to suit ourselves, our types and tastes . . . if we don't look our best, we have no one to blame but ourselves'

The dress of the moment is a tailored shirtwaister, the tight bodice belted over a full skirt and stiff petticoats. It is worn with a boater, a furled umbrella, and boot-shoes from Perugia. For a change, add a white piqué bib or revers, and increase the skirt with pleats.

In contrast, Dior produces his 'envol' line, super-imposing an angle of fullness upon an arrow-thin sheath. His jackets flare at the back to jut over tubular skirts, his dresses have apron fronts that curve up to a peak at the back above pencil underskirts. His tightest skirt has to be split for walking, and from the waist, day and evening, he gathers flying panels.

Coats are enormous triangles, pyramids of wool for day, faille for night, often cut short to show the tube skirts underneath.

In 1949 *Vogue* introduces Paris Original patterns so that readers can make their own Balmains and Schiaparellis. Zizi Jeanmaire, Roland Petit's ballerina, popularizes short hair cut in a ragged fringe, and *Vogue* notices a rush on strapless bras for evening dresses; jewellery shops are selling pearls in long ropes to wind tightly round the neck, and chandelier earrings to the shoulders, part and parcel of the 'gamine' look.

1   BALENCIAGA   Coffin

Left: Vogue's cover for June 1950, photographed by Irving Penn.
1. The shoulder-span hat: Balenciaga's grass-green faille with black wings.

1948-49

1
BRENNER   Lee Miller

2
CHRISTIAN DIOR   Coffin

NEW BEAUTIES *continued*

RENEE JEANMAIRE, newly risen star of Roland Petit's Ballets de Paris, electrified London and Paris by her dancing
in *Carmen*. She is small, dark, dazzling, with a nervous temperament in the finest sense of the word.

3
Hans Wild   4   Cecil Beaton

1. Striped seersucker blouse, pale blue
pirate-length jeans.
2. 'Pencil slim' black wool dress with a check
envol jacket, Peter Pan collar tied with a
black taffeta bow, a black-velvet beret tipped
over the forehead. Perugia's check wool and
patent leather boots.
3. Victor Stiebel's debutante dress in layers
of tulle. The make up: sharp, pink and white,
with pencilled eyebrows, streamlined eyes
and painted mouth. The hair, flattened to the
head as much as possible.
4. The gamine haircut, 1949, worn first by
Roland Petit's dazzling new ballerina Zizi
Jeanmaire.
5. Schiaparelli's slim silhouette with jutting
collar and peg-top skirt. Perugia's boots,
fitting like a stocking at the hemline.
6. Jacques Fath's lemon-yellow coat, a
tremendous triangle emphasized by the
buttoning; outsize collar.

The Tent
or the
Hourglass

5
Coffin

6   FATH

1950

Left: Irving Penn's portrait of Christian Dior's stylized, elegant mid-century woman demonstrated the acceptable *Vogue* way to smoke.
Right: Norman Parkinson's photograph of Enid Boulting in a Helena Geffers suit caused a sensation: American *Vogue*'s editor-in-chief cabled from New York SMOKING IN VOGUE SO TOUGH SO UNFEMININE!

1950

'Share the immense confidence of 1950, facing the
unknown half of our century'

The most confident and high-spirited fashion since the
mid-thirties, taking off from the New Look into
exaggerated, geometric shapes, boldly asymmetric and
stylized. The shirtwaister has competition in the new
sheath dress, swathed and draped for evening.
Balenciaga's sculptural formal designs for evening
dresses steal the thunder—stiff paper taffetas blown up
and rolled under into huge pumpkin skirts tipped up in
the front, bows the size of umbrellas wrapping up the
tightest sheaths, angles sharp as blades, buoyant
curving widths in the skirts.

Hair is pressed to the head and seldom seen in the
day without a hat, eyes become 'doe eyes', with
painted flick-ups of eyeliner at the outer corners,
complexions are made pink and white, lips sharp and
vivid. Collars are sharp, high and turned up, waists are
minimized by girdles that grip from rib cage to hips,
peplums jut out above the narrowest skirts. To make
skirts look even narrower at the knee, models are
photographed with one leg behind the other, and the
new trumpet skirt which flares out again below the
narrowest point turns full length evening dresses into
fishtail sheaths. The new shoe, day or evening, is the
sling-back with a rounded toe.

1. Short evening dress,
strapless lace corselet and
swathed silk skirt sashed at
the back. Sling-back lace
shoes.
2. Swinging redingote with
huge jutting collar, white
plush turban, black bamboo
umbrella.
3. Pumpkin evening dress of
blown-out satin taffeta.

HARDY AMIES   Don Honeyman

226   DIOR   Irving Penn   BALENCIAGA   Irving Penn

'Where has the waist gone? Anywhere but where you expect it'

'She's eighteen, and she chooses trousers because somehow one always seems to end up sitting on the floor in her room, what with the gas ring and the gramophone being there already. There will be spaghetti and "coke"'

'The long supple torso, the little neat head, the longer skirt, this is the season at a glance from both capitals'

In 1951, year of the Festival of Britain, *Vogue* produces a special Britannica number devoted to British achievements with an 8-page feature on 'The Rise of the Ready-to-Wear': the most fastidious and fashion-conscious woman can dress immediately for any occasion in ready-to-wear clothes.'

Christian Dior's and Balenciaga's spring 1951 collections have several points in common, tipping the fashion balance in favour of a Chinese look — coolie hats, flick-up eyes, wide barrel-shaped jackets, black and white as the favourite colour combination. This is Dior's first collection without stiffened and padded interlinings, and he launches his immediately successful 'princess line' with dresses fitted through the midriff, waist unmarked. Balenciaga on the other hand puts plenty of stiffening into his jackets, cutting them to curve like shells over the body, and indicating the waist with a loose bow or an indented curve; his new middy line drops the waist to the hips.

Dior produces a new bloused jacket for his princess dress — a battlejacket when it's short, a middy jacket when it's gathered onto a wide belt at the hips. His new jumper suits with sailor collars fit at the hips over flat pleated skirts. Jacques Fath, who invented the 'guipure' girdle, 'has become a steadier star and made a glowingly brilliant show', offering as an alternative to the middy line a crisp, young suit with a cropped matador jacket showing a cummerbund waist and a full skirt bolstered with stiff petticoats. 'Instant Paris' additions for *Vogue* readers are a stole to wear day and evening, a bathing cap with a piece of black veiling, long evening gloves worn pushed down to the wrist for day, glittering diamanté or rhinestone earrings and bracelets, a string of graduated pearls.

Two new couturiers open in Paris in 1951: Castillo, designing for Lanvin, and Jacques Griffe, designing for Molyneux now that Captain Molyneux has had to resign because of his failing eyesight. In 1952, Givenchy opens in Paris and Cavanagh in London. Givenchy began by designing for the Schiaparelli boutique, and starts his independent career with a boutique collection. *Vogue* notes, 'He has a brilliant hand with separates — skirts with built up waistlines and "laundered" white blouses with large ruffled sleeves. He uses tri-colour schemes: garnet, sea green, black; sand, turquoise, white.'

A totally new influence begins to make itself apparent in fashion as the teenage market demands a look of its own. The earliest indications in *Vogue* are the tapered trousers and the stiff ballerina petticoats, the flat shoes, the 'chunky' sweaters. In March 1952 Norman Parkinson photographs a spread of square dancers in spinning skirts and pumps, with strapless tops or sweetheart necklines, and in November, Anthony Denney photographs a blueprint teenager complete with ponytail and Coca Cola.

Rawlings

BALENCIAGA

Right: Spring suit in charcoal shantung with a collarless yoke, a loose white gilet, and coolie hat.

1

2. Night and Day
Make up, night. . . 'The natural complexion is masked and paled with a creamy cake foundation and a clear-toned powder. Glowing colour is painted on the lips, every curve accentuated, the eyes are made mysterious with eyebrow pencil and a dusky shadow, and strip eyelashes of nylon.'
. . . and day 'The lipstick is the same, but this time the true line of the lips is followed, and mascara is the only eye flattery. The natural complexion is not masked but softly veiled with a light foundation and fluff of warm-tinted powder.'

2

4

DIOR

BALENCIAGA

Randall

5

Blumenfeld 3 DIOR

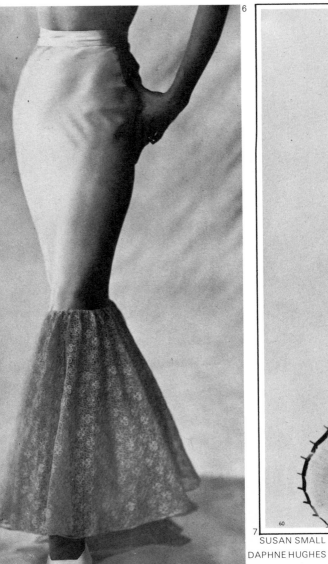

1. Agmar's suede bathing cap, hat of the moment, and the new emphasized eyebrows.

3. Accordion-pleated white crepe dress, Emba mutation mink coat, 1952.

4. Where is the waist? Under the arms, marked by a martingale in this Dior grey flannel dress and jacket. Beaver hat.

5. Where is the waist? Round the hips in this loose middy plaid suit by Balenciaga.

6. Trumpet skirt petticoat for evening.

7. Daphne Brooker, one of the winners of *Vogue's* first model contest in 1952 and now head of Kingston Fashion School, in a navy crepe jumper dress after Dior, with middy pleated skirt, sailor collar, Breton straw hat.

7 SUSAN SMALL
DAPHNE HUGHES

Anthony Denney

229

Irving Penn

2 DERETA   Cecil Beaton

1. Jacques Heim's wrapped bottle jersey
blouse, tapered blue and green velvet
pants and lilac cummerbund.
2. Dereta's three-quarter redingote of
ribbed wool with grosgrain collar and
pocket flaps. Grosgrain beret
by Pissot and Pavy.
3. Simonetta Visconti in one of her own
designs, a beaded faille house jacket
and calf-length taffeta pants. A great
exponent of the contemporary look,
Simonetta, though still in her twenties in
1952, streaks her hair with grey.
4. Prints make a comeback — Dior's
shantung dustcoat with side slits,
box-pleat back.

3   Norman Parkinson

4 DIOR   Randall

SUSAN SMALL   Spotted chiffon dress with a green straw hat
by Simone Mirman; photograph Antony Armstrong-Jones

Coronation year — 'and Norman Hartnell celebrates with a collection of white and gold evening dresses'

'The sweater has grown in importance and size. Buy it two sizes larger than usual for a casual look. Add a sweater scarf, or fill in the V with rows and rows of pearls'

The dropped armhole dictates the shape that dominates both student and Paris-based fashion.

The teenage look for daytime is the 'mansize chunky sweater' with drainpipe pants and 'flatties': for evening, a full circle skirt in a bright felt — probably turquoise or kingfisher blue — with a tight poloneck sweater or a scoop-necked blouse tucked in.

From Paris, the same dropped, rounded, bulky shoulderline for suits and coats, the loose neck rolling off the body like an oversized sweater. Dior reintroduces padding over the bust with his 'tulip' line, and captures headlines by shortening his skirts to 16 inches from the ground — still two or three inches below the knee. Women are by now used to wearing skirts almost to their ankles, and are nervous of a change that might date their clothes as suddenly as the New Look did in 1947: *Vogue* soothes its readers, 'Dior always emphasizes that skirt length is a matter of individual proportions: he lived up to his own maxim by putting his ultra-short skirts only on petite model girls. In any case, a major fashion change must first be put over at full strength and then modified for general acceptance . . . the probability is that women will have their autumn skirts a couple of inches shorter than they might otherwise have done, and be ready for further shortening in the spring.'

1

2

3

4

London couture, 1953. The members of the Incorporated Society of London Fashion Designers with key models from their spring collections, photographed by Norman Parkinson.

1. Elspeth Champcommunal at Worth
2. Norman Hartnell
3. Hardy Amies
4. Victor Stiebel at Jacqmar
5. Michael Sherard
6. Digby Morton
7. Peter Russell
8. Mattli
9. Michael at Lachasse
10. Charles Creed
11. John Cavanagh

Norman Parkinson

Norman Parkinson

1. Travelling clothes: beige wool jersey separates, pleated skirt, short sleeved blouse top, cardigan and Kangol beret.

2. White ottoman dress and fitted jacket at Harrods, Simone Mirman headband of grape hyacinths and white straw, fine strip sandals by Delman.

3. Evening make up, summer 1953, with liquid rouge the new ingredient, used over the temples and under the brows. The rest of the make up goes on like this: a moisture cream under a tinted foundation, a heavy powder on top, a dark brown eyeshadow, pencilled eyebrows and eyeline, mascara, lipstick. Time, 18 min. 45 second.

4. Claire Bloom, between *Berlin Story* and *Ophelia* for the Old Vic, photographed for *Vogue* in Simone Mirman's hat of white currants mounted on net.

5. 'More Taste than Money' — cardigan coat of bird's eye jersey lined with denim, £13.6s. Black suede shower-cap hat.

6. Sleeveless balloon jacket, pinspot silk with a black rose; bloused over a V-neck black dress with black suede gloves.

7. The ideal shape for a Dior dress — Lefaucheur's foundation with nipped waist, flat back and carved-in midriff.

DIOR'S BOLD SKIRT LENGTH: BULK UNDER BULK..

Bouché

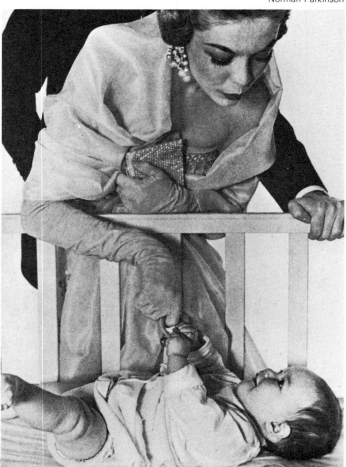

234

4.
SIMONE MIRMAN

Anthony Denney

5 DOBETT

Norman Parkinson

6. BALENCIAGA

Henry Clarke

7.

Frances McLaughlin

1954

'The biggest news is personality news; Chanel's reopening. Her collection is the talk of Paris, with opinion violently divided. At its best it has the easy liveable look which is her great contribution to fashion history; at its worst it repeats the lines she made famous in the 'thirties: repeats rather than translates into contemporary terms'

Talking to *Vogue* before her comeback collection, Chanel promised there would be no 'fifties horrors'. She is as good as her word. She makes a young, easy-moving dashing collection that is truly more modern than the 'contemporary terms' of Dior's careful sophistication or Balenciaga's sculptural formality.

Vogue shows clothes from the Italian and Spanish collections — Pucci's brash jazzy Palio shirts, Simonetta's casual at-home pants, and Pertegaz's evening looks, immensely formal like those of another Spaniard, Balenciaga.

Now that she's made *Sabrina Fair*, Audrey Hepburn's is the best-known and most copied of all faces, and the classic Fiona Campbell-Walter is acknowledged as the most beautiful *Vogue* model.

'Trifling hats — the small, whole difference.' Anya Linden, soloist of the Sadler's Wells Ballet, in turquoise velvet by Vernier.

VERNIER   Cecil Beaton

1. Chanel's return — her beautiful navy jersey suit with squared shoulders, tucked white blouse with a bow tie, and sailor hat tipped to the back of the head.
2. Wenda Parkinson, photographed by her husband in Michael's elegant tussore suit widened at the shoulders over a striped black and white 'football sweater'.
3. Dior's sailor suit in soft navy jersey trimmed with satin ribbon.
4. Emilio Pucci's Palio-print silk shirt and bright corduroy pants: the shirts are already collector's pieces.

2 MICHAEL   Norman Parkinson

3 DIOR   Henry Clarke

1

CHANEL   Henry Clarke

PUCCI.   Rawlings

237

1 PERTEGAZ   Henry Clarke

2 CHANEL   Henry Clarke

1. Emerald paper taffeta evening coat in tiers.
2. Chanel's shell pink jersey cocktail dress — 'Dresses are never gracious and flattering enough'.
3. Dior's flat-bosomed evening dress, skirt puffing from the hips.
4. Balenciaga's ball dress of spun-sugar net tied with ribbon.

3 DIOR   Coffin

4   Coffin

'A significant struggle is taking place in Paris. On the one side there are the designers whose achievement is to create clothes of so strong a shape that they look as if they could walk across the room alone . . . on the other side are the designers whose clothes are not superimposed on a body: they have no existence apart from it'

The first camp, designers of clothes with body and shape of their own, clothes popular with manufacturers and shops for their 'hanger appeal', are Dior, Givenchy, Balmain and Fath—now carried on by Jacques Fath's widow, Geneviève Fath.

Dior produces his new A line, a triangle widened from a small head and shoulders to a full pleated or stiffened hem. He uses stiff, strong fabrics such as tussore and faille. Variety comes from the placing of the crossbar waist—high for an empire line, below fingertip level at its lowest.

The second camp, whose clothes generally take their shape from the wearer in soft fabrics like jersey and silk tweed, include Chanel, Balenciaga's day clothes, Patou, Lanvin and Griffe.

An almost universal alternative to the A line is the slim tunic suit, sometimes called H and sometimes I, with the long jacket sometimes reaching to the knees over the even slimmer skirt. Chanel is the obvious exception to this hobble hem, with her easy jersey skirts widened with a deep inverted pleat.

Technological fashion assets now include one-size stretch stockings and lighter, softer stretch panti-girdles printed in vivid stripes or patterns.

Balenciaga's sinuous black I line tunic dress, great black fox collar giving weight at the top, and a flying panel from the shoulders.

1955

1. Working girl's wool jersey suit in bright red with a shirty top, pleated skirt.
2. Stockbroker pinstripes — Michael's suit that is really a jacket and pinafore dress, Charles Creed's fitted black and white suit with a wing-collared white piqué blouse.
3. Dior's H line, with the narrowest of skirts, photograph Vernier.

Opposite: Scarlet velvet toque by Otto Lucas, flannel suit, by Bazaar. Photograph by Norman Parkinson, who called it 'Van Dongen' after the painting 'The Lady Wants No Children', November 1959.

Over page, left: Jersey wrap and trousers by Lovable, hat by Malyard. Photographed in the Seychelles by Norman Parkinson, December 1971.

Norman Parkinson

MICHAEL   CHARLES CREED

1. Dior's evening A line, black faille with a straw cartwheel hat.
2. Givenchy's oatmeal tweed dress with a semi-fitted, diagonally seamed waistline; photograph Henry Clarke.

Opposite: '1960s Deco.' Twenties peach chiffon embroidered with silver bugle beads, from the Purple Shop, Chelsea Antique Market. Photograph by Norman Parkinson, December 1969.

DIOR

1

1956-57

Christian Dior's death in 1957: 'He is sure of a high place in fashion history . . . His mantle has fallen upon young M. Yves Saint Laurent'

'. . . the big story of the shrinking skirt-length — from just-below-the-knee at Lanvin-Castillo to just-on-the-calf at Dior'

Waists are raised by almost all the Paris dictators bringing in a new suit with a cropped jacket showing a small cinched waist—best at Dior—sarong dresses wrapped high to one side, and the innovation of a stiff four-inch waspie belt that has the effect of raising the waist and exaggerating the hips at the same time: it will become the most copied accessory for years. Fashion catches up with Chanel and her comfortable jersey cardigan suits; she goes one better with contrasting braid, and invents a casual new skirt wrapped to one side with a trouser pocket in the seam. Coats are the thickest, softest and warmest ever, rounded like beehives,

funnel sleeves lost in the bulk, linings of fur. Colours are black, geranium red, fuchsia and shocking pink.

Christian Dior's last collection leaves a legacy, the waistless shift or chemise dress that narrows towards the hem, a refinement of Givenchy's 'sack', called the 'spindle' or 'chemmy dress', shortly to be known as the sac.

The hat is half the point of any new look now, usually a flowerpot toque pushed right down over the forehead, or a modified sou'wester with black veiling added or wrapping the face in a mesh cage, with a rose topknot. Eyes and lips are heavily outlined, visible at a hundred yards, and exaggerated still more to show through veils. Long cigarette holders come back to keep the sparks away.

Guy Laroche is an interesting new arrival in Paris, Audrey Hepburn has grown out her fringe, and in London Elizabeth Seal stars in *The Pyjama Game*; Henrietta Tiarks is deb of the year.

Elements of the mid-fifties — the 'sloppy Joe', here sleeveless and shocking pink; the waffle cotton shorts, the Chianti bottle and the spaghetti, the long cigarette holder.

DORVILLE

William Klein

1. The flowerpot hat, pushed down to the browline, in coffee cream satin slotted with a brown ribbon.
2. The glamour of a cocktail hat: mop of uncurled black ostrich, and a long cigarette holder to keep the sparks at a distance.
3. The veiled face with eyes and lips heavily outlined to show through.

1 OTTO LUCAS   Donald Silverstein

2   Henry Clarke

1 DIOR

William Klein

2 FATH

3 DIOR

Francis McLaughlin

4

William Klein

1. 1957: Dior's sac dress from his last collection, falling straight and simple to a narrow hem.

2. Fath's fragile lilac pleating, cape sleeves, boat neck tied at the back. Worn with a tulle turban in the nostalgic mood of 1957.

3. The big wrap from Paris, bulky, barrel-shape, cocooning. Christian Dior's coat, half a cape, in Prudhomme's thick grey wool, the armholes so deep that the huge sleeves are inset to the elbows. Worn with the new veiled flowerpot hat.

4. Shoes by Perugia. The ones marked with a white dot were made for Poiret in 1918; the rest are from Perugia's 1956 collection.

5. Domino cotton beach outfit; big shirt with sleeves to push up, brief shorts.

6. The universal twinset, worn by Elizabeth Seal, star of *The Pyjama Game*, with jangling bracelets and rolled-up jeans.

7. The glistening black PVC coat — vinyl-coated raincoat just about to become a classic.

5   HARVEY NICHOLLS

1958

'Saint Laurent has saved France – the great Dior tradition will continue'

'Chanel, this perfect designer, whose first great period was in the twenties, seems more truly of today than many younger people'

'Chemise styles are in . . . trapezerie is gaining ground, and everywhere the high-rise influence prevails'

Yves Saint Laurent makes an enormous success of his first collection for Dior. *Vogue* reports, 'The newspaper sellers shouted "Saint Laurent has saved France" . . . the joy and relief were terrific — people cried, laughed, clapped and shook hands. For almost an hour no one could leave, and finally Saint Laurent had to appear in the street and wave to the cab drivers and passers by.' Backbone of his collection is the trapeze, 'the most important and fully formulated line in Paris', flaring gently from narrow shoulders to a shorter wider hemline just covering the knees.

By autumn the rest of Paris has adopted this length, only to find that Saint Laurent has dropped his hems to three inches below the knee—an unpopular move.

Only four years after her re-entry into the Paris couture, unrivalled now that Christian Dior is dead, Chanel's is the major fashion influence in the world. Her jersey suits and blazer jackets are copied all down the line to the local high street, and she is responsible for the popularity of men's shirts, jewelled cufflinks, gold chains and medallions, gilt and pearl earrings, Breton sailor hats, and sling-back shoes with contrasting toe caps. Because of her model-girls, women brush out their hair instead of flattening it to the head and have a fringe club-cut across the forehead.

Originating with Balenciaga and Givenchy there is the 'high-rise' waist, cinching the ribs above an almond-shaped skirt, gathered over the hips and narrowed at the hem. Bolero jackets are cropped to show the waist, and coats follow the same line when they are not flared into a trapeze.

Shaggy bright pink mohair jersey, sizes too big, with black needlecord drainpipes. Black Louis-heeled shoes piped in silver kid by Dolcis.

FENWICK   Norman Parkinson

1

2 KOUPY   William Klein

1. Chinchilla, for the first time worked horizontally in this cardigan jacket worn with a grey flannel Garbo hat, gold bangles.
2. Bright navy jersey lined with the navy spotted silk of the blouse and Breton hat, with pearl earrings, heavy gold bangle.
3. Saint Laurent's trapeze line,

backbone of his successful first collection for Dior. Simple black silk and wool dress, bow marking the high waist and hem raised to just cover the knee.
4. Grey and black striped wool trapeze dress in the London shops, 6 gns.

3

SAINT
LAURENT

4 BLANES

KIKI BYRNE

1. Antony Armstrong-Jones designed and photographed these ski clothes. Balloon anorak of orange and yellow proofed silk, with black leather knickerbockers.
2. The strapless evening-dress . . . Worth's in draped black chiffon.
3. Chanel's navy and white jersey suit hung with a mixture of gold chains.
4. The 1958 look, the Chanel look. Simple, unflattened hair, emphasis on the eyes, man's shirt with cuff links, heavy gold chains. Another 1958 development, the telescopic lens camera, taking in long-range details of Nelson's Column and Trafalgar Square.

2 WORTH

3 CHANEL   Henry Clarke

4 CHANEL   William Klein

Striped cotton bikini, photograph Antony Armstrong-Jones

'The waist is back! The sack has had its day'

'Dior's man can do what he likes . . . We won't show our knees' – *Newspaper headline*

'"A woman should be more important than her clothes" – the 40-year-old philosophy of the fierce, wise, wonderful Coco Chanel'

In his badly-received autumn collection, Yves Saint Laurent at Dior raises the skirt to the knees, belts every waist and pulls the skirt in to a tight knee-band. The confidence invested in him last year is swept away by the outcry of the press, directed mainly at the skirt. *Vogue* presents his collection in the kindest light, ignoring the shortest skirts and showing the hobble first in its 'least exaggerated . . . utterly unalarming' form before leading up to the 'extreme trendsetter'. 'When a new line is greeted with cries of indignation, it's a healthy sign . . . it means that the fashion world is alive and kicking.'

The acceptable line from Paris is the 'body line', a wide, loose look universally cinched by a four-inch belt, with the hem two and a half inches below the knee.

Chanel at the end of the fifties is re-established as the most constant and popular of designers, offering a real alternative to this or that shortlived 'line'. In a time of great insecurity about fashion, she provides a glamorous, easy-to-wear, recognizable head-to-toe look that doesn't date. Her cardigan suits with chain-weighted jacket hems, beautiful linings and real pockets made to hold cigarettes and keys free the wearer from clothes-worries and give enormous self-confidence.

The long-hair cult begins with evening hair, real or false, swept up loosely round the head and marked like a turban with a big central jewel. High bead chokers built up the neck are the corollary to boat necklines and loose rolled-back collars.

Grey flannel makes the simple dresses and suits that dominate young fashion all winter, and becomes the first 'craze' of the sixties. *Vogue*'s new young photographers and copywriters combine in 'send up' fashion features that will be a feature of the sixties.

249

1

Irving Penn

SAINT LAURENT

2

SAINT LAURENT

The waist is back

3
CARDIN   Henry Clarke

4
SAINT LAURENT   Henry Clarke

1. Yves Saint Laurent's autumn 1959 collection for Dior raises the skirts to knee level and introduces a provocative new line, belted, with a knee level pull-in. It causes the greatest fashion outcry since the New Look.
2. Yves Saint Laurent's black taffeta ruffled with lace, worn with pink satin winkle-pickers.
3. Pierre Cardin's navy worsted dress with a cuffed boat neckline, belted waist, and a barrel skirt with a deep front pleat. The huge rolled-back straw hat is almost Cardin's signature.
4. Pale blue shantung pleats, cape-collared and belted by Yves Saint Laurent for Dior's spring collection.
5. A new evening look, long hair — real or added — wrapped round the head and jewelled, a high Edwardian choker.
6. Princesse Odile de Croy in Chanel's cardigan coat, nubbly beige wool piped with navy blue silk.

5

6
CHANEL

Henry Clarke

1960-1969

David Bailey

The Revolutionary Sixties

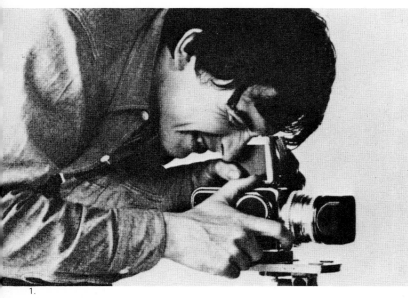

1.

Left: Jean Shrimpton in Mongolian lamb and over-the-knee boots, 1964.
1. David Bailey, 1965. 'They said that I wouldn't be a fashion photographer because I didn't have my head in a cloud of pink chiffon'.

'London is a city of and for the young,' wrote Peter Laurie in *Vogue* in 1964. 'Probably no other in the world offers us the opportunities that are here. Wherever enthusiasm, energy, iconoclasm or any kind of creative ability are needed, you'll find people in their mid-twenties or younger.' Britain had emerged from the turbulent last years of the fifties a changed country. 'In that period,' said American journalist John Crosby, writing for the *Daily Telegraph* colour supplement, 'youth captured this ancient island and took command in a country where youth had always before been kept properly in its place. Suddenly the young own the town.'

Everyone in the country who read the colour supplements or watched television could tell you who in particular owned the town, how they lived and the names of their friends. Yet the new social order was unrecognizable to members of the old establishment like Loelia, Duchess of Westminster, who told *Vogue*, 'London Society is a world which for better or worse no longer exists'. There was a new class system, and by the mid-sixties even *Private Eye* was referring – with disdain – to 'the new aristocracy'. They were all young, talented and concerned with the creation of 'image': pop singers, photographers, actors and model girls, pop artists, hairdressers, interior decorators, writers and designers. They came from all kinds of backgrounds. For instance, a cross-section of half a dozen, numbering David Bailey, Terence Donovan, Tony Armstrong-Jones, Alexander Plunket-Greene, Michael Caine and Terence Stamp, includes sons of an East Ham tailor, a Mile End lorry driver, an East End tugboat captain, a Billingsgate fishporter, a Q.C., and an organist. Because their prestige was founded on their talent, they shared a fierce respect for professionalism and treated any kind of amateurishness with contempt. They were aggressively self-confident, and – since nothing succeeds like success – became more so in the blaze of publicity. Any of them could have said in the words of Andrew Oldham, when joint manager of the Rolling Stones, 'I don't have to depend on other people's talents to get me on. I am good enough myself. I am good and I am going to get better.' There were no pretensions. When David Bailey published his *Box of Pin Ups*, designed by Mark Boxer and written by Francis Wyndham, he described the beginning of his career like this: 'I had a choice at this time, age 16, time Monday, 4.30 in the afternoon. I could either be a jazz musician, an actor, or a car thief ... They – from Mars or wherever they are – said I wouldn't be a fashion photographer because I didn't have my head in a cloud of pink chiffon. They forgot about one thing. I love to look at all women.' It was a feast for the press when he married French film star Catherine Deneuve in 1965, and the *Evening Standard* wrote, 'The bridegroom wore a light blue sweater ... and light green corduroy trousers', 'the bride

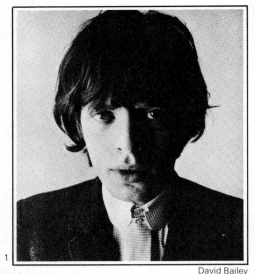

David Bailey

1

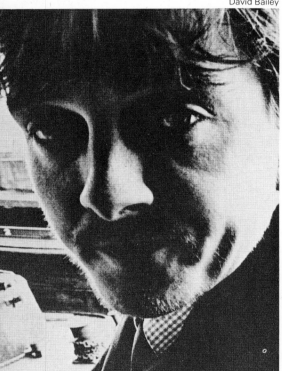

2

David Bailey

3

David Bailey

arrived smoking' and the best man, Mick Jagger, 'arrived with a blue denim suit and blue shirt with no tie'.

At every level, the sixties were a time of the young doing what they wanted better and more profitably than had been done before: a time of round pegs in round holes. Mary Quant had 'weathered the storm for the young designers' and in every field there were new opportunities to make revolutionary changes. Even in what had been the most reactionary circles, power was in the hands of the young. Roy Strong, talking to *Vogue* in 1967, when he was 'very young [at 32] to be the new Director of the National Portrait Gallery', was planning the first photographic exhibition in the museum's history. 'The great thing that all galleries have had to learn is that you have to go out to your public . . . Everybody's got it fixed in their mind that the National Portrait Gallery is terribly dull and dowdy, which, indeed, it was. Now the ordinary chap is coming in off the streets and saying, "Heavens, this is interesting, this is enjoyable." '

One thing Britain lacked, and felt the need of, was a young, dynamic political leader to fit the revolution, such as the U.S.A. had in President Kennedy. Between 1960 and 1963 the standing of Macmillan's government was falling sharply, and a note of envy

surfaced in *Vogue*, voiced by Mary Holland, who referred to America's 'new leader whose youth, vitality and firecracker energy make European statesmen seem like tired Victorians', and to 'the rest of us who still have old men at the top'. Part of *Vogue*'s interest in the President lay in his wife, Jacqueline Kennedy, who had won American *Vogue*'s talent contest in 1951 when, in answer to a question about People I Wish I Had Known, she had chosen Baudelaire, Oscar Wilde and Diaghilev. The good-looking and clothes-conscious Mrs Kennedy 'has resolutely eschewed the bunfight and the honky-tonk of the American political scene and is inclined, instead, to the gentler practice of painting, conversation, literature and fashion'.

Quite soon the youth cult was blown up out of all proportion by thousands of features in the magazines and newspapers. Arthur Jones, writing about the mods and mids in *Vogue*, said as early as 1964, 'There *is* a teenage society, there are new standards in England that are not quite local nor Standard English; but the whole hopeful, dynamic thing is frozen by the gorgon stare of the old, the rich, the powerful.' There was also a new language invented by and for the teenagers: not the 'pad', 'Daddy-oh' and 'real gone' that issued from the American teenagers, but, using Arthur

254

Duffy

1. Mick Jagger, photographed by David Bailey in 1964 when Baby Jane Holzer, New York socialite, was quoted by Tom Wolfe as saying, 'Wait till you see the Stones! They're so sexy! They're pure sex! They're divine!' etc.
2. David Hemmings, starring as the fashion photographer in *Blow Up*, Antonioni's film about London in 1966.
3. Terence Stamp, restauranteur with his restaurant manager Rex Tilt: the 'Trencherman' was 'down the far end of the King's Road — I mean really the far end — past the plexiglass and plastic palazzi, where London becomes English again after hesitating between more Contemporary Living and freaked out West Coast manqué'.
4. Mary Quant and Alexander Plunket-Greene, 1962, when they were *Vogue*'s 'Ultra front-room people'.
5. The royal marriage, 1960. Special acknowledgement for Brian Duffy, who photographed the glass coach as it returned to the Palace.
6. Mrs Kennedy drawn by Bouché, 1961.
7. President Kennedy, 'more presidential, less golden boy than usual in this portrait by Irving Penn'.

Irving Penn

1. Peter Hall, effective head of the Royal Shakespeare Company, 'the contemporary theatre's greatest entrepreneur and Britain's most versatile director'. Terence Donovan photographed him in 1965, the year he produced Schoenberg's *Moses and Aaron* at Covent Garden.
2. 'A new Nijinsky has been born'. The 23-year-old Rudolf Nureyev photographed by Irving Penn in 1961.
3. Harold Pinter who made his name with *The Caretaker*, 'Clinical recorder of the queasy maladies of society' in 1963.

Terence Donovan

Irving Penn

Jones's examples, 'Tone, nip up the G's and con the drummer for some charge so we can have a circus before charp.'

In the middle sixties *Vogue* ran headlines like 'The World Suddenly Wants to Copy the Way We Look. In New York it's the London Look, in Paris it's Le Style Anglais . . . Where fashion influence came from Hollywood, the Left Bank and Italian films, English girls now not only have the nerve to be themselves but can enjoy watching others copy them.' Britain had a new image all round. America's attention had been caught by British theatrical talent since Osborne's *Look Back in Anger* had been voted the best foreign play of the season on Broadway in 1958. Since then there had been plays by Brendan Behan, Lionel Bart, Robert Bolt and Shelagh Delaney, the tremendous success of *Beyond the Fringe* and the Establishment team, and Anthony Newley's *Stop The World, I Want To Get Off*: New York critics were talking about a 'British domination of Broadway'. At the 1963 Paris Biennale it was British artists who had stolen the thunder, particularly David Hockney, Peter Blake, Peter Phillips and Allen Jones, all from the Royal College of Art. When David Hockney's exhibition opened in New York the next year, it was sold out on the first day. The same year, Dame Margot Fonteyn and Rudolf Nureyev of the Royal Ballet dancing in Vienna received an ovation that beat all records, with 89 curtain calls. Britain was no longer a respectable bowler-hatted gentleman with a stiff upper lip: the last remnants of that image had been dissolved for ever by the Profumo affair.

More than anything, it was the phenomenal success of the Beatles' American tour within a year of President Kennedy's assassination that put anything British on top. When they arrived at Kennedy Airport the whole country became Beatle-obsessed. Hardly anyone noticed when Sir Alec Douglas-Home arrived there five days later. In March, American advance sales for the sixth record, *Can't Buy Me Love*, were 2 million, and the next month they held not only the first five places in the American Top Hundred, but also the first two places in the LP charts. If what Andrew Oldham said was true, pop music was taking the place of religion and the Beatles were gods. America's supreme accolade was to give them Carnegie Hall for the first pop concert in its history; England's, perhaps, was the serious evaluation by *The Times*' music critic, who said, among other things, 'one gets the impression that they think simultaneously of harmony and melody, so firmly are the major tonic sevenths and ninths built into their tunes, and the flat submediant key switches, so natural is the Aeolian cadence at the end of *Not a Second Time*' (the chord progression which ends Mahler's *Song of the Earth*) and admired 'the exhilarating and often quasi-instrumental vocal duetting, sometimes in scat or in falsetto, behind the melodic line; the melismas with altered vowels ("I saw her yesterday-ee-ay") which have not quite become mannered'.

Our other most popular export, the mini skirt, officially arrived in New York in 1965 with a British fashion show arranged by the Fashion House Group and held on board the *Queen Elizabeth*. The models in their thigh-high dresses stopped traffic on Broadway and in Times Square, and were seen on television all across the

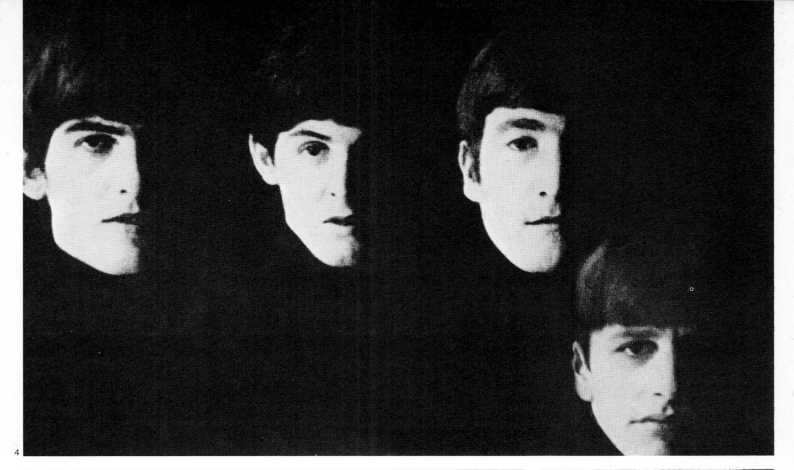

David Bailey

David Bailey

4. The Beatles, 1963.
5. Marianne Faithfull, discovered by Andrew Oldham at a party. How did he know she had a voice? 'He didn't. I haven't.'
6. Sandie Shaw, whose first hit song 'There's Always Something There to Remind Me' sold over a quarter of a million records. Daughter of a Dagenham welder, she became equally popular in France.

U.S.A. Mary Quant made a fortune there the same year when she took 30 outfits on a whistle-stop tour of 12 cities in 14 days, the models showing the clothes to a non-stop dance routine and pop music. She soon had a business worth a million pounds, selling to the U.S.A., France, and nearly every other country in the Western world, designing 28 collections a year. She received her O.B.E. for services to the fashion industry in 1966, and went to Buckingham Palace in a mini skirt.

Both the designers and the wearers were enjoying a new form of expression. The outlets were the pop-playing boutiques, packed with clothes ideas by and for the young. In 1960 an American girl fresh from campus told *Vogue*, 'I had a sort of idea things might be a bit stodgy here, but I couldn't have been more wrong. I have to put my hands in my pockets when I go around – especially all those small boutiques in Chelsea and Kensington.' You could try on as many clothes as you liked without being intimidated or reproached if you didn't buy: in fact it was sometimes difficult to find the assistant if you did want to buy. You never knew what you would find in a boutique. Seasonal cycles of stock were disrupted, and new looks arrived as soon as outworkers could get them finished, sometimes a few days after they had been designed. Girls who wanted to have first look at weekend stock learned to go along on a Friday evening when the boutiques took delivery and stayed open late. The fifteen- to nineteen-year-olds that had been a tiny fraction of the buying market in the mid-fifties grew in number until, in 1967, they were buying about half of all

1

the coats, dresses, knits and skirts being sold in the country. By then, to add to the deluge of ideas from home-grown designers, boutiques were selling every unusual thing in the world that you could wear, from rough Greek wool sweaters to saris; kimonos to harem pants; caftans to half-cured sheepskins from Turkey and Afghanistan. The fashion categories of the fifties, 'formal' and 'casual', had ceased to have any meaning. In 1960 *Vogue* photographed Mary Quant's dark striped pinafore with a black sweater for day, and on its own for going out to dinner. By 1965, the women at any smart party would be divided into two groups: half in the shortest skirts, half in full-length evening dresses, and neither feeling out of place.

One boutique that stands out from the rest because of its immediate and continuing popularity is Biba. Its originator and fashion designer, Barbara Hulanicki, began the original mail-order business in 1964, calling it after her sister. Her husband, Stephen Fitz-Simon directs all the business aspects and runs the Biba empire. As a boutique, Biba started in undistinguished two-room premises off Kensington High Street. What made it different from the start was its dark, exotic, glittering interior, jumbled clothes, feathers, beads and Lurex spilling out over the counters like treasure in a cave. Its gimmick was the incredible cheapness of the clothes. There were no price tickets, but the poorest student could afford to say 'I'll have it' before asking 'How much?' In 1966, for £15, the price of a Mary Quant party dress, you could walk out of Biba in a new coat, dress, shoes, petticoat and hat. Stephen Fitz-Simon says, 'We could always spot a member of the trade turning a dress inside out to see how it was possible to sell it for so little.' Biba was often so crowded on a Saturday that there would be a queue waiting to be let in one by one as customers left, and Barbara Hulanicki remembers, 'We had to go out every day with a damp cloth to wipe the nose marks off the window.' By the end of the sixties the clothes were no longer so cheap and Biba was an all-in-one store, but it had more than a gimmick, it had an immediately recognizable image of its own. This is hard to define, being derived from Art Nouveau and Art Deco but, in the mood rather than the style, having more to do with the current idea of what they were like than the reality.

The sixties made Britain into a fashion leader and the most inventive country in the world. A million and one young designers were spilling out of the art schools, bursting with new ideas and practical expertise. As *Vogue* said in 1962, in a feature called Fresh Air in the Rag Trade: 'For the first time the young people who work in the rag trade are making and promoting the clothes they naturally like: clothes which are relevant to the way they live ... ours is the first generation that can express itself on its own terms.' As David Bond put it, 'I tend to design clothes I'd like to see my girl friends in.' An unprecedented flow of talent was coming from the Royal College of Art under the aegis of Professor Janey Ironside – Zandra Rhodes, Marion Foale and Sally Tuffin, Bill Gibb, Ossie Clark, Graham Smith, Christopher McDonnell, Anthony Price. 'She taught by the tone of her voice,' said Graham Smith. 'She never told us that something was terrible. She didn't have to. She gave us the know-how and then left us the greatest freedom.' Not all the talent went into the boutiques. Jean Muir, for instance, our leading classic fashion designer, went to Jaeger for six years, and was backed by Courtaulds when she opened as Jane & Jane in 1962. She emerged independently with a unique standard in line and proportion – her clothes are meticulously controlled, demure, and reveal every line of the body. Zandra Rhodes finally found at Fortnum & Mason the freedom to extend her prints into clothes, making floating chiffons and crinoline nets coloured with a painter's palette. They are at the same time delicately executed and the last word in upstaging technique – you can't miss a girl in a Zandra Rhodes dress. Woollands 21 Shop, under the clever guidance of Vanessa Denza gave a boost to many of the best designers, including Ossie Clark, who made them a special collection while he was still at the Royal College of Art. Many, too, went to the best chain fashion shops such as Wallis: Jeffrey Wallis was a key figure in the recognition and promotion of British designing talent. He had already made the Chanel suit almost a uniform among well-off working women, and had kept the distinction and comfort of these suits by using the identical fabrics that Chanel had chosen. Equating good design with good profits, he told *Vogue*, 'The rise of positive thought that's strongly and independently creative is one of the most exciting things that's happened in England. Today a market exists of around 5,000,000 people in America, Europe and England all on the same fashion wavelength. Today the provinces are places like Texas, not Manchester. Young designers are springing up all the time; industry is creating the climate for them, top buyers the right type of background.'

Meanwhile in the face of this tremendous competition, the British couture members were growing fewer and fewer. In 1966 when they numbered seven, the hard facts were that a suit, with three fittings, came to between £90 and £200: a best-seller would not exceed an edition of 25. Even Michael, who dressed the most Parisian-minded of London's couture market, would have found it difficult had he not had an arrangement with Marks & Spencer, supervising their fashion design. Here and in Paris the couture began to turn to boutiques and ready-to-wear – Nina Ricci, Yves Saint Laurent, Cardin and Lanvin among others.

By 1967 fashion had finished with the 'space age' look, and designers began to see the future in terms of the present again. In the Courrèges heyday geometric haircuts, creaking welded plastics, silver and chalk white had become almost a uniform. 'Courrèges clothes are so beautiful,' said Andy Warhol. 'Everyone should look the same. Dressed in silver. Silver doesn't look like anything. It merges into everything. Costumes should be worn during the day

2
Robert Freson

with lots of make-up.' Fashion had embraced brutalism and gone off at a wild tangent. In reaction there was a passion for the most romantic of dressing-up clothes. There were three schools of fashion – the flower power school, the ethnic peasant look, and *Viva Maria* ruffles and ringlets. By the end of the decade, nostalgia reigned; people turned back to the recent past for looks from the most heavily stylized and most easily identifiable decades. Girls were wearing slippery culottes, square-shouldered suits with scarlet lipstick, and beaded twenties dresses found in the antique markets. Bernard Nevill, whose Jazz Collection fabrics for Liberty had given the mood so much impetus, told *Vogue*, 'Initially Art Deco 69 was influenced by the flat florals and geometrics of Art Deco 25, which designers find fit so well the mood of Pop Culture. Now the trend is spreading in other directions as people collect the furniture, jewellery, ceramics and graphics of the period. And converging with this interest – a nostalgia for the 30s and 40s styles which are equally relevant now.' He emphasized the difference between Art Deco 69 and Art Deco 25. So much gets in the way of the reconstruction of a look from another time – the way you stand, your make up, how you want to appear, the underclothes you wear, the air you breathe – making the most careful copy only a parallel. The style that Aldous Huxley had described as 'A mixture of greenhouse and hospital ward furnished in the style of a dentist's operating chamber' was now the inspiration for the interiors of the smartest Chelsea houses and Regent's Park flats.

The scope of the fashion revolution can be seen at a glance in men's fashion. From the revival of Edwardian dandyism in the fifties via longer hair, printed shirts and no ties, polo-neck sweaters and skintight jeans, men were dressing in satin, chiffon, frills and lace by the end of the sixties. Mick Jagger wore a white organdie dress (with trousers) for an open air concert, and the mods appeared in high heels, with handbags and plucked eyebrows. Even the men who had changed their appearance least had changed a lot. Plain grey suits turned out close at hand to be made of rainbow weaves. 'Hooray Henrys' wore sheepskins, cavalry twills and paisley cravats: their trousers were cut in a slim backward curve, and their trouser hems were cut to lift over the instep. John Taylor of the *Tailor and Cutter* attributed it all to sex: 'It's simple; men want to look younger and more attractive now. England is not such a man's world as it was.' *Vogue* attributed it to women: 'The hand that rocks the cradle is at last having some influence on the droopy fawn cardigan and the grey socks round the ankle', and found that 'The Englishman's view that to be at all dandified is effete – or worse – is changing. After-shave lotions are established, deodorants a necessary commonplace, and colognes are catching on.' Fancy dress reached its height in 1968, when Christopher Gibbs urged *Vogue* readers to buy and wear the Diaghilev ballet costumes being auctioned at Sotheby's: 'There is nothing wrong in loving young men (though loving everyone is where it's at) . . . I'm sure Diaghilev would have been delighted to see his extravaganzas clothing the supple limbs of young Voguesters, bringing a pinch of the glory of All the Russias to dowdy gimcrack London . . . Come in colours, and the grey pox will never catch you. Heed only the poets and the painters and you'll never go wrong.'

Running away from the grey pox was a recurring theme of the decade. When Kenneth Tynan gave the name satire to the humour of *Beyond the Fringe*, a university review on the outskirts of the Edinburgh Festival in 1960, he remarked, 'England is complacent and the young are bored. There is the desire to hear breaking glass.' Humour had grown cruel and subtle since the early days of the rollicking moon-mad Goons, and it became the favourite weapon of the press. Peter Laurie was not entirely free of satirical intent himself when he wrote in *Vogue*, 'The intellectually aware will no doubt have noticed a new journalistic commodity in vogue among the cultured press: satire.' He pointed out that the Angry Young Men had quickly exhausted the value of sheer protest, but had uncovered a mine of social material which they had scarcely had time to work. Jonathan Miller said that the English seemed unable to be funny in their own voices, but in turning their attention to the target instead of the audience, the satirists found a new lightness of touch. 'There is an assumption that we are moderately well read and moderately familiar with what more serious artists and thinkers are doing,' said Peter Laurie, and Mary Holland wrote about *That Was The Week That Was* as 'this anarchic, unkind, uneven and often downright sick arrival to B.B.C. television . . . It is certainly not well-intentioned. It is sharp-tongued, cruel, sophisticated, and, praise be, firm in its belief that the audience is as clever as itself and capable of enjoying the same jokes.' Satire depended on a supply of targets ripe for sustained attack, and as these fell away towards the end of the sixties, this particular vein ran dry.

In the cinema, the decade began with long queues for foreign films. Londoners lost their interest in Cinerama, Todd A-O and Cinemascope, and went instead to the *nouvelle vague* films of Louis Malle, Claude Chabrol and Jean-Luc Godard, or the new Antonioni or Fellini from Italy. 'In the windy chill of London's Westbourne Grove,' said *Vogue* in 1960, 'people queue past the baker's shop and down the side street to see *Hiroshima Mon Amour*. There are four shows a day, all packed; no seats are bookable and

Peter Laurie

3   Peter Laurie   Peter Laurie

1. 'The attic dressers' drawn by Roger Law: dandies who dress in frilly shirts and frock coats from the Portobello Road, striped Edwardian suits from the attic and panamas, silver-topped canes and watch chains.

2. *Private Eye:* 'Its strength is that the editors write solely to please themselves'. Christopher Booker, William Rushton, Richard Ingrams.
3. David Frost of *'That Was The Week That Was'*.
4. Cabaret at The Establishment, Jeremy Geidt, John Fortune, John Bird and Eleanor Bron.

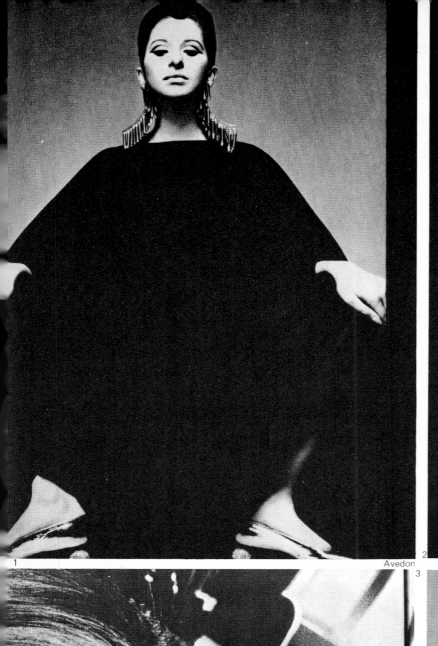

1

2

Avedon

Cecil Beaton

David Bailey

4

3

the telephone is permanently engaged. With this, his first feature film, director Alain Resnais joins the ranks of the new French film-makers who make us stand in line while many cinemas are half empty.' Resnais followed up with *Last Year in Marienbad*, developing the use of flashbacks to introduce the past into the present and give a feeling of *déjà vu*. Foreign films had a great influence on British directors, and the birth of neo-realist films like Karel Reisz's *Saturday Night and Sunday Morning*, produced by John Osborne's and Tony Richardson's Woodfall Films. 'With this film,' said Francis Wyndham, 'the British cinema has really grown up at last, indeed one might argue that this is the first British film ever made. It is about working class life today.' There followed a remarkable series of British films including *A Taste of Honey*, *The Loneliness of the Long Distance Runner*, *A Kind of Loving* and *Billy Liar*. Directors of all nationalities were aware of each other's work and films became much more cosmopolitan. To take three key films of the sixties, Richard Lester's Beatles vehicle *A Hard Day's Night*

and Joseph Losey's sinister *The Servant*, with brilliant performances by Dirk Bogarde and James Fox, were both made by Americans living and working in England, and Antonioni's *Blow-Up* by an Italian in London. A characteristic of the sixties was the fantasy fulfilment theme followed by a nightmarish ending – as in *Jules et Jim*, *Lolita* and *Bonnie and Clyde*.

'To those who say, "what was good enough for my father is good enough for me",' said the catalogue of the John Moores Liverpool exhibition, 'modern methods will not commend themselves in art as well as in transportation or heating.' After the 'British Painting of the Sixties' show at the Whitechapel, Edward Lucie-Smith introduced the work of a handful of dissimilar painters to *Vogue* readers and explained how wariness, toughness, worldliness and a scrupulous professionalism were now part of an artist's equipment. David Hockney, he said, 'has had the good fortune to find himself at the head of a well-defined new school of painting – the so-called "Pop Art" movement. What nobody seems to have

1. Avedon's portrait of *Funny Girl* Barbra Streisand in Grès navy linen poncho, and Roger Vivier's gold ball-heeled slippers. Barbra Streisand ('that second A, who needs it?') was made for success and fought for it. *Vogue* said, 'When she is being bothered — or thinks she is — she doesn't allow irritation to show; she simply darts out a beam of pure poison and lodges it in the annoyer.'
2. Audrey Hepburn in an Ascot dress designed by Cecil Beaton for *My Fair Lady:* all white and black. 'The costumes must step ahead of the past to have influence', said Cecil Beaton, 'but the ghost of my Aunt Jessie is present in all of them. I remember her as she returned from Paris with enormous five-foot-square boxes filled with hats and glittering finery', and Audrey Hepburn said, 'He makes you look the way you have always wanted to look' and asked for one of the costumes to keep.
3. Pauline Boty, 26, actress, painter, beauty, a distillation of the 1960s, who died tragically young.
4. Jane Asher, friend of Paul McCartney but also a considerable actress, with a dozen features and television films already behind her in 1964.
5. Frederico Fellini with a *Vogue* model, photographed by William Klein beside the 'gigantesco' poster for *La Dolce Vita*, the 'biggest and most controversial success in Italian movie history', 1960.

William Klein   263

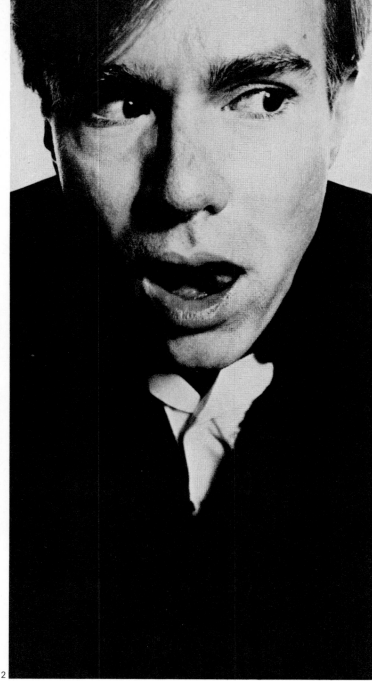

David Bailey

noticed is that Hockney is at his best just where he is least closely affiliated to Pop . . . he is a true narrative painter.' Howard Hodgkin was 'representative of a more sober kind of figurative painting . . . the nearest thing to a really classical artist'. Eschewing fashion in a fashion magazine, he told readers to look at a painting they would like to buy and see it as it would look in ten years' time – 1973 – 'just at the moment when it is most out of fashion, most *déjà vu*'. When *Vogue* interviewed Andy Warhol in 1965 he was more interested in Minimalism than Pop, and delivered to Polly Devlin a non-interview to go with his intentionally empty art-works. 'Edie is with us,' he informed her. 'The film with Edie for the festival is very beautiful. Half of it's out of focus and she does nothing . . . I flick on the switch and the film makes itself . . . Movies are so boring and you can sit and watch mine and think about yourself or whatever you want to think about. I don't know what I'm doing either. It keeps us busy.' He ventured that Tennessee Williams had written a script for him: 'Really only a title. It's "F and S". That's all. He wrote it. I'll make a film of it when I get back.' 'What does it mean?' 'What does it mean to you?' Does Warhol collect anything himself? 'All this art is finished . . . Squares on the wall. Shapes on the floor. Emptiness. Empty rooms . . . Redundant. That's what my art is all about.'

A year later, Elaine Dundy interviewed another celebrity of the sixties, Tom Wolfe, whose *Kandy-Kolored Tangerine-Flake Stream-line Baby* arrived in England via Jonathan Cape. His way of writing, his feud with the *New Yorker* and his extravagant form of dress had made him a V.I.P. in the U.S.A., and here he had a considerable impact on journalism, particularly on magazine and advertising copywriting. The new Wild Man of American literature, he had savagely attacked the *New Yorker* style, 'which requires that whenever you mention, say, an actor's name, you give the play he was in at the time, the cast, the theatre, and the length of time it ran and you get a fact-stuffed sentence that's quite beside the point . . . People only write in careful flowing sentences. They don't think that way and they don't talk that way.' Elaine Dundy described his clothes – a pale grey sharkskin suit and a tie twice as wide as usual with clowns dancing on it . . . 'It is necessary to refer to his clothes because he ascribes almost magical properties to them. "If that shirt and that shirt were running a race," he will say, pointing to what appear to be two identical shirts, "that shirt would win."' His style was hyperbolic, colloquial and immediate.

> I shall burst this placid pink shell
> I shall wake up slightly hungover,
> Favoured, adored, worshipped and clamoured for.
> I shall raise Hell and be a real
> Cut-up.

1. Edward Lucie-Smith's chosen painters, 1963. *Left*: David Hockney leaning on 'Two Friends'. *Centre above*: John Howlin below his 'I'll remember April'. *Centre below*: Ian Stephenson in front of 'Panchromatic'. *Right:* Howard Hodgkin and his 'Julia and Margaret'.
2. Andy Warhol, 1965.
3. Tom Wolfe, 'Wild Man' of American literature. Elaine Dundy said that he dressed to give offence to his viewers — to 'shake 'em up'. He himself said 'Everything's wrong with my coat . . .

too wide lapels, too much shoulder-padding and more buttons than a policeman's uniform', but he looked good in his clothes, as he was well aware.
4. *Hair*, America's Tribal Love-Rock Musical. Avedon photographed the writers James Rado and Gerome Ragni with Lynn Kellog who played Sheila.
5. Portraits in the style of new painters, photographed by David Montgomery. Looking like a Lichenstein, Charlotte Rampling.

3   Jack Robinson

4   Avedon

5   Montgomery

'The idea of what is news today is still a nineteenth-century concept,' he said. 'Perfect Journalism would deal constantly with one subject: Status.'

The dynamic turmoil of the late fifties and early sixties had become the nervous stimulation of the mid-sixties. In reaction to the orgy of commercialism that had characterized the decade, there was the alternative society of the idealists, the flower people using words like 'love' and 'freedom' in a woolly way. But it soon became evident that the alternative society was just as ripe for exploitation as any other. Underground magazines were paid for by record advertisements. *Hair* ('What do you want to be, besides dishevelled?') supposedly genuinely hippy, had an advance ticket sale of $250,000. In the U.S.A. flower-power was turning ugly in the heat of anti-Vietnam agitation: among the serious demonstrators were every kind of provocative revolutionary. In London the hippies found they could not live and buy pot by making candles and Batik prints alone. Rather than take National Assistance, a few dropped out and went to farm in the remotest parts of the country. For the most responsible and constructive thinkers – the Des Wilsons and the Naders – the conclusion seemed to be that we must do the best we can with what we have, working from inside the system to redress the balance and make good. With exploding populations and shrinking resources, the question already was, 'Is it too late?'

JEAN SHRIMPTON

Jean Shrimpton, top model and international figure of the 1960s, was the first high fashion model to be a favourite pin-up too. She was the most natural of models, and made the elegant and expensive clothes relate to the whole world of girls of her own age and type. She began modelling in 1960, and was only 19 when David Bailey's pictures of her began to dominate *Vogue* a couple of years later. *Vogue* called her 'just marvellously pretty' but it is a fact that it was almost impossible to take a bad picture of her — even in her passport picture she looks a great beauty. Barry Lategan says, 'She always looks as though being photographed is exactly what she wanted to do.' Jean Shrimpton told 'About Town' in a 1962 interview, 'I'm not a classical beauty. Nor beatnik really. But nearer beatnik than classical. I've been lucky, but I'm riding the crest of a wave. In a year everyone might be against my type of looks.' However she continues into the 1970s to have an uncontrived glamour that hasn't tarnished. She got out at the top, and lives in the country refusing modelling assignments and working at photography. She shows signs of real talent at the other side of the lens.

1. 1972.
2. Jean Shrimpton in New York: navy blazer suit by Slimma in a Chinatown telephone box, a pagoda in red, green and gold, 1962.
3. In a black dress by Fredrica, 1962.
4. Wallis cotton piqué suit, 1965.

2
SLIMMA   David Bailey

3

4
David Bailey

John Encome

2

Avedor

VANESSA REDGRAVE

1. Vanessa Redgrave at the party following the première of *Isadora* in 1969. She is the daughter of Sir Michael Redgrave, and had been on the stage for several years before she made her film debut in *Morgan*, 1966. With her appearance in *Blow-Up* a year later she was hailed as 'the intellectual woman: withdrawn, neurotic and sexy'. *Isadora* was her first star vehicle, followed by the film *The Seagull* and *Oh What a Lovely War*. Politically minded, independent and revolutionary, she has never conformed to a star image: Norman Parkinson says, 'her heart has always ruled her head'.

CATHERINE DENEUVE

2. Perfectly beautiful Catherine Deneuve, photographed by Avedon. 25 in 1969, she had just completed her twenty-sixth film, *La Sirène de Mississippi* for Truffaut. *Vogue* said, 'A cool independence and iron will have singled her out from a bourgeois background to the amoral medium of the modern cinema, from a beautiful heroine to an actress with the enigmatic quality that makes her unique in the field, from a French star to an international one.' Francis Wyndham called her 'a cool combination of the virginal and the vicious'. She has evolved a school of acting so transparent and effortless that it's almost non-acting.

VERUSCHKA

3. Veruschka, top model, her face painted by Antonio, 1968. Face and body painting were a feature of the late 1960s, and no one did it better or more often than this tall and beautiful German countess.

JEANNE MOREAU

4. Jeanne Moreau, French actress of stage and screen who became well-known in England through films of the early 1960s like *Les Liaisons Dangereuses, La Notte* and *Jules et Jim,* which had a great impact on young fashion in 1961. A year later *Vogue* showed this photograph by Dave Budnick and called her 'latest in the long line of sadder but wiser girls in the French cinema'. She starred with Brigitte Bardot in *Viva Maria* in 1965, another film that influenced fashion when it arrived in Britain.

JULIE CHRISTIE

5. Julie Christie, international English film actress, made a great impact with a passing appearance in *Billy Liar*, 1963, starring Tom Courtenay *Vogue* called her 'a kooky blonde' and 'one of the best things in the film'. From drama school and a job in a bottling factory, she became a star in her own right and went on to secure her fame in films like *Darling, Dr Zhivago* and *Far From The Madding Crowd* — she made eight well-known films in the 1960s. Photographed by Roberta Booth in 1967.

SOPHIA LOREN

6. Sophia Loren, internationally famous Italian film star and beauty, with one of her two sons. The Ponti family live in complete seclusion in a large sixteenth-century villa half-an-hour's drive from Rome. Sophia Loren told *Vogue* about her day: she gets up at 5.30, has a cup of black coffee, exercises for ten minutes, spends the morning with her children in the garden and reading scripts. She has lunch with her husband, takes a siesta, and goes to bed at 7.30, often skipping dinner. She says, 'I only spend my time doing things which I consider worthwhile' and never goes shopping or to films, has no interest in clothes, jewels or cars. Her make up takes 20 minutes.

Snowdon

ELIZABETH TAYLOR

Elizabeth Taylor is perhaps the last of the great world-famous movie stars, complete with diamonds, private planes and yachts, and a chain of husbands — Conrad Hilton, Michael Wilding, Michael Todd, Eddie Fisher and Richard Burton to date. British born, she evacuated with her family to Hollywood during the war and became a child star in such films as *Lassie Come Home* and *National Velvet.* She was posing for cheese-cake pictures when she was fifteen, and her amazing violet-eyed black-and-white beauty was already undeniable. Elizabeth Taylor and Richard Burton were the world's most spectacular couple in the 1960s, and could guarantee an audience for any picture they played in. Even so, the blockbuster *Cleopatra* almost sank Twentieth Century Fox — to break even, it was said, the film had to bring in over 40 million dollars. By 1969 she had made 38 films, including her shattering performance with Burton in *Who's Afraid of Virginia Woolf.* In private life, she is extremely generous with her money where children's charities are concerned, donating around a million dollars a year, and has a large family of her own both by marriage and by adoption. 'Liz Taylor is 40,' ran *Life*'s cover in 1972,'. . . and all of us are suddenly middle-aged.'

1. 1953.
2. 1965.
3. In a wig designed to match her dog, 1972.
4. With Richard Burton at the 'Proust' ball given by Guy de Rothschild, 1972. She was dressed as Ida Rubinstein, in black taffeta and lace, emerald roses and a black egret cockade, all by Valentino; the Burton diamond on a black velvet ribbon around her neck.

1

2

William Klein

3

Cecil Beaton

Norman Parkinson

270

'Brevity is the soul of fashion'

'The beat look is the news at Dior . . . pale zombie faces; leather suits and coats; knitted caps and high turtleneck collars, black endlessly'

'St Tropez has burgeoned into one of the great playgrounds of the western world. It's Bardot and Sagan territory . . . an odd mixture of slightly scruffy insouciance and tremendous chic. Fashions started here one year are worn on beaches round the world the next'

'Young' begins to appear as the persuasive adjective for all fashions, hairstyles and ways of life: Bazaar's new clothes are prominent and after Bardot's pink gingham and *broderie anglaise* summer, even Paris begins to take St Tropez into account. Hair is backbrushed and waved, a long spiky fringe is brushed over the forehead, and eye make up begins to steal attention from lipstick. Best 'young' fashion investments are a pinafore, striped or flannel, to wear with or without a tight black sweater, and a leather suit, more tempting than a fur coat. Young Idea shows dark plaid knitted stockings, rainshirts, kneelength jeans worn inside a full unbuttoned skirt. The 'art student' look is everywhere, always qualified by *Vogue* 'not beat, not scruffy, but pretty'.

From Paris there are formal evening dresses, Chanel's rough white tweed cardigan suits edged with wide navy and scarlet braid — much copied, and a Wallis shops best seller — and Yves Saint Laurent's collection for Dior: a short skirt, gathered over the hips and tightened at the knee. At its most exaggerated, it's called the 'puffball' skirt. His 'beat' collection is the most unpopular look in Paris, and his last for Dior.

Page opposite: Patti Boyd wears Thocolette's topless Liberty lawn nightdress; photograph by David Bailey.
1. The art student pinafore from Bazaar, Young Idea's 1960 essential: grey and black stripes, worn with a tight black sweater and black stockings for day . . . and by itself for the evening, with a patent purse and stilettos.

1960

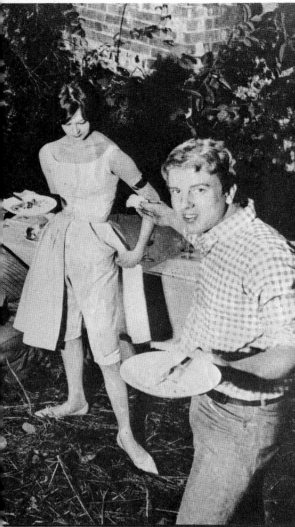

Duffy

McLaughlin-Gill

3

1. Blue and white striped kneelength jeans and matching skirt, wide-necked top and pointed pumps.
2. The bouffant hairdo, worn with pearls, white gloves, black broadtail jacket.
3. The 1960s leather suit. Sun spectacles are a new accessory.

KIKI BYRNE

Claude Virgin

4 | SAINT LAURENT   Penn

5 | CHANEL   Penn

6 | TRACY   Duffy

7 | DIOR   Duffy

8 | JEAN ALLEN   Duffy

4. Saint Laurent's unpopular last collection for Dior. 'The beat look, the Left Bank, is the news at Dior . . . pale zombie faces; leather suits and coats; knitted caps and high turtle-neck collars, black endlessly.'

5. Chanel's much copied 1960 suit: rough white tweed bound in navy braid.

6. Tom Courtenay, fresh from Konstantin in *The Seagull* at the Old Vic, said, 'I don't like that', to which the model, dressed in a gold lurex jersey cardigan suit replied, 'Well, try to like it.'

7. Kenneth More took time off from *The Greengage Summer* for the photograph. He liked the model's

Christian Dior dress: 'the bed jacket drape's wonderful'.

8. Lionel Bart working on *Blitz*, a follow-up to *Oliver* and *Fings*, said, 'It's amazing how I don't notice clothes . . . but she looks slightly off-beat, which I like.' The model is wearing a brown silk faille dress.

1961-62

'Young Idea is Gone on Moreau – clothes with the kind of tough gamin charm sparked off by Jeanne Moreau in the film *Jules et Jim*'

'What to wear with your new wig; chiffon culottes'

The 'Twist' arrives from France and is danced first at the Saddle Room. The Truffaut film *Jules et Jim* sets a fashion for grandmother spectacles with round wire frames, long mufflers, gaiters, boots, kilts, Gorblimey caps and knickerbockers. The culotte skirt is a new look, in suede, in tweed or chiffon. Bazaar and Kiki Byrne make sleeveless jumpersuits with pleated skirts, Mary Quant's in soft grey tweed bound with wide black braid. Girls are saving their money for the new coats — V-neck black leather cardigans, suede trenchcoats, or Gerald McCann's rabbit coat, the cheapest fur at 35 gn. Foreign buyers are becoming aware of the explosion of new British fashion talent: the London Fashion Week produces more than a million pounds worth of additional export business. In March 1962 *Vogue* applauds Edward Rayne's success in capturing the American press and buyers, bringing them over from Paris to see the shows of the Incorporated Society of London Fashion Designers, and getting them back in time for the Saint Laurent collection. Mary Quant makes a highly successful trip to America.

In Paris, 'The most heartfelt sounds during collections week were the bravos, ecstatic tears and kisses that greeted Marc Bohan after his first showing at Dior. It was the succès fou of Paris. Back again was the old Dior tradition of desirable, wearable clothes, each new design drawing choruses of oohs and aahs from the enraptured spectators.' Meanwhile Saint Laurent opens his independent couture house, and *Vogue* photographs a plain white dress with a cut out back and a circus pony turban, bought by Fortnum & Mason. His autumn collection brings the Left Bank look into the couture with total success. No one can deny the new elegance of his black ciré satins with ruffs of black mink, his rajah coats and tubular dresses worn with turbans and dark stockings, his long pulled-down tops and barrel skirts, all decorated with rich dark jewellery. Balenciaga makes a deep country suit in soft thick tweed with flat leather boots to the knee, and a slim city suit with belling peplum and hem. Bohan at Dior makes a dress that blouses over the waist, and bases a whole collection on matchbox seams, squaring off the silhouettes of suits and coats.

Wigs begin to edge into the fashion picture. Most hairdressers, *Vogue* reports, are telling their staff to cut down on back combing and advising clients to buy false pieces instead. Everyone wants more hair, adding thickness and height, whether the cut is short and curly or long, heavy and swinging. Lipsticks begin to pale down as eye make up gets heavier.

The new fluid all-in-one creams are the biggest make up revolution right now, giving an unpowdered matt complexion.

Jean Shrimpton and the *Jules et Jim* look: knickerbockers and Jackie Coogan cap, black leather jerkin and white cotton shirt.

Duffy

1 SAINT LAURENT   Penn

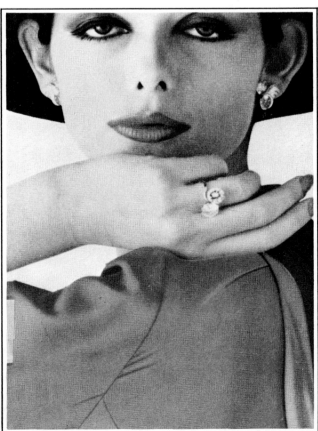

1. The Left Bank look makes good now that Saint Laurent finds his independent fashion identity: black ciré satin cuffed in black mink.
2. Nine-tenths rabbit coat, 'affordable fur'.
3. Make up at full power in 1962, with the new all-in-one foundation creams.

2 GERALD McCANN   Peter Rand   Claude Virgin   277

1961-62

1
POLLY PECK   Duffy

2   David Bailey   3 MOSBROOK   ANELLO & DAVIDE   Duffy

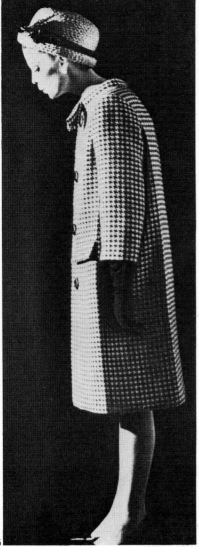

4
SUSAN SMALL   Peter Rand

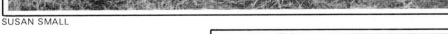

5 MARC BOHAN   William Klein

1. *Jules et Jim*'s influence on Young Idea: here, grey cardigan suit with a V neck over a black leather sweater.

2. By 1962, the concensus among top hairdressers like Raphael and Leonard, André Bernard, Aldo of Aldobruno, Raymond and Steiner is that false pieces add height and bulk more satisfactorily than back-combing, which breaks the hair.

3. Yellow and black tartan kilt, with yellow shantung shirt and black high-heeled boots.

4. Instead of the little black dress, the schoolmarm blouse in tucked cotton with a black bow, long grey flannel skirt.

5. Marc Bohan's matchbox coat for Dior, in black and white check tweed with the bow of the dress showing at the neck.

6. From Yves Saint Laurent's first independent collection, a white silk crepe dress with a swimsuit back, a circus pony turban.

6
SAINT LAURENT   Helmut Newton

1963

'Boots, boots and more boots are marching up and down like seven leaguers, climbing to new leg lengths and taking with them stockings and kneesocks in thick depths of textures'

'The rule for dressing this winter: legs first'

'People are talking about . . . the secret rouging of knees above white socks'

Saint Laurent brings leather indoors, 'makes brass studs smarter than rubies' and shows women how to dress for their boots. He makes boots in alligator, covering the whole length of the legs to the thighs. Every woman who owns a tweed suit is buying a pair of boots, and there are dozens of heights and shapes to choose from. When legs show, they are covered in cables, paisleys, rugger socks, diamonds and tartans. 'There's a positive preoccupation with the fear of an arctic winter,' says *Vogue* in autumn, and it helps to sell Victorian vests and long underpants in stripes or diamonds edged with lace and made in stretchy Helanca, red flannel nightshirts and fur hats pulled down over the ears. In this year of the Profumo affair and Beatlemania, all the new looks are tied up with Vidal Sassoon's important new haircut — very hard, very architectural, a thick chopped bob that's shaped to bare the top of the neck, or falling a little longer in limp curves, straight as silk. Vidal Sassoon's talk of bone structure and head shape leads to rethinking in make up and a new interest in hats. *Vogue* talks of rouge being used not so much for colour as 'contouring the cheekbones', and James Wedge designs a collection of hats to go with the Sassoon cuts, sold from boutiques in the hair salons. Boo Field Reid makes more anti-establishment hats, including Bardot headscarves, Jules et Jim caps, and tweed baseball caps. The newest shape is the helmet fitting the head like a bathing cap, with a chin strap, in white fur by James Wedge, in black satin with a cartwheel brim by Dior. Herbert Johnson are selling as many bowlers to women as to men, in stitched dark velvets.

The Look for winter. Muffling brown check suit, with a skunk busby and boots of brown suede and patent leather, patterned tights and leather gloves.

David Bailey

MATITA

False eyelashes are an essential part of make up, but *Vogue* shows how to shape and trim them so that they only add a little thickness to the outer corners of the eyes. 'The beat look, left-bank pallor and the Cleopatra eye are off the beam: paint eye contours on with a thin line, using a tiny brush.'

1963 brings new young designers into *Vogue:* Foale and Tuffin from the R.C.A., with their cut-out shift dress; Roger Nelson, also from the College, with his designs for Woollands; Clive Evans who opens his couture house this year, and French designer Emmanuelle Khanh, working in Paris on her *'nouveau classique'* look. Her suits are meticulous and architectural, narrow and fitted tightly to the shoulder, every line curving. Onto this careful structure she adds exactly proportioned cuff and shoulder widths, revers and flaps curling away like petals. Her look is called 'the droop', and goes with the Vidal Sassoon haircut, and owl

spectacles. Within a few months of *Vogue*'s first pictures, many ready-to-wear dresses and suits sprout long spaniel's ear collars.

Mary Quant launches her new Ginger Group — a collection of cheap clothes to be collected piece by piece and put together in endless variations. From Paris, bias shift dresses, Saint Laurent's peasant shirt and painter's smock, and Cardin's cut-out smocks baring the skin or the close-fitted dress beneath. Bohan makes a pinstripe suit for Dior, with leg o'mutton sleeves and kilt skirt, his signature a white gardenia worn with everything. Chanel goes from strength to strength: her newest suit is in rough rainbow tweed, thick as a thick-knit sweater. Saint Laurent's black and white geometric shifts are the easiest of all French looks to copy: in April, *Vogue* shows two spreads of them from the British ready-to-wear.

MARY QUANT   Terence Donovan

2   Peter Rand

1. Mary Quant's sailcloth
sand-coloured dungarees with a
black shirt.
2. The Vidal Sassoon haircut.
3. Emmanuelle Khanh, young French
designer discovered by *Vogue*, wearing
one of her own '*nouveau classique*'
suits: cream checked Harris tweed, the
silk shirt echoing the falling revers of
the jacket.
4. New all-stretch corselette in
Lycra net.

4 WARNER   281
   Henry
   Clarke

David Bailey

CHANEL

Penn

MISS
POLLY

282 3

TUFFIN
& FOALE

4

Carapetian

5
SAINT LAURENT   Penn

6
SAINT LAURENT   Penn

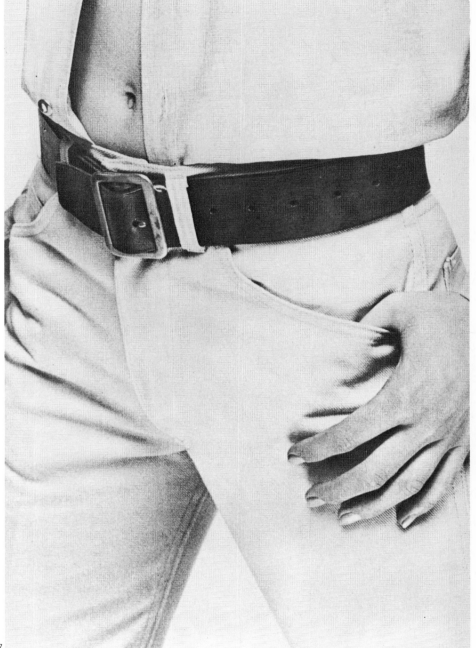

Terence Donovan

7

1. Bohan's leg o'mutton sleeves,
kilt skirt in chalk stripe navy wool,
with bowler and gardenia.
2. Chanel's navy jersey blazer suit
worn by Anouk Aimée, who loves
Chanel clothes on and off
the screen.
3. After Saint Laurent — piebald
dress from the London ready-
to-wear.
4. Royal College of Art fashion
students Sally Tuffin and Marion
Foale have an early success with
this simple shift dress cut out in
a circle under each arm.

5. Black ciré smock and
thigh-high alligator boots.
6. Saint Laurent's beautiful
country tunic, bulky and loose with
a narrow skirt, in Bernat Klein's
mohair and wool tweed, worn with
knitted wool stockings and flat
walking shoes.
7. Jeans, the out-of-uniform
uniform for the young.

283

1964

'Some of the occasions designers
apparently have in mind haven't
happened yet'
'Courrèges's skirts are the shortest in Paris'
'Courrèges invents the moon girl'
'White sets the pace at Courrèges'

The year of Courrèges. An expert tailor
trained at Balenciaga, he has been
producing his own collections since 1961,
but with his spring collection he suddenly
comes to the front of the Paris couture. To
the throbbing of tom-toms in his hot white
showroom on the avenue Kléber he parades
clothes that seem to be the projection of a
space age far ahead. *Vogue* says, 'White
sets the pace at Courrèges — tweeds,
gloves, kid boots, shoes, tunics, coats,
trousers are all white. Trouser suits are
lean, the trousers curved up at the ankle in
front, dipped over the heel at the back;
overblouses are straight and squarish,
jackets single breasted with a back half-
belt; skirts are the shortest in Paris —
above the knee. Coats are seven-eighths.'
From now on sixties fashion will revolve
round bare knees, the trouser suit, outsize
sunglasses, white leather boots, white and
silver.

This is also the first year of the ribbed
sweater and the small Liberty print, false
eyelashes with filaments added to give an
illusion of thickness and length. *Vogue*'s
pages are full of tawny tigresses like 'Baby
Jane' Holzer, wealthy jetsetter and
companion of Andy Warhol, and of the
Beatles' girl-friends Jane Asher and Patti
Boyd. In California, it's the year of Rudi
Gernreich's topless dress; in New York, of
Andy Warhol's camp culture and
underground movies.

1. Courrèges's 'moon girl': silver sequin pants tied with white satin
ribbon, white faille coat and suntanned midriff.
2. Courrèges makes his mark with his spring collection. Seven-eighths
coat in camel reversing to white gabardine over a white gabardine
dress, and trouser suit of white cotton matelasse with straight slit
trousers. Both worn with 'space helmets' and white kid boots.
3. Baby Jane Holzer demonstrates the craze for hair — the greatest
volume that can be contrived.
4. Jane Birkin wears a beautiful caramel wool coat by Dejac,
buttoned and half-belted, pleats at the back.
5. 1964 version of the Marlene Dietrich trouser suit in beige shantung,
trousers cut loose and straight, Canadian mink dropping off
the shoulders.

1
COURRÈGES

Penn

2

COURRÈGES

David Bailey

3

David Bailey

4

5 RICCI

David
Bailey

David Bailey

ELMA   David Bailey

GERNREICH   David Bailey

1. White leather suit worn with white lace stockings and white kid Courrèges copy boots.

2. Rudi Gernreich's brave new world — the Californian originator of the topless bathing suit turns to camelhair and checks, felt yashmaks and suede balaclavas. His model wears scarlet eye make-up.

3. Jane Asher, 'the envy of millions. The Beatles are her fans,' in mustard and black spotted cotton by Sally Tuffin and Marion Foale.

4. Madame Grès's beautifully draped evening dress of angora jersey, striped in grey, blonde and white.

5. From Emmanuelle Khanh's collection for Frank Usher, a white rayon suit piped in bright red. Petalled piqué bonnet, James Wedge.

6. The new cling sweater in sock ribbing, pulled down hard in schoolboy grey wool, tucked into a grey flannel skirt.

TUFFIN & FOALE

1964

KHANH   Helmut Newton

6
JOHN LAING   David Bailey

GRÈS
Penn

1965

JOHN BATES   Duffy

Skimp cotton bikini dress in terracotta and navy,
netted together in navy.

Opposite: Dresses, *left to right*, by Nettie Vogues,
Diorling. Grace Coddington, fashion editor, in the water.
Photograph by Helmut Newton, October 1973.
Over page, left: Make up by Christian Dior, felt cap by
Charles Batten, heart necklace from Butler & Wilson.
Photograph by Norman Parkinson, December 1973.
Over page, right: Face painted by Gil of Max Factor with
a silk scarf by Karl Lagerfeld. Photograph by Clive
Arrowsmith, November 1970.

'The world suddenly wants to copy the way we look.
In New York it's the "London look", in Paris it's
"*le style anglais*"'
'Every kind of English girl seems now to have the
self-assurance praise and admiration give; every girl's
an individualist – and a leader'
'Bras have been like something you wear on your
head on New Year's Eve' – *Rudi Gernreich, American
designer of the 'no bra' bra*

The Fashion House Group takes mini-skirts to America
with a show on board the *Queen Elizabeth* berthed at
New York. In Australia, Jean Shrimpton shocks race-
goers with her mini-skirt four inches above the knees.

Skirts rise to mid-thigh, girls change over from
stockings to tights and the London look becomes
international. On the Continent and in America girls are
approximating to 'the leggy, soft-skinned English blonde
in country shoes, classic raincoat and grey flannel'. New
examples of the type may come from anywhere:
Françoise Dorléac, Françoise Hardy, Jane Birkin, Daliah
Lavi, Jane Fonda. In March *Vogue* features 'The Attic
Dressers', boys 'without the funds for Carnaby Street'
who are dressing in dandy Victorian or Edwardian
fashion from the street markets, Portobello, Brixton, or
Church Street, Paddington, and out of dusty suitcases
discovered in relations' attics. Ad men, with the money
to pursue the look, are having made suits with
waistcoats in pinstripes or grey flannel, which they wear
with gold fob watches on chains, bow ties, and — if
daring — a gangster hat. For evening, there are frilly
shirts and velvet dinner jackets.

The dress of the moment is the see-through dress,
with a netted midriff or made entirely of white crochet,
necessitating another novelty, the invisible body
stocking, flesh coloured and undecorated, pioneered in
this country by Warners. Rudi Gernreich's soft 'no bra'
bra firms the natural line without altering the shape or
adding uplift; and this year, Mary Quant branches out
into foundation-designing too.

Ossie Clark leaves Janey Ironside's fashion department
at the R.C.A. this year and is quickly featured in *Vogue*.
Ossie — 'After the war my father moved to a town
called Oswaldtwistle and I've been called Ossie ever
since' — began to make his name by designing a
special collection for Woollands while still in his final
term at College. Jean Muir, whose 'Jane & Jane'
designs are constantly photographed in the magazine,
begins to emerge with her own name on a small
collection of beautifully simple maternity dresses.

In Paris, Edward Molyneux comes out of retirement,
but only to sell to the trade. Yves Saint Laurent's
Mondrian collection is based on a plain white jersey
shift with lines and blocks in black and primary colours:
the easiest thing in the world for the ready-to-wear
market to copy. The first op art fabrics appear in the
summer, versions of Bridget Riley's paintings.

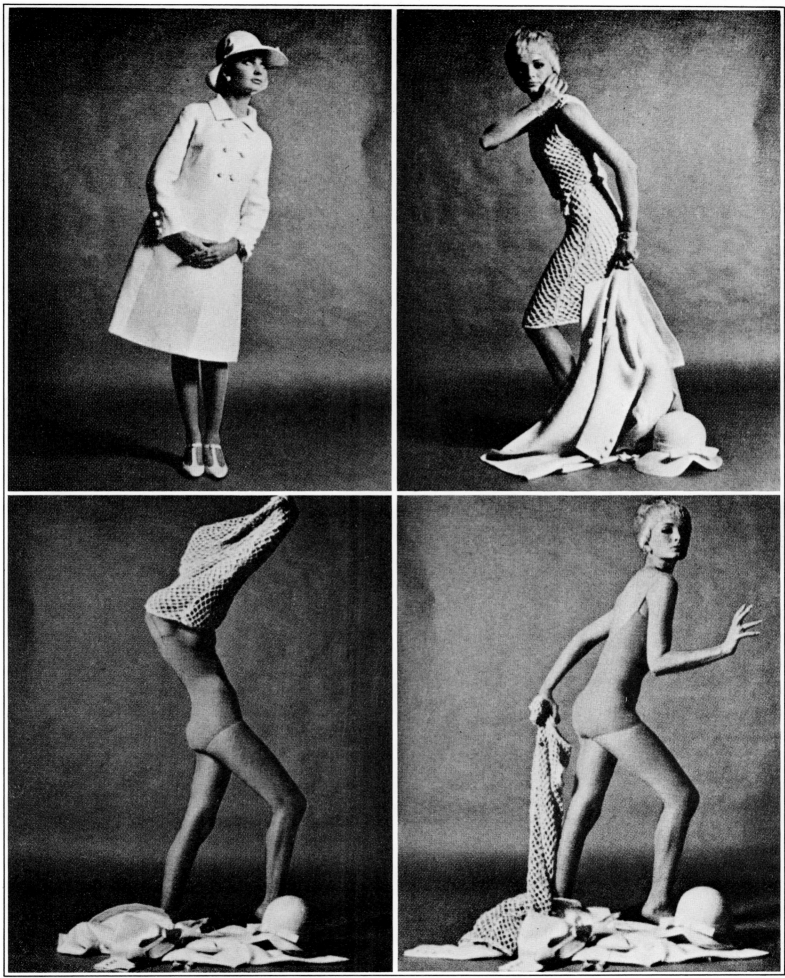

David Bailey

1965 layers: coat by Liza Spain, chenille dress by
Susan Small, Warners body stocking.

Opposite: Bianca Jagger in a box at the Théâtre de
France, with masked and white-powdered face by Serge
Lutens. Photographed by Eric Boman, March 1974.

1   W.H.I.

2   Penn

3   BONNIE CASHIN   Norman Parkinson

5
OSSIE CLARK   David Bailey

1. The crochet dress, made by Women's Home
Industries to be worn over skin-coloured body
stockings or camisole slips.
2. Diamanté mesh, Lord & Taylor, New York.
3. Blackberry leather tracksuit lined in silk, with a
hooded jersey sweater.
4. 'Hypnotical Illusions': op art stripes designed by
Getulio Alviani for Marucelli of Milan, photographed at
the Temple of Rameses II on the west bank of the Nile.
5. New talent from the R.C.A., 23-year-old Ossie
Clark, and his black and white quilted silk coat.

4

Henry
Clarke

1966

'Suddenly everyone's talking about Paco Rabanne, and his plastic fashion sculpture'
'Space projections . . . plastic, chrome, Dynel . . . everything silver, from visor to stockings and shoes'

The craziest fashion year of the sixties — a year in which make up becomes pure decoration, and you wear silver leather and plastic chain mail, skirts that show the whole length of your legs, mops of artificial hair coloured pink, green and purple, chrome jewellery, and visor sunglasses.

Paco Rabanne's plastics, small tiles linked together by chain, steal the show in Paris. Nearly all designers are infected with the mirage of 'space age fashion.' Cardin's dresses are half sculptures, little shifts suspended from ring collars, or cut out discs and squares. Saint Laurent makes his shifts in sheer organza, transparent except where they are striped or chevroned with silver sequins. Everywhere, from the couture to the ready-to-wear, the favourite dress is the briefest triangle, taking no account of the waist. It's worn with the shortest hair — Leonard cuts Twiggy's right back to the skull, shorter than a little boy's — huge plastic disc earrings, silver stockings, silver shoes laced up the leg, bangles of clear plastic and chrome. Silver leather or shirred silver nylon make the new jackets. Foale & Tuffin are just one of the shops selling suits with skirts and trousers matching the jackets, silver or contrasting corduroys. The craze for false hair reaches its peak with great mops and switches of Dynel, and eye make-up is designed to be seen from 100 yards, in streamlined eyeliners, black and white used alternately, and false eyelashes made still thicker with filament mascaras. Mary Quant's new make up is based on the face-decoration of 11 top models, and Verushka, America's surreal top model, is painting her body and face with flowers or colour abstractions.

These extreme looks need an extreme new kind of model girl, and *Vogue* photographs the Paris collections on the thinnest and most angular of them all — the spider-limbed black Donyale Luna, Ford plant manager's daughter from Detroit.

As alternatives to this new fashion brutalism, there are two new looks, Saint Laurent's gypsy print shifts or shirts-and-skirts with kerchiefs covering the hair, and the caftans that women are buying in Morocco or from the Indian boutiques in London. The caftan is undemanding, exotic, and a collector's piece and now becomes a classic. By the end of the sixties very few fashionable women won't have one.

Saint Laurent's autumn collection includes a few jokes, chiefly the pop dresses inspired by Andy Warhol, with vivid profiles of a face or a body scrawled over them in positive-negative contrast.

PACO RABANNE

David Bailey

1. 'The neon-lit kite coat', plastic diamonds on white crepe, by Paco Rabanne for Venet.
2. The Look: Dynel hair used in impossible thicknesses and colour combinations, and theatrical eye make up using alternate lines of black and white.
3. Front-zip silver Vinyl shift.
4. Scarlet kid coat and dress ruffed in racoon and lined in fleece.

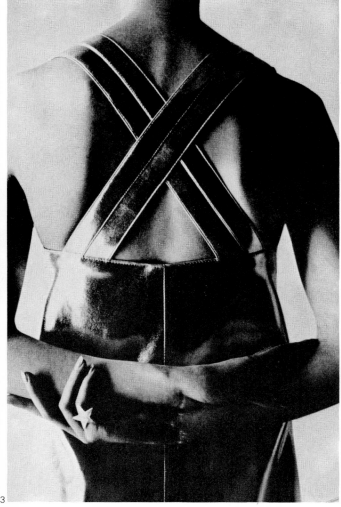

BONNIE CASHIN

Helmut Newton

JAN FINCH

David Bailey

1966

FOALE & TUFFIN   Traeger

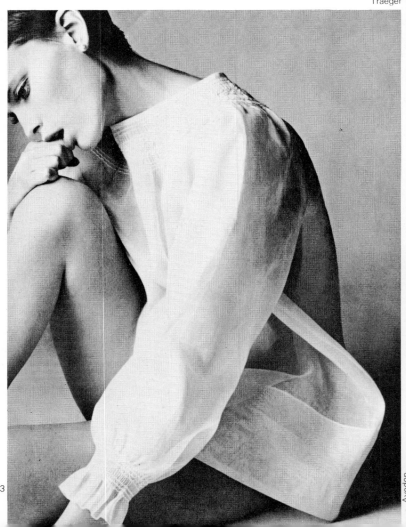

JULIAN ROBINSON   Bob Richardson

1. Grey and rust corduroy suit. Hat by James Wedge.
2. Dynel coat of powder-pink fluff.
3. Mia Farrow cuts her hair back to the skull, wears tiny pearl studs in her ears, and sets a new style.

Avedon

3

JOHN MARKS   RHONA ROY   David Bailey

4. Long white wool coat, worn by Susannah York, here with Warren Beatty.
5. Lady Egremont wearing a sky blue caftan embroidered in white, from northern Nigeria.
6. Patti Boyd (Mrs George Harrison) and her sister Jenny Boyd in buckled red cotton dungaree dress by John Marks and navy spot shirt, white crepe skirt by Rhona Roy.

1967-68

'On gusts of balalaika music from the Balkans, from hurdy-gurdy gypsy camps in Varna and the Ukraine, from straw-roofed Chechen villages, comes pure theatre for evening fashion. Give full rein to instincts for display and munificence with tinselled finery, brilliant skirts, silk embroidery, gold lace, tall boots, pattern used with pattern'

Hair arrives in London: 'Long, beautiful, gleaming, steaming, flaxen, waxen, curly, fuzzy, naggy, shaggy, ratty, matty, oily, greasy, fleecy, down-to-there hair like Jesus wore it halleluyah, I adore it hair!'

These two years mark the change in direction from futurist to romantic fashion. In reaction to the uniformity of geometric haircuts and 'functional' fashion, stiff carved tweed shifts and creaking plastic, women want to dress up and look wild and beautiful. The word 'romantic' now covers three kinds of dressing, all based on this wish to dress up again. The youngest is the flower power school, its prettiest exponent Patti Boyd, Mrs George Harrison, with her Red Indian leather fringes, headbands, and colour mixtures in layers of crepe and brocade — a kind of rag dressing mixed with bells, tassels and tinsel. Hair is loose, plaited or Afro fuzz, like Marsha Hunt's, star of *Hair.* The jetset version of this look is the wealthy ethnic gypsy, Ukrainian wedding dresses, Indian pantaloons, Afghan coats mixed with sheepskin and gold embroidery. In London you find it in the new Indian and middle-eastern boutiques that spring up all over the city and as special departments in the big stores. The last of the romantic looks is the ruffle-and-ringlet vogue, partly inspired by the Bardot/Moreau film *Viva Maria*, released last year, and it is available at shops like Annacat and Mexicana. By day it borrows kneebreeches and velvet suits from men, with ruffled shirts and long curly hair, by evening it becomes long demure dresses in fragile fabrics, frilled and tucked, with full milkmaid sleeves, bib fronts, and lace edgings. The hair is worn in ringlets or shoulder length curls, tied with bunches of ribbons.

The pop revolution burns out with a crackle of paper dresses. Expendable dresses come in poster prints or fabric patterns, in packs costing from 16*s.* to 22*s.* 6*d.* Biba sell a silver paper suit for £3, and there is a metal-sprayed Melinex dress that won't rip, tear, flare, crack or scratch, but makes such a noise that you can hear it in the next room. The micro skirt shrinks even more and becomes shorts, in grey flannel like a schoolboy's with shirt, tie and waistcoat for day, in organdie for one-piece shorts-dresses for the evening.

Ossie Clark's satin dresses with fabric prints by Celia Birtwell make the most revealing evening dresses in London, slashed or flowing against the body to show

1
DELISS   David Bailey

every line. Beside these hothouse dresses, which become a kind of status symbol, he turns to the recent past for fawn jersey tailored suits with square shoulders, a forties-through-sixties-eyes look.

Jean Muir, undiverted, develops her own tradition of simple, immaculate, intellectual fashion: dresses in Macclesfield silk, pyjama stripes or dressing gown paisleys, trouser suits made by an expert dressmaker.

1. Linen and lace peasant dress from Yugoslavia, pleated and embroidered in red silk, with a wide hem of flowered lace.
2. The Romantic evening look of the year, Viva Maria tucked and lacy cotton from Mexicana, blouse and bloomers.
3. Pale fringed doeskin, wrapped and tied.
4. Beginning of the hippy look: The Fool's painted walls at Apple, for the Beatles, and their clothes, clashing crepes, pieces of brocade, tassels and belts.

The Romantic Look

2

3 LESLEY   Traeger

MEXICANA
David Bailey

4 FOOL   Traeger

1
RICCI   David Bailey

2
CARDIN   Avedon   3
UNGARO   Penn

1. Navy braided suit with a monogrammed white silk shirt, navy scarf and hat.
2. Silver cast metal neck-sculpture supporting a sheath of black crepe. Sculpture by G. Mannoni.
3. Ungaro, trained at Balenciaga and Courrèges, opened independently in 1965, with 'another leap into space'. Here his yolk yellow canvas coat, blue pleat dress, and thigh-high Vinyl boots.
4. Watered purple velvet dress with white crepe tab and cuffs.
5. Saint Laurent's shock piece, sheer black chiffon with ostrich hips, a gold serpent wound round the waist.
6. Slimming by machine, a new form of faradism evolved by a Dr Hawkins in South Africa.

4
JOHN BATES   David Bailey   5   SAINT LAURENT

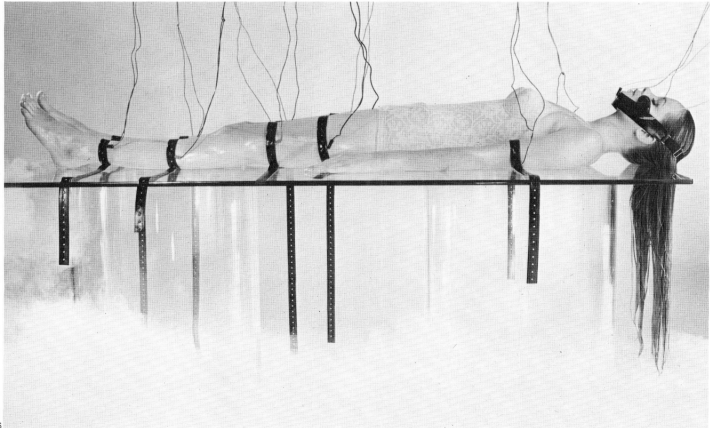

6

Helmut Newton

299

1969

'In fashion, the revolution is over. A new quiet reigns. There has been an explosion of energy and excitement, linking together all the visual arts. A national upheaval, it has had international repercussions. It has brought us to the brink of space-age clothes, and stopped short at the notion of silver suits and transparent visors. Will it be like that? No, because what it will be like is growing now out of the life we lead'

'Brevity is the soul of fashion'

'The beat look is the news at Dior . . . pale zombie faces; leather suits and coats; knitted caps and high turtleneck collars, black endlessly'

Complete nudity is now permitted on the stage, and incomplete nudity in fashion: the most extreme looks from Paris, from Cardin, Ungaro, Courrèges, are now about the body instead of the space suit. By the autumn collections there is a freedom and wearability about all the important looks. Skirts are mini, knee-length, midi or maxi, 'Everything goes so long as it works for *you*.' There is Saint Laurent's frogged fitted hussar coat, or his caped highwayman coat to wear with trousers. Dior makes the easiest coat of all — just a wool dressing-gown wrapped and tied, with a big collar. All the tweeds are worn with crochet pudding-basin-hats pulled down to hide the hair, and long matching mufflers. Eyes are made up in technicolour, stockings are black, shoes are nanny's lace-ups.

Pop gives way to the pale pre-Raphaelite, hair in Ophelia ripples, eyes painted icing green or harebell blue, dresses are fantasies by Zandra Rhodes or Ossie Clark. The King's Road looks like a Russian ballet, and twenties beaded dresses with handkerchief points are treasured pieces. Art Deco is given impetus by Bernard Nevill's beautiful Jazz Collection prints for Liberty, and the antique clothes market opens up. You can dress as you please in any look, any length, and passers by don't turn a hair.

British fashion has never before had the world prestige it commands at the end of the sixties. In a fashion sense, it's as important, as sophisticated and more international than Paris. Buyers from all over the world look to the British ready-to-wear for the new tricks, and in London you

Avedon

can buy Saint Laurent ready-to-wear, Cerruti trouser suits, Missoni knits, Scandinavian cottons, the best couture and ready-to-wear from the Western world and every kind of exotica from far-away places. The indigenous talent discovered and trained in the art schools has produced Jean Muir, Ossie Clark, Mary Quant, Zandra Rhodes and Barbara Hulanicki of Biba, to name a few of the best British designers, and American painter Kaffe Fasset is living in London and inventing a new tapestry of patterns for knitting.

1. Pale, ethereal beauty Ingrid Boulting, photographed with her hair wet-plaited and combed out when dry.
2. Pale chiffon dress with a shamrock print by Celia Birtwell.
3. Cobra print georgette, brown suede waistcoat appliquéd with the real thing.
4. Kaffe Fassett's tapestry pattern knit cardigan coat and stripe sweater, with suede trousers by Beged-Or.

2
OSSIE CLARK

Norman Parkinson

3 JEAN MUIR

4 KAFFE FASSETT

David Bailey

301

1   LESLIE POOLE   Barry Lategan

1. Tiered silk dress, ice cream pinks and blues, photographed with Bernard Nevill's Jazz Collection fabrics for Liberty, the Ideal Standard House door frame saved by Bernard Nevill, and part of his Deco collection.

2-4. Winter Collection: 'Everything goes (mini, midi, maxi) so long as it works for *you.*' Photographed by David Bailey.

5. Beautiful evening dress of mother-of-pearl printed panne velvet.

6. Cerruti's unisex look, well cut classics made for men and women. Here, scarlet and white paisley silk jackets and waistcoats with gabardine pants.

7. Clove wool dressing-gown coat.

2   UNGARO   3   SAINT LAURENT   4   GIVENCHY

5
SAINT LAURENT   David Bailey

6
CERRUTI   Patrick Lichfield   DIOR   David Bailey   303

1970·1975

Waste not, want not   Arthur Elgort

The Uncertain Seventies

Eva Sereny

'The million dollar girl next door.' Lauren Hutton, the highest paid model in history —
two hundred thousand dollars a year in America for personifying Charles Revson's
Ultima beauty products. Not in spite of, but because of her gap teeth and her 'banana
nose', she is one of the beauties of our time.

Five years into the seventies, it seems that fashion has undergone a fundamental change. Even in the revolutionary sixties fashions were either 'in' or 'out': the differences were patently in the looks and lengths, the pace, and the fashionable age-group. Today the role of fashion has changed: the word 'fashion' itself conveys a multitude of different things to different people. Women now have lived through more fashions than at any other time. In 1970 and 1971 clothes became pure decoration – 'decoration, not labelling', *Vogue* emphasized – and the decorative revival spread outward from the houses of fashion designers to theatrical and movie circles, with hand-painted murals, ceilings sprayed with words and slogans, tigerskin-sprayed cars, cut-out tree silhouettes for the edges of rooms, pop-painted walls, toadstool chairs and flocked tea sets. Now, in London, you can find the whole range of fashion within a stone's throw – tweedy, ethnic, Hollywood, classic, glamorous, executive, nostalgic, pretty or international. Fashion has turned into repertoire. If clothes are modes of expression, fashion is a vocabulary. This is a point that has been emphasized again and again in *Vogue* during the 1970s: 'The real star of the fashion picture is the wearer, the real star of the issue is you . . . Done right, fashion now is the expression of women who are free, happy, and doing what they want to be doing . . . One woman lives dozens of different lives – one at home, another at work, another out in the evening, another in the country, another in the city, and at least two more for fun.' In 1971 *Vogue* made a point of breaking all the old fashion rules,

beautifully, finally asking, 'Is bad taste a bad thing?' This is a great milestone in the history of fashion. Enjoying this new freedom, women are no longer set pieces, arranged differently for each situation according to who will see them. In the Christmas 1974 issue, *Vogue* photographed Lauren Hutton, the highest paid model in history ($200,000 a year in America for personifying Charles Revson's Ultima beauty products), make-up-less, gap-toothed, tousle-haired, a 'million dollar girl next door'. In a previous issue, *Vogue* showed a kitchen gardener in beret, muffler, wrinkled wool tights, loose mohair knitted coat, and said, 'The clothes aren't smart, but they're very much in fashion. They obey the first rule of dress which is that clothes must be appropriate.' Replacing the worn-out dress roles of the past, women are pleasing themselves and giving pleasure to others by the originality and variety of their appearance, seldom conforming to anyone else's idea of what elegant means. In spite of the formidable talents of the best designers of our day – including Karl Lagerfeld, Yves Saint Laurent, Missoni – the people who really make today's look are the women who wear the clothes. It is safe to say that things will never be the same again.

Free as we seem to be, we are never without limits and boundaries. There are plenty of clothes we would *not* wear. The fashion of the too-recent past, for instance – which seems in the mid-seventies to begin in the mid-sixties; and no woman with her eyes open would walk about now in the skins of a rare animal and be the butt of raised eyebrows and uncomplimentary remarks. Fashion seems set

Left: 'The clothes aren't smart, but they're very much in fashion'. Printed wool skirt
by Daniel Hechter, with a mohair cardigan coat by Krizia and woollen stockings.

Henry Clarke

to evolve between the limits of the financial crisis and all its repercussions. In the 1960s clothes hinged on age. In the 1970s they will hinge on price. The fashion market is beginning to resolve itself between, on the one hand, the dead cheap – viz. the clothes in *Vogue*'s 'More Dash Than Cash' feature – and on the other hand, the expensive fashion investment. This category will not in the 1970s be confused with luxury – things you want but do not need. Luxury like fashion has changed its meaning, since the greatest luxury is always the thing in shortest supply. Luxuries today are, perhaps, time and peace. Fashion investments were redefined in *Vogue* in 1974 in a profile of an imaginary woman, the new fashion collector: 'She spends more money on her clothes than most women, but, when they're searching around for something to wear, she's already perfectly dressed. When their clothes are beginning to look wrong, hers are right. So in the end, she probably spends no more than they.' Simplicity and quality do not become devalued – they are the only two fashion properties to hold their worth in *Vogue*'s fashion copy since 1916 – but in the 1970s they are not the whole story. Simple can also be plain and boring. An investment is really something that continues to give pleasure long after the novelty is over, and that means beautiful cloth, faultless cutting and making, and great discernment on the part of the designer and the buyer. One of *Vogue*'s chief functions today is to provide all that is necessary to give a reader this discerning eye. As one well dressed woman with very little money told a newspaper the other day, 'I always buy *Vogue*, that's my main extravagance'.

Alongside the noisy fashion revolution of the 1960s and early 1970s there has been a quiet revolution. The most fashionable clothes are for the first time being seen in context and on a par with the other arts, even to the point of holding their value long after their day is over. There have been increasing signs of this since the Victoria and Albert Museum's exhibition in 1960 of Heather Firbank's clothes, 'A Lady of Fashion', but as early as 1954 Richard Buckle's Diaghilev exhibition in Edinburgh and London displayed costumes as works of art, something over and above artefacts. A

pioneer private collector, Mrs Doris Langley Moore, who showed her fashion collection to the public whenever and wherever she could get accommodation for it, was offered a permanent site in 1959, and opened the Museum of Costume four years later in the beautiful Bath Assembly Rooms, where the clothes are charmingly arranged and displayed. The most recent important fashion exhibition has been Sir Cecil Beaton's 'Fashion', at the V & A in the winter of 1971–2. He showed a collection of 350 remarkable clothes dating from the 1880s, each one a milestone in fashion because of its origin or fabric, because of the design or the way it summed up the mood of its decade, or because of the woman who wore it and on what occasion. Dazzled by Balenciagas, Poirets, Vionnets, a Fortuny and a mass of Chanels, women gasped with horror at Cecil Beaton's story of how, six weeks before he had approached a Chicago millionaire whose deceased mother and wife had been famously fashionable, the widower had made a bonfire of all their clothes, many still unopened and unworn in their Paris boxes and tissue paper, dating back to the 1890s. A few decades ago this story would have been a joke: now, when that sort of perfection has almost disappeared (and with it many social injustices), it is a tragedy. Today dealers charge up to a hundred pounds for rare and beautiful clothes in perfect condition, and Sotheby's and Christie's regularly include costumes in their sales at which private collectors bid against museums.

A recent development in English middle-class life, a keen interest in food and good domestic design, has made Terence Conran a wealthy man. Say 'Habitat people' and everyone knows what you mean. Terence Conran himself admits that you could call the Habitat style 'Packaged Good Taste', but its success can be measured by the 22 Habitat stores in Britain, and the 18 scheduled to open up in France over the next five years, with the bourgeoisie panting for Le Style Britannique d'Habitat. 'His eye for design,'

1. Yves Saint Laurent and Madame Catroux in the white drawing room of his Paris apartment.
2. Engagement photograph by Norman Parkinson. Princess Anne in riding clothes and Captain Phillips in No. 1 dress uniform of his regiment, The Queen's Dragoon Guards.

3. John Lennon and Yoko Ono, 1971.
4. Terence Conran photographed by David Bailey, interviewed by Antonia Williams. 'Life is simple for Terence,' says a friend, 'he just wants the whole world to have a well-designed salad bowl.'
5. Germaine Greer whose intelligent and beautifully written book *The Female Eunuch* came out in America with a first printing of 75,000 copies, accompanied by serialization in three leading American magazines, and the attention of Norman Mailer and David Frost.

David Bailey

David Bailey

said Antonia Williams in her interview with him, 'stems from his great love for the architecture of the Industrial Revolution, the factories and railways, locks and machinery, the work of Brunel and Morris and Mackintosh . . . the basement life of Victorian and Edwardian England when things were beautiful because they were economical, because they were practical and because they were functional and because they weren't simply decorated to add grandeur to them.'

Whoever emerges in the second half of the seventies, it is sure that Germaine Greer will be remembered as a key figure of the decade. Her intelligent and beautifully written book, *The Female Eunuch*, gave rise to a great deal of journalistic debate and dinner-party bickering, but no one has yet added anything significant to what she had to say. Her argument is that women do not suffer from penis envy as Freud taught, but from the castration and distortion of the natural female personality. *The Female Eunuch* came out in the U.S.A. with a first printing of 75,000 copies, and serialization in three leading American magazines: it provoked swipes from Norman Mailer (whose *Prisoner of Sex* had recently been published). Kathleen Tynan interviewed Germaine Greer for *Vogue*, and found her 'boldly dressed and bra-less, with a long Pre-Raphaelite face, and a voice that can be coaxingly soft or stridently vulgar . . . funny, outrageously coarse and direct about her pleasures . . . a born teacher', who had once told her students, 'A teacher is yours to plunder'. Miss Greer, then lecturer in English at Warwick University, underground journalist, singer, dancer, actress, argues that it is not reform we need but a revolutionary change in our social structure. What we have to do is open up a bigger landscape, 'retrieve our power of invention', unleash our particular female energy on a world badly in need of it. 'To be *in* love is to be in dead trouble and to be deficient in the power of living and understanding the other person,' she says. 'The warning signal is when you're more anxious about losing the other person than seeing that they're happy, for then you lose your power of benevolence. What I'm supporting is a tenderness in sex which doesn't involve that edge of insecurity which makes you clutch, where you're only meant to take hold.' Her aim is to get the message of women's lib across, whether it means writing about the hazards of going to bed with Englishmen who are likely to suggest, 'Let's pretend you're dead', or 'not losing your temper when people ask you for the millionth time, "Do you hate men?"' Another liberationist, Midge Mackenzie, describes Germaine Greer as a 'phenomenon, a super-heroine . . . who raises the possibilities for

Snowdon

1

2

Snowdon

other women. Although some of them feel that there is only room for one girl who both enjoys sex and has a Ph.D.'

With all this in the air, the Losey/Mercer film version of Henrik Ibsen's *A Doll's House*, made in 1973, acquired an extra edge of interest. Anthony Haden-Guest went to Roros in Norway, where the million-dollar production was being shot, and wrote that it was the scene of a few 'skirmishes in the sex-war'. The Ibsen conflicts came to life with Jane Fonda, 'fresh from anti-Vietnam peregrinations that have caused some of her fellow countrymen to demand her impeachment for treason'; her husband-to-be Tom Hayden, Vietnam activist and 'conspirator' with the Chicago Seven; Nancy Ellen Dowd, who had worked with Jane Fonda on a previous film *F.T.A. – Fuck the Army*; Delphine Seyrig, star of *Marienbad* and Buñuel's *The Discreet Charm of the Bourgeoisie*, active liberationist, accompanied by Michèle Richer who had fought alongside her on various abortion platforms; director Joe Losey who had left Hollywood during the Communist purge of the fifties; and playwright Joe Mercer, Marxist. Anthony Haden-Guest concluded that the director was not dealing with Jane Fonda alone, but with Nora Helmer herself. At the traditional end-of-the-film party, attended by the actors, the unit and several hundred citizens of Roros, all dressed up to the nines, Jane Fonda turned up in workforce jeans and industrial-strength boots.

Peter Brook's conception of *A Midsummer Night's Dream*, performed at Stratford in 1970, was one of the most astonishing theatrical productions of the early 1970s. Marina Warner, *Vogue*'s

3

4

features editor, wrote, 'Peter Brook's production dives straight into the audience's imagination . . . shakes the play to pieces, makes it astonishing and unrecognizable, yet loses none of Shakespeare's poetry.' Actors became acrobats in a set that was a stark white box, with ladders, firemen's poles, trapezes, swings and ropes. Titania's bed was a flying quilt of scarlet ostrich feathers, with coiled wire trees, fairies in sackcloth. The flower drug 'love-in-idleness' was a zinc plate spinning on a Perspex rod tossed back and forth between Puck and Oberon, and the play went on to wild percussion music from two bands seated high in the gallery, 'banging, whistling and shaking metal sheets, hissing and clicking'. As Marina Warner pointed out, it was a case of Theseus' own contention about theatre in the play scene that closes the *Dream*: 'The best in this kind are but shadows, and the worst are no worse, if imagination amend them.'

In films, the musical lived again in *Cabaret*, 'the film of the musical of the film of the play that was called *I am a Camera*, of the book that was called *Goodbye to Berlin* by Christopher Isherwood'; and lived again as self-parody in Ken Russell's *The Boy Friend*, launching Twiggy with Christopher Gable 'among lollipops and teddy bear kitsch and imitation Busby Berkeley routines'. It was an odd choice for Ken Russell after *The Devils*, set in the superstition-seized seventeenth century. His most recent venture is *Tommy*, The Who's rock opera: as Alexander Walker said in the *Evening Standard*, 'Ken Russell will try anything'. In the mid-seventies, directors of the *nouvelle vague*, François

1. Liza Minnelli in *Cabaret* 'hitting her stride at last as the lusty Sally Bowles'.
2. George Melly, photographed by Snowdon, 1973. 'Some of his turns on stage are famous, 'notably Frankie and Johnnie, a one-man melodrama in which he sings, acts, changes sex, makes love, shoots himself, staggers about, collapses and dies into the audience, singing all the while.'
3. Michael White, impresario who has put on several successful 1970s shows, including *America Hurrah!*, *Oh Calcutta!*, and *The Rocky Horror Show*.
4. Ken Russell and his daughter Victoria. 11-year old Victoria played a groupie in her father's film of The Who's *Tommy*.

Truffaut, Jean-Luc Godard, look like the living aristocracy of the cinema. In 1971 Truffaut talked to *Vogue* about his life in the cinema, and the split between Godard and himself since the days when they had grown up together as critics on the influential *Cahiers du Cinéma*. They made their first important films in the same year, 1959; Godard *Breathless*, and Truffaut *The 400 Blows*. Today Godard denounces Truffaut as conventional and frivolous, and Truffaut comments, in all kindness: 'Fundamentally, Godard's a dandy, struggling against his dandyism . . . He finds it difficult to express himself, to find a language.' Truffaut himself, 'trim and small and solemn in a careful suit, smoking a Gitane and avoiding drinks or coffee because they disturb his sleep', lives a life dedicated to the cinema, has no home, and lives in a suite at the Georges V in Paris.

If *Death in Venice* has been the most beautiful film of the 1970s so far, it is not so easy to name the most exciting or the most vicious: there is plenty of competition. Small-budget films with unknown people for stars turn out to be better, often, than big-

budget ones: quicker and funnier and more surprising. Whatever the film, it is more than likely to have at least one scene put in for shock. 'Villains are heroes now,' said *Vogue* in 1971. 'Communication is brief, actions summary, titles terse. The beaten up and the beaters up, the mean and the sluttish are in the sun.'

Reflecting the focus of general concern, *Vogue* has in the early 1970s put emphasis on the pollution–conservation–preservation message. Since 1970 features have included the discovery of black holes in space, the origins of life, power and where it lies today, the reasons for advocating the Big Bang theory as the beginning of the universe, recycling, the possibility of life evolution on other planets, craftsmanship today and what happens to design students when they leave college, endangered buildings and what can be done to save them. In fashion captions for country clothes you read: 'Are they chopping down the trees? Ring your local C.P.R.E. branch. Is the river filthy? Ring Friends of the Earth. Plant your

1. Bjorn Andresen, the beautiful boy in Visconti's film of Thomas Mann's story *Death in Venice*.
2. Graham Palmer of the Waterway Recovery Group.
3. In 1972 when this picture was taken, David Essex was Jesus Christ in *Godspell*. Vogue said, 'He times his punch lines beautifully, dances disarmingly, and moves the audience to tears.' David Essex said, 'the only time I started to read the Bible was after I got the part'.
4. Marc Bolan, star singer of Tyrannosaurus Rex. When he went to Decca in 1965 they told him, 'With your face, boy, we'll make you a star.'
5. Francis Bacon photographed by Francis

Goodman, 1971, the year of his retrospective at the Grand Palais in Paris, an accolade only before accorded to one living painter, Picasso. John Gruen, in an interview with him for *Vogue*, said, 'The uniqueness of his style is based on a vision that concerns itself with precise yet never photographic observation.' Francis Bacon told him, 'I'm very interested in trying to do portraits, which now is almost an impossible thing to do, because you either make an illustration or a charged and meaningful appearance . . . how are you going to make a nose and not illustrate it?'
6. Allen Jones's drawing room, with his wife and two plastic dollies, 1970.

David Bailey

Richard Gloucester

Clive Arrowsmith

own trees for posterity, nurture the dandelion and the buttercup . . . hang on to the butterflies and birds, the wild flowers and the free range animals.' The Friends of the Earth point out from *Vogue*'s pages that every year this country consumes a forest the size of Wales to make paper, most of which goes into dustbins, or that, although metals are amongst the simplest of materials to recycle, we throw away enough cans each year to make a pile 45,000 miles high. And James Cameron reminds us that 'There is no mystery, for example, about how to cure poverty, rationalize education, abolish road accidents, and eliminate the causes of war, and probably ninety-nine per cent of people want exactly these things. The only missing factor, as every sociologist has pointed out for donkey's years, is the ability to put the collective will and the available machinery to work.' If that factor cannot be reversed, 'toleration of the unacceptable will be replaced by acceptance of the intolerable'.

5

Francis Goodman

4   Richard Imrie

6   Norman Parkinson   311

THE CHANGING FACE

BIANCA JAGGER

Bianca Jagger, wife of Mick, mother of Jade, calls herself the only person who has become a star without having done a thing. She has a degree in political science, drinks tea in nightclubs, and is prepared to spend hours a day exercising and grooming herself for an evening appearance: she is known for making late and spectacular entrances, always looking beautiful.

1. 1973
2. 1974

OSSIE CLARK

David Hockney

Peter Sellers

LIZA MINNELLI

Liza Minnelli, who was 'bounced up and down on some of the finest knees in the motion picture business' is the daughter of Judy Garland and the hysterical star of *Cabaret*. A natural actress who can't stop, keyed up to a high pitch of energy, she is made to hold attention — a real star. Everyone is waiting for her to make another film: at the moment she's making a fortune in cabaret with a small c. Photographed here by Peter Sellers in 1973.

David Bailey

GRACE CODDINGTON

Grace Coddington, fashion editor and model, exerts considerable
influence on the style of the 1970s through designers, who like her to
wear their clothes, photographers, who like to photograph her, and
models, who have copied her. She is able to change her style
completely from time to time, through discipline and a make up
technique only matched by Barbara Daly, and today wears her hair
blazing red and frizzy with curls, her make up light, and her clothes by
Saint Laurent, Sonia Rykiel, Jap, interspersed with one or two things
from the antique markets. (See also the colour photograph opposite
p.288).

Pablo and Delia's drawing of themselves, *left*, and Grace
Coddington, *right* (twice) in their own designs, 1972.
Hair tucked away under a beret, in a biscuit crepe suit by Jap with a
bow-neck blouse, photographed at Ajaccio harbour in 1974.
As she looked in 1966.

3

Traeger

TWIGGY

Twiggy (Lesley Hornby), was still a child when *Vogue* began photographing her, a schoolgirl model with a naturally sophisticated and refined face: 'Lately,' said *Vogue* in 1972, 'she has grown up and into her face. Her eyebrows have changed into the finest of arches, her eyelashes have become silky, she wears a little shadow at the outer edges of her eyes and draws the cupid's bow of her mouth even sharper.' She is quick-witted and original, with a guffawing laugh and great charm. From model via dress- and sweater-design, she became a singer, tapdancer and film star with *The Boy Friend*. She says, '*The Boy Friend* changed things for me — after that, people began to take me a little more seriously. I loved modelling at the beginning, it was all I wanted, but I couldn't think of doing it now.' Already established in films, she had a television series of her own in 1974 and was Cinderella in the 1974-75 Christmas pantomime. As *Vogue*'s Cinderella, photographed by Barry Lategan, Twiggy was the cover of Christmas 1974 *Vogue*.

1. Twiggy in the seventies.
2. In black shorts and brown lizard waistcoat, 1967.
3. *Vogue* cover, Christmas 1974.

Barry Lategan

MARISA BERENSON

Marisa Berenson, jetsetter, heiress and model, is the grand-daughter of Schiaparelli. She took leading roles in *Cabaret*, *The Female Condition*, and looks like becoming a real star in Kubrick's *Barry Lyndon*, made on location in Ireland, playing opposite Ryan O'Neal.

1. 1972 by Avedon.
2. 1970.

David Bailey

Helmut Newton

DOMINIQUE SANDA

Dominique Sanda, international film star who began as a model, was discovered by Bresson for *Une Femme Douce*, and made her name with Bernardo Bertolucci's *The Conformist*, quickly followed by Vittorio De Sica's *The Garden of the Finzi-Continis*.

Recent projects were *Steppenwolf, India Song*, and *Nove Cento* for Bertolucci. She told *Vogue*, 'Between the cinema and me it was, instantly, love.' She has a son, Ian. Here, in Saint Laurent's suit *à la Russe*.

'Clothes are a different thing from what they were. They are purely for decoration (not labelling) and they have more to do with you in particular than anything in general'

'What better time to paint your face, paint your clothes, paint your hair, your boots, your body?'

This year fashion becomes decoration, clothes become cosmetic. Hair is fuchsia pink or lime green, dresses are overlapping painted leaves or chiffon wisps trailing feathers, faces are painted in a rainbow of stripes or flowers (see pictures overleaf), necklaces are fringed leather bands painted with butterflies. This is the year of the embroidered Spanish shawl, the hand-painted boot, the layered haircut. Pablo & Delia, art students from Buenos Aires, arrive in London and tell *Vogue,* 'We are painters, and we have chosen fashion because it is a very, very lively manifestation, and we want to make free things, to create all the possibilities, in the language of fashion.' Leonard cuts the first important hairstyle of the 1970s, a cap of layered wisps following the shape of the head and blown dry instead of being set. By the end of the year it has become both longer and shorter — a short feathery cut with a thin veil of long hair covering the neck and shoulders, lightened or streaked in brilliant colours.

Everything is painted — necklaces, faces, hair, boots — and *Vogue* photographs models with picture faces: flowers, stripes, even parachutes. The fantasy continues to operate on the mass market level, designers aren't thinking 'This is for women in the AB income group'; they are thinking 'This is for a woman in a gypsy holiday mood'. Hats are right back in fashion for day and evening, and Liberty prints are collectors' items, to wear two or three at a time.

In the summer *Vogue* announces, 'The long skirt is here — and the first *Vogue* with not a short skirt in sight.' Jean Muir's collection provides an object lesson in the new lengths and how they depend on the balance of shape: the theme is tension at the top, freedom in the skirt. The proportion 'begins and ends with your body,' meaning a natural line, soft fluid fabrics and the bosom God gave you . . . 'Don't let them know you wear a bra,' says *Vogue.*

Far left: Pinafore and shirt by Pablo & Delia; photograph by Arthur Elgort in 1974.
Left: Pagoda dress of turquoise velvet with fur boots.

ZANDRA RHODES   Clive Arrowsmith

1

320

DIOR

Clive
Arrowsmith

GRAHAM PRICE

Clive Arrowsmith

2

BILL
GIBB

Clive Arrowsmith

3

JEAN MUIR

Clive Arrowsmith   JEAN MUIR

4

5

Barney Wan

LEONARD   Clive Arrowsmith

7

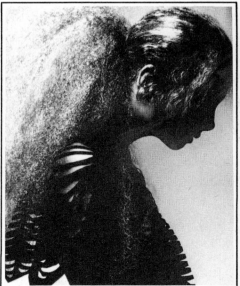

ARA GALLANT   Avedon

8

1. Dior's new coat proportion for trousers: tight bodice, bell skirt to mid-calf. In navy wool bound in braid.

2. Velvet knickerbockers and chiffon spot shirt loaded with decoration — bronze velvet shawl from The Purple Shop, cockade and hat, silk roses added to the shoes

3. Ziggurat pigskin jacket over knife pleats of jersey and tweed checks.

4 and 5. 'The long skirt is here': Jean Muir's collection says it all. *Left*, tucked and ribboned suede shirt. *Right*,

Barney Wan draws the new proportions from her summer show.

6. 18-year old *Vogue* beauty of the year, Lady Caroline Cholmondeley. Silver and enamel disc necklace by Dorothy Hogg of the R.C.A.

7. Leonard's haircut of the 1970s, layered and wispy, like a mob cap with a frill of fringes all round. Ends lightened by Daniel at Leonard.

8. Frizzed hair by Ara Gallant of New York.

321

6

Barry Lategan

1971

'Is bad taste a bad thing?'
'Fresh options, fantastic changes, breakthroughs . . .'
'There are no rules in the fashion game now. You're
playing it and you make up the game as you go . . .
you write your own etiquette, make up your face your
own way, choose your own decorations, express
yourself . . . faites vos jeux'

This year marks the height of fashion anarchy, when
there is no leading right look, but every style adds to
the vocabulary of the fashionable women — even 'bad'
taste. Women are dressing to amuse themselves, not to
improve their status or attract men, and *Vogue* runs a
leading summer feature on the end of etiquette in
fashion, asking 'Is bad taste a bad thing?'

There have never been so many different looks in
fashion. The biggest category by far is the sensational:
Zandra Rhodes's fantastic follies, Chloé's pastiche tap-
dancers in silk gym-knickers, Thea Porter's oriental
treasures, Pablo & Delia's baggy appliqué felts, Bill
Gibb's elaborate patterns piled on together, and a new
Japanese influence, tucked and quilted white cottons
from Kenzo Takada of Jap, and Kansai Yamamoto's
Kabuki theatre satins.

The forties and fifties craze, successor to the twenties
and thirties, adds pedal-pushers, turban bows, red
lipstick and box jackets to the repertoire, and flashy
wedge-heeled platform shoes with peep toes and
anklestraps appear with almost every look in the book.

A gentler nostalgia deepened by a sense of loss
brings in a summer-in-the-country mood, with a flavour
of early Colette, in shady straw hats with wreaths of
poppies, flowered pinafores and aprons, faded cotton
skirts, bonnets, collarless Liberty print blouses with full
sleeves, bare feet in clogs. 'This is not a maternity
feature,' writes *Vogue*, introducing calico and gingham
smocks in spring, 'but what a great year to be
pregnant.'

Shorts make a new appearance worn with puff-
sleeves blouses, bows in the hair, lots of make up,
fishnet tights and platform shoes — a joke tap-dancing
look. 'Shorts are a sort of holiday from fashion,' warns
Vogue. 'They look great on the right shape, in the right
place,' but soon 'hotpants' are so popular that they are
being worn by secretaries in city offices. Other
alternatives to a skirt are dungarees in denim or quilted
satin, worn with T shirts printed with the words 'Kiss
me quick', 'Hallo sailor', 'Pow!' etc. The dandy trouser
suit is by now a classic, three-button with a waistcoat
or doublebreasted in tweedy checks.

Prints have never been better and there is a new way
of wearing them. Saint Laurent puts spotted shirts with
tile-pattern kilts and adds a patchwork-knit vest,

STIRLING COOPER   Arthur Elgort
Toggled tent coat and drainpipe trousers in green and brown plaid

Missoni puts a Spanish shawl print with brilliant stripes,
and ready-to-wear designers everywhere are mixing up
the Liberty cottons. In the same way, sweaters get
more interesting. The new vest top that goes over the
top of a long-sleeved sweater comes in colourways and
patterns that relate, but do not match. Women begin to
think in families of colours and pattern groups when
they put their clothes together. In Italy Missoni takes
this kind of dressing furthest, importing painters to
experiment with effects in his modern Milan factory,
and his many-coloured many-patterned layer dressing
shows the way to a knitting revolution.

1
SAINT LAURENT   Barry Lategan

2 SYNDICA   Guy Bourdin

3 BUS STOP   BIBA   Jonvelle

PATRICK HUGHES   DAVID HOCKNEY   ELIZABETH FRINK   ALLEN JONES

1. Printed shirt, printed wool skirt, plaided patchwork vest:
a new kind of mixture from Saint Laurent Rive Gauche.
2. Layers of bubble-knit sweaters in mushroom pink, blue
and maroon.
3. Trouser suits for 'new tweedy people'.
4. 'Art can be a wearing business.'

323

1971

1. White cottons designed by Kenzo Takada for Jap.
2. 'If all the world were summer.' Jonvelle's photograph of a Provençal country picnic, with Colette clothes.

JAP   Duc

Jonvelle

JAMES DREW   Clive Arrowsmith

The new look: fresh, sharp, crisp, with tidy short hair and a simple white shirt.

'Dress like a lady, in hat, gloves, ribbed cardigan and pleated skirt'

'Wear at least one thing you wouldn't be seen dead in – pearlised puce nail polish, little white embroidered gloves, a really hatty hat, a neat and tidy crisp summer dress'

'If you think you know all about sweaters, think again' Sweaters, trousers and shoes dominate the fashion picture. Sweaters have become batwing or kimono-sleeved at Jap, wildly striped and patterned, bright as paint, and layered over other sweaters equally unconventional. Grainy speckled cardigans and knitted matching skirts give the effect of Donegal tweed, a winter favourite. Trousers are Oxford bags, pleated in to the waistband with side pockets and big turnups: by autumn, put with the new windcheater jackets, gathered onto striped elastic cuffs and waistband, they are a new kind of trouser suit. The summer look, blueprint Saint Laurent, is a combination of wide white gabardine trousers with cutaway red or navy vest, worn with cotton fishing hat and bright espadrilles. The jacket is loose and gathered from a yoke, a controlled smock shape. An alternative, easier to put together from the cheaper end of the ready-to-wear market, is the sailor suit, loose top with a sailor collar edged in navy or red stripes. 'All the nice girls love a sailor suit' says *Vogue*, and the shops are full of sailor sweaters, anchor-print shirts, spotted and striped trousers and T shirts with yachting motifs.

Shoes are preposterously high and vivid, the thick platform adding inches to already tall heels. Saint Laurent's rope-soled wedge espadrilles in primary colours lace up over bright contrasting tights, and for bare legs there are the new corksoled sandals. Best sellers at the Chelsea Cobbler are their high scalloped peeptoes with leather roses and anklestraps.

The wilder shores of fashion recede into evening fantasies, make up is lighter but just as bright, with less emphasis on the eyes, and Leonard's smooth short bobbed hair evens up the last of the layered ends. The condition of hair becomes a fetish and hairdressers lay in stocks of henna, which brightens the colour and adds shine and weight. In the summer there's a new fortyish hair style, brushed up into a curly topknot over the forehead, or a forehead roll with waved shoulderlength hair. Pillbox hats with veils go well with pinned-up hair and widened shoulders, and the period look is completed by the high anklestrap shoes. Newest equipment for model girls are the new coloured contact lenses, to give bright green or violet eyes.

'Try dressing like a lady' suggests *Vogue*: and Saint Laurent provides the greatest incentive with his long ribbed cardigans, bownecked silk shirts and striped or spotted shirtwaisters.

325

1   MIURA   JOHN CRAIG   DANIEL HECHTER   JEFF BANKS   Clive Arrowsmith

3   OSSIE CLARK   Clive Arrowsmith

1. New sporty sweaters.
2. Spots-and-stripes cakefrills, jacket and
baggy trousers.
3. Dusty blue velvet trouser suit,
peak-shouldered, wasp-waisted,
Oxford-bagged.

2
SALLY TUFFIN   Clive Arrowsmith

MISSONI Barry Lategan

Peter Knapp

ZANDRA RHODES Jonvelle

4. Missoni's new way to dress. Emerald checked knitted shirt worn over larger checked shirt, under square-necked jerkin with short checked sleeves.

5. Grainy wool cardigan and knitted skirt to match, with a bowneck shirt.

6. 'Change the colour and the shape of your hair.'

7. Zandra Rhodes's first sweater, pink, green, blue, with bat sleeves and duck tails, and her black silk jersey skirt with a lampshade frill.

Henry Clarke 327

ALBINI   Guy Bourdin

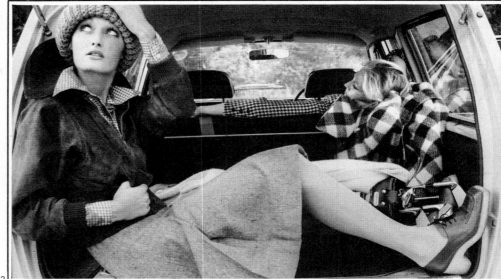

2 SAINT LAURENT   Norman Parkinson

3 WALLIS   Zachariassen

1. Walter Albini's new classic with a new painted look: striped big-buttoned twinset, check shirt and button-through skirt.
2. The 1972 Saint Laurent look: knitted pudding basin hat, batwing suede windcheater with ribknit collar and cuffs, Donegal tweed skirt and crepe-soled lace ups.
3. Scarlet corduroy dolman jacket.
4. *Left*, loose white trousers, tight wrap bodice of green and white taffeta checks, cream straw hat. *Right*, long loose jacket and wide trousers in cotton.

4 SAINT LAURENT   Peter Knapp

'Do your clothes get along well together? Are they well related? Do they mix? They will now'

'The best looks now are simple and glamorous . . . classics with a difference'

'Clothes for the life you lead – and we're speaking to *you*'

'*Vogue* is a glossary of all the clothes for all the lives you lead concurrently,' says the magazine. 'We're speaking of dressing up and getting dressed in 5 minutes, driving the car and getting the shopping done, going away for the weekend and out for lunch.' As life gets more hectic, fashion gets simpler. Separates look new because they look uncontrived and easy: jackets, skirts and trousers in different colours and mixtures to put together with shirts and sweaters. 'Colourings make their effects by the combinations of colours in groups . . . Not just misty green for instance, but a greeny oatmeal cardigan over a lavender silk shirt and trousers checked with all three.' Even suits begin to look as though you'd picked each piece separately, with a jacket of one fabric put with a skirt or trousers of another. Jackets cue all the looks, simple and fitted or a bloused windcheater shape, in ciré, speckled velvet, checks with knitted edges, piqué for summer, sequins or fake fur for winter.

The sailor jersey gives way to the cricket sweater with shawl collar and striped edges, and tapestry jacquard knits join the mixture of patterns in the shops. From Paris and Italy come new ideas in knits, Saint Laurent's extra long cabled cardigan with V neck and cuffs ruffed with fur, and Missoni's soft knitted suits in bias plaid, fine sweater with a heavier cardigan and skirt.

There are hats for morning, noon and night: tam o' shanters and berets, thicknit pull-ons, skull caps of Lurex and pillboxes of sequins with a mist of black veiling.

There is an out-of-uniform uniform for students and school-leavers: floppy-brimmed hat, long straight hair, full-sleeved shirt or smock, and cotton skirt to the ground. Girls of this age flock to the new Biba, in the palatial premises of the former Derry & Toms in Kensington High Street, with acres of marble floor and glittering dark caves heaped like treasure with Lurex sweaters, satin cushions and slinky dresses — 'a Nickleodeon land of Art Deco with potted palms and mirrored halls'. Bibaland is a new centre where the young can go to read magazines and listen to records, try on clothes, do their food shopping, and eat or have a drink with friends.

1. Mink coat and jeans.

1
KATHERINE HAMNETT   BRENT SHERWOOD   David Bailey

1973

AVANT
GARDE

1
LEONARD

Clive Arrowsmith

2

David
Bailey

3
BUS STOP   Bruce Laurence

COLETTE BREZAN   Norman Parkinson

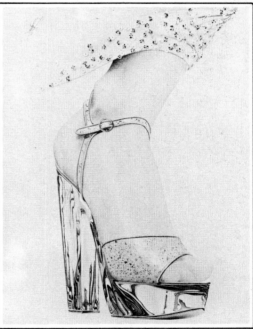

6
RICHARD SMITH   Michael English

1. Leonard's shaded chalky beige-white ducktail hair, cropped, brushed up and forward. Colouring by Daniel at Leonard.
2. Long cabled cardigan furred in grey fox, pale grey to go with grey flannel pleats.
3. Dog's tooth checks on wool and acrylic, windcheater jacket bloused onto cream knit edges, with a shawl collar.
4. Beige and plum trellised twinset edged in stripes, Burgundy cord velvet skirt, and feathered velvet hat.
5. Twiggy in Biba sequins with matching mittens and skull cap, Deco necklace, photographed at the bar in Biba's Rainbow Room.
6. A highheeled speckled leather shoe on a perspex platform.

5   BIBA   Justin de Villeneuve   331

1973

1. Brown and black plaid knitted suit, rib-waist sweater belted over the skirt, and long loose cardigan with ribbed edges.
2. Jap's cream wool cricket sweater, shawl collar and cuffs striped in navy and wine.
3. Clean cut velvet jacket, spotted and dotted with grey, elastic bringing the waist in.
4. Navy jersey jacket, short sleeved white wool shirt, camel trousers, with a cream felt hat from James Drew.

1 MISSONI   David Bailey

2

JAP   Rose JANICE WAINWRIGHT   David Montgomery   SAINT LAURENT

3   4

Barry Lategan

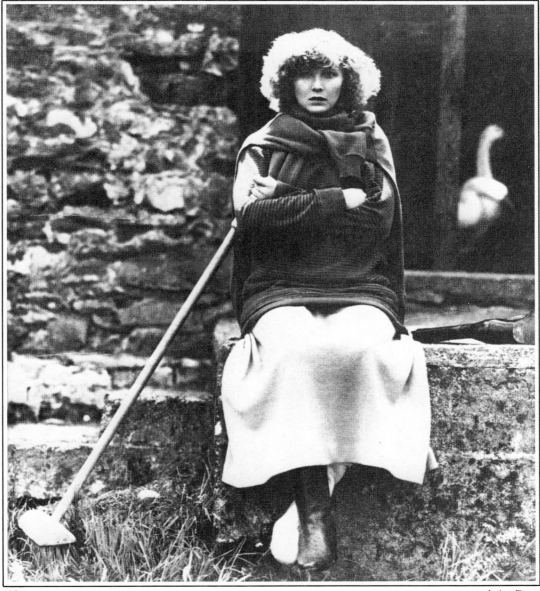

JAP

Arthur Elgort

'Cleanliness is next to godliness. Keep the country country, hang on to the butterflies and birds, the wild flowers and the free range animals. Use your own energy and initiative unstintingly to protect the things you love. Are they chopping down the trees? Ring your local CPRE branch. Is the river filthy? Ring Friends of the Earth. Plant your own trees for posterity, nurture the dandelion and the buttercup.' Long loose striped wool polo-neck, brown and black, baggy brown wool V neck sweater round shoulders, beige wool skirt, all by Jap.

'The real star of the fashion picture now is the wearer'

'[Gardening clothes] The clothes aren't smart, but they're very much in fashion. They obey the first rule of dress which is that clothes must be appropriate'

'Meet the new fashion collector. She spends more money on her clothes than most women, but, when they're searching around for something to wear, she's already perfectly dressed. When their clothes are beginning to look wrong, hers are right. So in the end, she probably spends no more than they'

The utterly simple, the wrapped and layered, the nostalgic and the quite fantastic are all equally fashionable, and women use these categories as a kind of repertoire to pick from. No designer today can tell just how his look will be worn and changed by the wearer. Designers try to ensure their look by putting it together in great detail, with special hats, jewellery, shoes, make up — only to find that women take them apart again and make their own look from the pieces. In other words, any very fashionable woman now has to be a bit of a designer herself. Even the simplest Aquascutum coat looks quite different with frizzed red hair, kohl-rimmed eyes, two mufflers and a pixie hat. All the 'classics' are new looks, as can be seen by comparing a trench coat now with an original. Nostalgia in fashion takes many forms, from the junk market dress that looks 1975 with today's hair and make up to the new pastiche, but its most important contribution is an emphasis on quality, a quality that has almost disappeared from the affordable horizon. Pure fantasy is always with us in fashion as a way of bringing dreams to life, usually as evening looks, but lately also as country clothes for the city.

333

1 STEPHEN MARKS

David Bailey

2 SAINT LAURENT

Guy Bourdin

CHLOÉ

Helmut Newton

334

DIOR

Barry Lategan

Barry Lategan

1. The loose overdress to wear with or without a shirt, in denim blue cotton gathered from the yoke.
2. Black crepe with marguerites, print by Eric Boman with a white collar and white straw hat.
3. Pale rose-print dress with a cakefrill neck, cut on the bias, with shredded print flowers.
4. Crin hat with a veil for a brim.
5. 'More Dash Than Cash.' A whole winter's outfit for £34 27p.
6. Jap's glazed honey coloured cotton cape, cream silk shirt, cotton trousers and bowler.

Clive
Arrowsmith

SAINT LAURENT

David Bailey

1. Perfectly simple and simply perfect white gabardine
jacket and fly button skirt, black and white striped
T shirt inside.
2. Blackberry bouclé shirt-tailed smock by Sheridan
Barnett, wool by Dormeuil. Cowled dickie, leg warmers,
skull cap and cotton satchel by Jap.
Photograph by Willie Christie.

BIBLIOGRAPHY

Battersby, Martin, *The Decorative 20s*, Studio Vista, 1969
Beaton, Cecil, *Fashion, an anthology*,
    (Catalogue to the V & A Exhibition, October 71 - January 1972)
Beaton, Cecil, *The Glass of Fashion*, Weidenfeld & Nicolson, 1954
Blythe, Ronald, *The Age of Illusion*, Penguin Books, 1963
Booker, Christopher, *The Neophiliacs,* Collins/Fontana, 1969
Cartland, Barbara, *We Danced All Night*, Arrow, 1970
Chamberlain, E.R. *Life in Wartime Britain*, Batsford, 1972
Contini, Mila, *Fashion*, Paul Hamlyn, 1965
Dormer, Jane, *Fashion in the 20s and 30s*, Ian Allan, 1973
Ewing, Elizabeth, *History of 20th Century Fashion*, Batsford, 1974
Flanner, Janet, *Paris was Yesterday*, ed. Irving Drutman, Viking, 1973
Garland, Madge, *Fashion*, Penguin Books, 1962
Garland, Madge, *The Indecisive Decade*, Macdonald, 1968
Graves, Robert, and Hodge, Alan, *The Long Weekend*,
    Faber & Faber, 1940; Penguin Books, 1971
Griffiths, Richard, and Mayer, Arthur, *The Movies*, Spring Books, 1957
Hadfield, John, ed., *Saturday Book 28*, Hutchinson, 1968
Hillier, Bevis, *Art Deco of the 20's & 30's*, Studio Vista, 1968
Hopkinson, Tom, ed., *Picture Post 1938-50*, Penguin Books, 1970
Laver, James, *Between the Wars*, Vista Books, 1961
Laver, James, *The Jazz Age*, Hamish Hamilton, 1964
Levin, Bernard, *The Pendulum Years (Britain in the 60s)*, Pan, 1970
Montgomery, John, *The Fifties*, George Allen & Unwin, 1965
Sissons, T.M.B. and French, P., eds., *Age of Austerity 1945-51*,
    Hodder & Stoughton, 1963
White, Palmer, *Poiret*, Studio Vista, 1973
Woolman Chase, Edna, *Always in Vogue*, Victor Gollancz, 1954

ACKNOWLEDGEMENTS

Many people have shared the burden of this book. I should like to thank Sheila Murphy, who had the enviable task of sifting through fifty-eight years of *Vogue* and choosing one-fiftieth of the material as a starting point, and Alex Kroll, Peter Carson and Eleo Gordon for the patience and care with which they gradually cut the book down to a manageable size.

I am grateful to Beatrix Miller and Georgina Boosey for their good advice and guidance, not to say forbearance when work on the book eclipsed my other work, and to Norman Parkinson and Sheila Wetton for their great help and long memories. Over the years a great number of gifted people have worked on *Vogue* and given the magazine its character and distinctive flavour in each decade. It has proved impossible to acknowledge them individually but to them belongs the credit for everything *In Vogue*.

I am grateful to Faber & Faber Ltd and Harcourt Brace Jovanovich Inc. for permission to quote from T.S. Eliot, *The Waste Land*; Faber & Faber Ltd and Random House Inc. for permission to quote from W.H. Auden, *Poems*.

I lastly want to thank my family who have lived with *In Vogue* for a year and a half: Michael, Thomas and particularly my mother, Gwen Howell, without whose unfailing help in times of crisis I should never have finished the book.

NOTE ON *VOGUE*

Vogue was founded in New York in 1892 as a society magazine and bought by Condé Nast in 1909. He turned it into America's leading fashion magazine and founded British *Vogue* in 1916. Edna Woolman Chase joined *Vogue* in 1895 and stayed for sixty years. She became editor of American *Vogue* in 1914 and later editor-in-chief. British *Vogue* was edited by Elspeth Champcommunal (1916-22), Dorothy Todd (1922-26), Alison Settle, O.B.E. (1926-35), Elizabeth Penrose (1935-40), Audrey Withers, O.B.E. (1940-60), Ailsa Garland (1961-64). The present editor is Beatrix Miller.

Many of the illustrations in this book had to be reproduced from the magazine as the original documents were no longer available. We hope that the interest of the subject matter will compensate for the occasional lack of quality.

INDEX

343